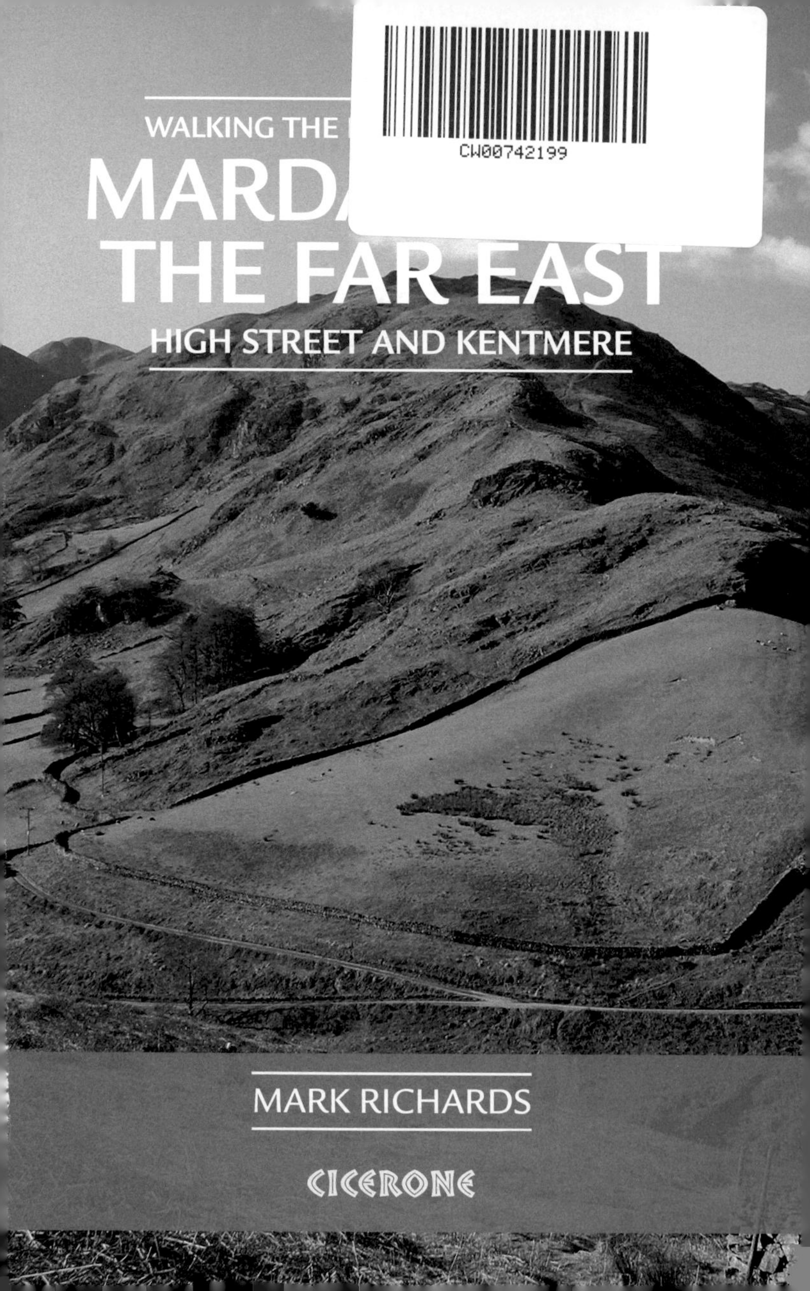

WALKING THE

MARDA

THE FAR EAST

HIGH STREET AND KENTMERE

MARK RICHARDS

CICERONE

© Mark Richards 2020
Second edition 2020
ISBN: 978 1 78631 035 4

Originally published as Lakeland Fellranger, 2013
ISBN: 978 1 85284 547 6

Printed in China on responsibly sourced paper on behalf of Latitude Press Ltd

A catalogue record for this book is available from the British Library.
All photographs are by the author unless otherwise stated.
All artwork is by the author.

Maps are reproduced with permission from HARVEY Maps, www.harveymaps.co.uk

Updates to this Guide

While every effort is made by our authors to ensure the accuracy of guidebooks as they go to print, changes can occur during the lifetime of an edition. Any updates that we know of for this guide will be on the Cicerone website (www.cicerone.co.uk/1035/updates), so please check before planning your trip. We also advise that you check information about such things as transport, accommodation and shops locally. Even rights of way can be altered over time. We are always grateful for information about any discrepancies between a guidebook and the facts on the ground, sent by email to updates@cicerone.co.uk or by post to Cicerone, Juniper House, Murley Moss, Oxenholme Road, Kendal, LA9 7RL.

Register your book: To sign up to receive free updates, special offers and GPX files where available, register your book at www.cicerone.co.uk.

Front cover: Ill Bell range from the Knowe (photo: Maggie Allan)
Title page: Beda Fell from the slopes of Hallin Fell

CONTENTS

Key to route maps and topos

 Route on a defined path

Route on an intermittent or undefined path

🔟 **Starting point**

4 **Route number** (on topos)

▲ **Fell summit** featured in this guide (on maps)

 Fell summit featured in this guide (on maps)

❸ **Route number** (on maps)

N

0   500

m

1:40,000

Harvey map legend

Lake, small tarn, pond

River, footbridge

Wide stream

Narrow stream

Peat hags

Marshy ground

> Contours change from brown to grey where the ground is predominantly rocky outcrops, small crags and other bare rock.

Improved pasture

Rough pasture

Fell or moorland

Open forest or woodland

Dense forest or woodland

Felled or new plantation

Forest ride or firebreak

Settlement

Boundary, maintained
Boundary, remains

> On moorland, walls, ruined walls and fences are shown. For farmland, only the outer boundary wall or fence is shown.

Contour (15m interval)

Index contour (75m interval)

Auxiliary contour

Scree, spoil heap

Boulder field

Scattered rock and boulders

Predominantly rocky ground

Major crag, large boulder

O.S. trig pillar, large cairn

Spot height (from air survey)

Dual carriageway

Main road (fenced)

Minor road (unfenced)

Track or forest road

Footpath or old track

Intermittent path

●   ●   Long distance path

+—+—←— Powerline, pipeline

▪•■ ▫ᵘ▫ ⊤ Building, ruin or sheepfold, shaft

> The representation of a road, track or footpath is no evidence of the existence of a right of way.

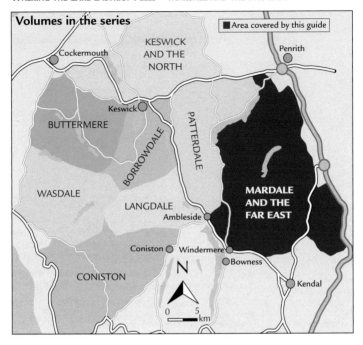

Volumes in the series

■ Area covered by this guide

Cockermouth

KESWICK
AND THE
NORTH

Penrith

Keswick

BUTTERMERE

BORROWDALE

PATTERDALE

WASDALE

LANGDALE

MARDALE
AND THE
FAR EAST

Ambleside

Coniston ○ Windermere

○ Bowness

CONISTON

N

○ Kendal

0   5
km

Caudale Quarry backed by Dove Crag

The popular pitched path up to Wansfell Pike from Ambleside

AUTHOR PREFACE

This land of living dreams we call the Lake District is a cherished blessing to know, love and share. As we go about our daily routines, we may take a fleeting moment to reflect that someone, somewhere, will be tramping up a lonely gill or along an airy ridge, peering from a lofty summit or gazing across a wind-blown tarn and taking lingering solace from its timeless beauty. The trappings of modern life thrust carpet and concrete under our feet, and it is always wonderful to walk the region's sheep trods and rough trails, and to imprint our soles upon the fells. This series sets out to give you the impetus and inspiration to make space in your schedule to explore them time and again, in myriad different ways.

However, the regular paths of long tradition deserve our care. Progressively many of the main paths are being re-set with cobbles and pitching by organisations such as Fix the Fells, to whose work you have contributed by buying this guide. But in many instances, the best consideration we can give these pathways is rest. The modern fellwanderer should show a new 'green' awareness by choosing to tread lightly on the land and to find new ways around the hills. One of the underlying impulses of this guide is to protect these beloved fells by presenting a diversity of route options for each and every fell – and also, in this new edition, recommending 'fell-friendly' routes to each summit which are less susceptible to erosion.

Another feature of this latest incarnation of Fellranger, apart from the smaller size to slip in your pocket or pack, is the addition of a selection of inspiring ridge routes at the end of each volume for those of you who like to spend a little longer with your head and feet in the heavenly realms, relishing the summit views and the connections between the felltops, as well as some accompanying online resources for readers with a digital bent.

Mark Richards

Location			GR [NY... unless otherwise indicated]	Access	Ascents described from here
1	Kirkstone Pass	large but popular car park	401 081	FP, B	Caudale Moor
2	Caudale Bridge	layby for several cars W of road a few hundred metres S of the bridge and E of road just before the bridge (403 115)	402 112	FP, B	Caudale Moor, Hartsop Dodd
3	Hartsop	large but popular car park (donation requested for Patterdale School)	410 131	FP, B	Angletarn Pikes, Brock Crags, Caudale Moor, Gray Crag, Hartsop Dodd, High Street, Rampsgill Head, Rest Dodd, Thornthwaite Crag
4	Deepdale Bridge	small layby by old phone box	399 144	FP, B	Angletarn Pikes
5	Patterdale	car park to E of road S of Patterdale Hotel	396 159	PP, B	Angletarn Pikes, Place Fell, Rampsgill Head, Rest Dodd
6	Martindale	some off-road spaces just past the church before Christy Bridge	434 184	FP	Angletarn Pikes, Beda Fell, High Raise, Steel Knotts, Wether Hill
7	Sandwick	some off-road spaces to E of road before the turnaround	424 196	FP	Angletarn Pikes, Beda Fell, Hallin Fell, Place Fell
8	The Hause	small off-road car park opposite the church at the top of the pass	435 193	FP	Angletarn Pikes, Beda Fell, Hallin Fell, Steel Knotts
9	Fusedale	some off-road spaces just over the cattle grid, beside the beck	445 194	FP	Arthur's Pike, Bonscale Pike, Hallin Fell, Loadpot Hill, Steel Knotts, Wether Hill
10	Roehead	verge parking at the end of the single-track road	479 236	FP	Arthur's Pike, Loadpot Hill

Location		GR [NY... unless otherwise indicated]	Access	Ascents described from here
11	Askham	small parking area before the cattle grid at the W edge of the village	507 235	FP	Arthur's Pike, Loadpot Hill
12	Helton	off-road parking beside fell road	497 215	FP	Arthur's Pike, Loadpot Hill
13	Helton Fell	off-road parking beside fell road	487 206	FP	Arthur's Pike, Loadpot Hill
14	Cockle Hill	off-road parking beside fell road	495 195	FP	Loadpot Hill
15	Bampton	parking at memorial hall (honesty box)	516 183	PP	Wether Hill
16	Moorahill	verge parking across from farm	493 182	FP	Loadpot Hill, Wether Hill
17	Burnbanks	small parking area S of road at entrance to village	508 162	FP	High Raise, Wether Hill
18	Mardale Banks	verge parking to E of road	479 119	FP	Branstree, Selside Pike
19	Mardale Head	small car park at road end	469 107	FP	Branstree, Harter Fell, High Raise, High Street, Kidsty Pike, Mardale Ill Bell
20	Swindale	verge parking to W at end of fell road	522 143	FP	Branstree, Selside Pike
21	Wet Sleddale	reservoir car park at SE corner	555 114	FP	Branstree
22	Shap Summit	long stretch of layby E of the A6	554 063	FP, B	Grey Crag, Winterscleugh
23	Huck's Bridge	large layby on E of the A6	553 037	FP, B	Whinfell Beacon, Winterscleugh
24	Hollowgate	small area of verge parking beside hen huts opposite farm on old road above (W of) A6	548 032	FP	Grey Crag

Location			GR [NY... unless otherwise indicated]	Access	Ascents described from here
25	Bannisdale Bridge	verge parking on out- side of bend on back road via Jock Scar that turns off A6 just south of bridge	543 014	FP	Grey Crag
26	Plough Lane	verge parking on W before culverted stream	SD 530 999	FP	Grey Crag
27	Greenholme	rough parking in centre of hamlet	597 057	FP	Winterscleugh
28	Tebay	roadside parking out- side the primary school and a little further S on edge of the village	616 043	FP	Winterscleugh
29	Low Borrowbridge	off-road spaces on S side of Borrow Beck, off a track leading off A685 (also a layby 0.5km further S on E of A685 at 607 007 at Hause Bridge)	606 015	FP	Grayrigg Forest, Whinfell Beacon, Winterscleugh
30	Grayrigg	verge parking north of Grayrigg Hall Farm over bridge	SD 579 976	FP	Grayrigg Forest, Whinfell Beacon
31	Sadgill	rough parking at end of road	483 056	FP	Branstree, Grey Crag, Harter Fell, Kentmere Pike, Shipman Knotts, Tarn Crag
32	Ullthwaite Bridge	verge parking just N of bridge	456 012	FP	Sallows
33	Kentmere	little on-road parking but extra fields opening up for (pay) parking at busy times	456 041	PP	High Street, Ill Bell, Mardale Ill Bell, Sallows, Thornthwaite Crag, Yoke

	Location		GR [NY... unless otherwise indicated]	Access	Ascents described from here
34	Hallow Bank	large layby on right-hand bend just before Stile End bridleway	464 050	FP	Harter Fell, High Street, Ill Bell, Kentmere Pike, Mardale Ill Bell, Shipman Knotts, Yoke
35	Moor Howe	a few verge spaces at the entrance to Dubbs Lane	423 006	FP	Sallows
36	Woundale	small layby on S side of Kirkstone Road (other verge parking nearby)	405 068	FP, B	Caudale Moor, Wansfell
37	Town Head	small layby on W of Kirkstone Road just north of Troutbeck	415 040	FP, B	Caudale Moor, Froswick, Thornthwaite Crag, Troutbeck Tongue, Wansfell
38	Church Bridge	spaces along river on Green Gate just south of church	413 026	FP, B	Sallows, Yoke
39	Town End	large layby on S of road	405 019	FP	Wansfell
40	Low Fold	small council car park, Ambleside	377 038	PP, B	Wansfell
41	Rydal Road	large council car park, Ambleside	374 047	PP, B	Wansfell

FP – free parking
PP – pay parking
B – on a bus route (in season)

Summit cairn on the top of Mardale Ill Bell

INTRODUCTION

Valley bases

If you're looking for a taste of wilderness in the Lake District, Mardale and the Far East may be the area for you. Bounded by Ullswater and the River Lowther to the north, the twists and turns of the famous Kirkstone Pass (A592) to the west and the spectacular gorge of the River Lune on the M6 at Tebay to the east, these quiet fells rise above myriad secluded valleys north of Windermere and Kendal, among them Mardale, Troutbeck, Kentmere, Longsleddale and (Westmorland) Borrowdale. Here the high peaks of the central range fade away to extensive rambling moorland stretches in the east, leading to views of the silky flanks of the Howgill Fells of the Yorkshire Dales, close relatives of these eastern fells.

This is an area for those who find beauty in solitary but intimate, dale-head surroundings and exquisite secret valleys threaded by sinuous narrow roads ill-suited to hasty travel, none more enchanting than the almost landlocked Martindale. Peace pervades the area. There's a sense of being far from the madding crowd, albeit just a few miles away from the honeypots of Ambleside and Bowness.

↑ *High Street from Twopenny Crag at the head of Riggindale*   15

Nanny Lane on the Troutbeck flank of Wansfell (photo: Maggie Allan)

Facilities

The majority of walkers visiting this area base themselves as close to the walks as they can. Those arriving by public transport, are, however, limited to staging posts along the A592 and A591; Howtown on the southern shore of Ullswater, by steamer; and Troutbeck, by the Kirkstone Rambler (in season). For those arriving by car, there is a good choice of hotels, B&Bs or self-catering cottages, as well as hostels and camp sites, scattered across the area, from Kendal in the south to Pooley Bridge in the north, and from Tebay in the east to Ambleside in the west. (The Visit Cumbria website (www.visitcumbria.com, click Accommodation) seems to have the best database or you could just use a search engine.)

Getting around

Bus services are confined to roads to the west and north. The 555 service from Kendal through by Windermere and Ambleside to Keswick can be relied on all year and the 108 service from Penrith to Patterdale, likewise, leads through the Ullswater vale to serve a string of communities year-round. The Ullswater Steamer adds to the repertoire specifically for Howtown and the Martindale fells. The scenically adventurous Kirkstone Rambler from Bowness-on-Windermere to Patterdale is also very handy in season. Trains run regularly from Oxenholme/Kendal to Windermere, sometimes halting at Staveley (for

Kentmere), but these only take you into the National Park rather than to the foot of any these fells.

Parking is not to be taken for granted anywhere in this popular park. Always allow time to find an alternative parking place, if not to switch to a different plan for your day or just set out directly from your door – perfectly possible if you find accommodation within any of the main valleys. Also take care always to park safely and only in laybys and car parks, not on the side of the narrow country roads. Consult the Starting points table to find out where the best parking places (and bus stops) are to be found. Note that although, in general, one preferred starting point is specified for each route, there may be alternative starting points nearby (for example in the vicinity of Hallin Fell) should you arrive and find your chosen spot taken.

Fix the Fells

The Fellranger series has always highlighted the hugely important work of the Fix the Fells project in repairing the most seriously damaged fell paths. The mighty challenge has been a great learning curve and the more recent work, including complex guttering, is quite superb. It ensures a flat foot-fall where possible, easy to use in ascent and descent, and excess water escapes efficiently minimising future damage.

The original National Trust and National Park Authority partnership came into being in 2001 and expanded with the arrival of Natural England, with additional financial support from the Friends of the Lake District and now the Lake District Foundation (www.lakedistrictfoundation.org). But, and it's a big but, the whole endeavour needs to raise £500,000 a year to function. This enormous figure is needed to keep pace with the challenges caused by the joint tyranny of boots and brutal weather. The dedicated and highly skilled team, including volunteers, deserve our sincerest gratitude for making our hill paths secure and sympathetic to their setting. It is a task without end, including pre-emptive repair to stop paths from washing out in the first place.

Mindful that a metre of path costs upwards of £200 there is every good reason to cultivate the involvement of fellwalkers in a cause that must be dear to our hearts... indeed our soles! Please make a beeline for www.fixthefells. co.uk to make a donation, however modest. Your commitment will, to quote John Muir, 'make the mountains glad'.

Using this guide

Unlike other guidebooks which show a single or limited number of routes up the Lakeland fells, the purpose of the Fellranger series has always been to offer the independent fellwalker the full range of approaches and paths available and invite them to combine them to create their own unique experiences. A valuable by-product of this approach has been to spread the effects of walkers' footfall more widely over the path network.

This guide is divided into two parts: 'Fells' describes ascents up each of the 36 fells covered by this volume, arranged in alphabetical order. 'Ridge routes' describes a small selection of popular routes linking these summits.

Fells

In the first part, each fell chapter begins with an information panel outlining the character of the fell and potential starting points (numbered in blue on the guide overview map and the accompanying 1:40,000 HARVEY fell map, and listed – with grid refs – in Starting points in the introduction). The panel also suggests neighbouring fells to tackle at the same time, including any classic ridge routes. The 'fell-friendly route' – one which has been reinforced by the national park or is less vulnerable to erosion – is also identified for those particularly keen to minimise their environmental impact.

After a fuller introduction to the fell, summarising the main approaches and expanding on its unique character and features, come the route descriptions. Paths on the fell are divided into numbered sections. Ascent routes are grouped according to starting point and described as combinations of (the red-numbered) path sections. The opportunities for exploration are endless. For each ascent route, the ascent and distance involved are given, along with a walking time that should be achievable in most conditions by a reasonably fit group of walkers keen to soak up the views rather than just tick off the summit. (Over time, you will be able to gauge your own likely timings against these figures.)

In many instances a topo diagram is provided, alongside the main fell map, to help with visualisation and route planning. When features shown on the maps or diagrams appear in the route descriptions for the first time (or the most significant time for navigational purposes), they are highlighted in **bold**, to help you trace the routes as easily as possible.

As a good guide should also be a revelation, panoramas are provided for a small number of key summits and panoramas for every fell in this guide

The summit outcrop on Place Fell from the west top

can be downloaded free from www.cicerone.co.uk/fellranger (see 'Additional online resources' below). These name the principal fells and key features in the direction of view.

Advice is also given at the end of each fell chapter on routes to neighbouring fells and safe lines of descent should the weather close in. In fellwalking, as in any mountain activity, retreat is often the greater part of valour.

Ridge routes

The second part of this guide describes some classic ridge routes in Mardale and the Far East. Beginning with an information panel giving the start and finish points, the summits included and a very brief overview, each ridge route is described step by step, from start to finish, with the summits highlighted in bold in the text to help you orientate yourself with the HARVEY route map provided. Some final suggestions are included for expeditions which you can piece together yourself from the comprehensive route descriptions in 'Fells'.

Appendices

For more information about facilities and services in the Lake District, some useful phone numbers and websites are listed in a 'Useful contacts' appendix. 'A fellranger's glossary' offers a glossary to help newcomers decode the language of the fells as well as some explanations of some of the most intriguing place names that you might come across in this area. 'The Lake District fells' is a comprehensive list of all the fells included in this 8-volume series to help you decide which volume you need to buy next!

Safety and access

Always take a map and compass with you – make a habit of regularly looking at your map and take pride in learning how take bearings from it. In mist this will be a time, and potentially a life, saver. The map can enhance your day by showing additional landscape features and setting your walk in its wider context. That said, beware of the green dashed lines on Ordnance Survey maps. They are public rights of way but no guarantee of an actual route on the ground. For example, on High Street's Rough Crags ridge east of Caspel Gate the green dashes beeline off the crest close to the precipice edge. A mist-blinded bearing based on such a line would indeed be dangerous. Take care to study the maps and diagrams provided carefully and plan your route according to your own capabilities and the prevailing conditions.

Please do not rely solely on your mobile phone or other electronic device for navigation. Local mountain rescue teams report that this is increasingly the main factor in the incidents they attend.

The author has taken care to follow time-honoured routes, and kept within bounds of access, yet access and rights of way can change and are not guaranteed. Any updates that we know of to the routes in this guide will be made available through the Cicerone website, www.cicerone.co.uk/1035, and we are always grateful for information about discrepancies between a guidebook and the facts on the ground, sent by email to updates@cicerone. co.uk or by post to Cicerone Press, Juniper House, Murley Moss, Oxenholme Road, Kendal, Cumbria, LA9 7RL.

Additional online resources

Summit panoramas for all of the fells in this volume can be downloaded for free from the guide page on the Cicerone website (www.cicerone. co.uk/1035). You will also find a ticklist of the summits in the Walking the Lake District Fells series at www.cicerone.co.uk/fellranger, should you wish to keep a log of your ascents, along with further information about the series.

1 ANGLETARN PIKES 567M/1860FT

Climb it from	Patterdale **5**, Deepdale Bridge **4**, Hartsop **3**, Sandwick **7**, the Hause **8** or Martindale **6**
Character	Two craggy crests provide a cracking objective above Angle Tarn
Fell-friendly route	7
Summit grid ref	NY 413 148
Link it with	Beda Fell, Brock Crags, Place Fell or Rest Dodd
Part of	Martindale Round

Angletarn Pikes merits all the time you can give it. Most striking from afar perhaps is its unusual summit arrangement – two parallel spine ridges of hard volcanic rock 200 metres apart vying for supremacy, defended to the north by a peaty hollow. But get a little closer and discover its most enchanting feature – the eponymous Angle Tarn, sitting in a high basin south of the summit, with three little islands, one linked to the shore by an isthmus and well-known to wild campers. On the secret eastern flank you can also find Heck Crag and Cove, wild places more than matched by the tarn's outflowing beck into the Goldrill vale.

Photographers will love the opportunities the tarn provides, especially as a foreground for a reflected vista of the Helvellyn range. Birds, too, find the lake

↑ Angletarn Pikes viewed from High Hartsop Dodd 21

alluring, and on occasion geese can be encountered honking rowdily. With a bit of good fortune, you might also catch a herd of red deer grazing nearby on the Nab.

The Pikes are most commonly climbed from either Patterdale (1–2) or Hartsop (3–5) but ascents also spring from Boredale (6) or Martindale (7–8) offering the opportunity for compact fell-rounds taking in Place Fell or Beda Fell.

Ascent from Patterdale 5

Via Boredale Hause →*2.9km/1¾ miles* ↑*400m/1310ft* ⏱*1hr 20min*

The popular natural line from Patterdale

1 Head south through the narrow street between the village shop and White Lion Hotel to bear left with the no through road leading over **Goldrill Beck**. This leads by a cluster of properties and bears left to reach gates. Guided by the slate sign 'Angle Tarn, Boredale Hause' go through and after 50 metres swing up right. Climb the steep bracken slope, keeping to the lower of the two adjacent paths to reach **Boredale Hause**. On meeting a path rising from the right, ford **Stonebarrow Gill** above the fold and bend south with the path, which has some pitching as it leads through a gill notch. As you reach a fine bird's-eye view down over the Goldrill Beck valley to Brothers Water, the path forks. Take the higher path. It runs under the summit bastion which you can then climb easily from the south.

Ascent from Deepdale Bridge 4

Via Boredale Hause →*3.2km/2 miles* ↑*400m/1310ft* ⏱*1hr 30min*

Another clear and accessible, if slightly less travelled, route to the top

2 From the road bridge follow the short lane east between cottages to a kissing-gate and cross the meadow by way of a stile, kissing-gate and finally a stile onto an open track. Keep on to cross the **Goldrill Beck** bridge and swing left to an acute track junction. Bear right signed 'Hartsop'. After 70 metres come to a further acute track junction and here break up left on a path engineered during the laying of the Hayeswater aqueduct pipeline. The ascent is only gradual for a while but then climbs more earnestly to reach **Stonebarrow Gill** and turn east and then south, falling into step with Route **1**.

Martindale

alehead

·577
The Nab

Ascent from Hartsop 3

Via Angletarn Beck → *3km/2 miles* ↑*440m/1445ft* ⏱ *1hr 40min*

A fascinating little-tried gorge ascent but a little steep to be suitable for every walker

3 Begin at the wooden signpost 30 metres west from the car park, and walk up a concrete roadway, via a gate, that provides access to the outside world for two elevated bungalows. Enjoy the views before dipping to a three-way fork. Keep ahead, guided by a yellow waymark, and pass Grey Rigg along a confined passage to a hand-gate. Here the path starts to decline on rocky ground and through a small ford of the ambitiously named **Eden Beck**. Go through a hand-gate and ford **Angletarn Beck** beneath an impressive set of leaping falls. (**4** Alternatively, avoid the early ascent by following the

Fall Crag and the upper falls of Angletarn Beck

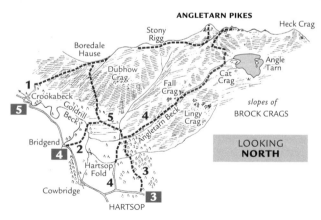

24

approach road to the car park back towards the main valley road and turning right just before at a white house, Langton Adventure Centre, along the
byroad signed 'Hartsop Fold'. After the chalet park this becomes a confined
path leading to a gate, ford and footbridge spanning Angletarn Beck.)

After crossing the beck, bear up right on the north bank to meet a fording lateral path. The ascent is obvious, although there are moments when
a steady step is needed as you work up the rocky flank that accompanies a
sequence of lovely cascades. **Fall Crag** eventually intervenes, and you are
obliged to ford the beck and carry on with a wall close left. As Angle Tarn
comes into view bear up left coming onto the regular path rising from the
tarn's shore. Go left then right to claim the northwest top and true summit.

Via Boredale Hause →*4.2km/2½ miles* ↑*450m/1475ft* ⏱*1hr 50min*
5 From the footbridge over **Angletarn Beck** follow on with the open track that
conceals the Hayeswater aqueduct pipeline. Walk along the line of partially-
channelled **Dubhow Beck** until a ford brings the path beside a wall. After a
while the path arrives at the point where the aqueduct begins its climb to
Boredale Hause. Join the rising track (with Route **1**).

Ascent from Sandwich **7** *off map* N or the Hause **8** *off map* N

Via Boredale Hause →*6km/3¾ miles* ↑*450m/1475ft* ⏱*2hr*

A back-door route from peaceful Boredale

6 From either start point set out along the minor country road into Boredale
to approach the furthest farmstead. A permissive path veers up right short of
the gate entry into **Boredale Head**, avoiding disturbing the environs of the
farmstead. Climb to a ford and contour above the tree-sheltered dwellings to
connect with the open bridle-track (which otherwise runs through the farmyard). The track comes up beneath a lead mine retaining wall to where the
old path hairpins right. Keep on through the stony gully, passing inspection
covers on the Hayeswater aqueduct, and arrive onto the undulating **Boredale
Hause**. Turn left on a bridle-path, being sure to keep right at a cairn, where
the route turns south to ford Freeze Beck. The path draws left onto the saddle.
Here find a path that bears right to avoid a peaty hollow and continue to the
summit ridge.

Ascent from Martindale 6

Via Bedafell Knott →*3km/2 miles* ↑*355m/1165ft* ⏱*1hr 45min*

Strike up the eastern flank of Beda Fall to a remote stretch of ridge-walk.

7 Walk 2.5km across and up Martindale from the church, along the road, to the road-end farm at **Dalehead**. Go right by the deer notice at the turning point, ford the gill and go through the hand-gate. Bear up left above the farmstead enclosure and go over a plank-bridge to rise with the green track and come beside the field-wall. Quickly spot a sign directing up on a lateral path, which is little more than a sheep trod at this point. After fording a tiny gill this becomes more substantial as it rises to a gate/stile where a fence meets the wall of an insular enclosure. The bridle-path mounts steadily on a long diagonal course. Ignore the quad track which takes a short-cut up the flank of the fell to the skyline ridge; it is better by far to keep with the age-old inter-dale route. High up, come upon the lower walls of a bothy overlooking Heck Cove. Reach the ridge at a tiny cairn at the cross-paths. Turn left and follow the lovely ridgeway south-southwest. Rise above **Heck Cove** to follow a

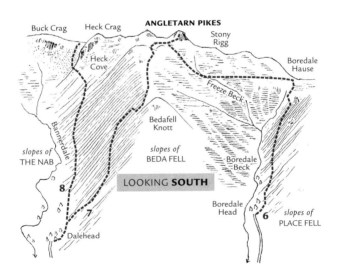

West top looking to the east top

comparatively minor branch path right, which quickly beelines to the shapely summit ridge of the west peak.

Via Heck Crag →3.8km/2½ miles ↑360m/1180ft ⏱1hr 50min

A scenically surreptitious ascent, ill suited for descent

8 Begin as Route **7**, but keep the intake wall close left on a level course. After a fence-gate the green-way leads on into **Bannerdale**, looking down on a sycamore-shaded field barn and then a ruin incorporated in the adjacent wall. The path drifts slightly away from the wall as it approaches a gate (do not go through). Traverse the steep slope with patches of scree on a very narrow trod – **watch your footing**. As next Buck Crag dominates the view ahead, the path climbs to come beside the higher section of the wall. Duly, and, after much anticipation, the path comes over the brow. Bear right with the regular path, forking right again to keep with the rising path going north as it heads back towards the top of **Heck Crag** (whose summit cairn may be visited). Depart from the ridge path left to reach the summit on a thin path over marshy ground.

The summit

The eastern top has a cairn, but concedes a few metres to the western top, which has the better view, too, with the fells surrounding Deepdale especially impressive.

Safe descents

The popular path skirting round to the S and E of the summit bastion (**6**) offers the best line of escape in inclement weather; veer north to reach Boredale Hause for Patterdale.

Ridge routes

Beda Fell →2.9km/1¾ miles ↓135m/445ft ↑80m/265ft ⌚40min
Head E off the summit ridge, crossing the marshy ground to join the ridge path. Now turn N, with a consistent path all the way. Watch your step in negotiating Bedafell Knott and in coping with some marshy ground on the approach to the summit.

The Helvellyn range in view across Angle Tarn

Heck Crag

Brock Crags →2.2km/1½ miles ↓105m/345ft ↑100m/330ft ⏱45min
Head E to unite with the path from Beda Fell. This path declines SE and, joining the popular path from Boredale Hause, runs on above the eastern shores
of Angle Tarn. Rising behind Buck Crag find a path forking right, short of an
intervening wall; this leads down to a gateway, but don't go through. Bear
right (W), with the wall first to the left and then right, before stepping over and
through a pool-filled hollow to reach the summit cairn.

Place Fell →2.7km/1¾ miles ↓180m/590ft ↑270m/885ft ⏱1hr 10min
Depart E to connect with the minor path crossing W–NW into the headstream of Freeze Beck. Coming down, merge with the bridle-path straddling
the Beda Fell ridge from Bannerdale. Stride over the undulating saddle of
Boredale Hause and link onto the reinforced path winding onto Place Fell.

Rest Dodd →3km/2 miles ↓90m/300ft ↑220m/720ft ⏱1hr 25min
Follow the path to Brock Crags. Here keep to the regular path, crossing a wall
and the awkward bedrock on top of Satura Crag, after which the path splits.
Take the left-hand option, rising from E to NE onto the grassy ridge. Keep
climbing where the path forks again, mounting over the brow to find the summit cairn lurking beyond a peaty step.

2 ARTHUR'S PIKE 533M/1749FT

Climb it from	Roehead **10**, Askham **11**, Helton **12**, Helton Fell **13** or Fusedale **9**
Character	A scarp-topping cairn with a stunning view over Ullswater
Fell-friendly route	1
Summit grid ref	NY 461 207
Link it with	Bonscale Pike or Loadpot Hill

Viewed from the foot of Ullswater Arthur's Pike has a strong identity, rising above a western shield of impregnable crags, all but lost from other angles. Strictly it is no more than the leading shoulder of Loadpot Hill but all the same, many's the walker who ventures to this grand little summit and turns tail, content with the view and rejecting the lure of Loadpot. Little wonder, for this is one of the most sensational spots above Ullswater and, being a good distance from a convenient road, it's a good leg stretch over open country to reach it from most approaches.

Askham, the furthest flung of those starting points, is one of Cumbria's prettiest villages, with well-tended cottages decorating an irregular green, two pubs, a village shop and a delectable tea room.

↑ *Arthur's Pike from Geordie's Crage*

Routes rise from Roehead (1–2), Askham (3) or Helton (4–5) or you can savour the perfect harmony of lake and fell to the full by taking the steamer from Pooley Bridge or Patterdale to Howtown and climbing via Bonscale Pike (6).

Ascent from Roehead 10

Via the Cockpit →*4.7km/3 miles* ↑*320m/1050ft* ⏱ *1hr 40min*

Spurn the Roman road to take a less-travelled route, just as high and dry, to the top.

1 Pass through the gate at the end of the single-track road and follow the open track all the way up to the cairn, almost on the brow. Here bear off right on the firm dry path which leads to **the Cockpit** stone circle. Keep right with the main path, immediately cross a ford and walk on to a second ford where you will find a small cairn that marks your point of departure (left) from the popular bridleway. After about a kilometre and a half this path inexplicably swerves left as the summit hoves into view – keep your eye on the knoll and pace off the trail to the top cutting through a maze of dog-walking paths and sheep tracks on your way.

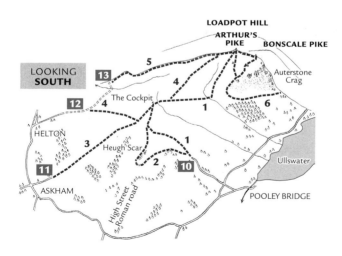

Via Heughscar Hill →5.8km/3½ miles ↑320m/1050ft ⊕2hr 10min

An attractive extension brings a bonus limestone hill-scarp into the equation.

2 A hundred metres above the gate on the open track find a rough trod breaking half-left up the slope and climbing to where the wall turns a corner under a bower of mature trees. The grass path continues northeast to join a better-used grass track beyond the prominent limestone outcrop of **Heugh Scar**. Bear up right easily onto the scarp-top and follow the brink, with evidence of surface clints, to where a path forks right, declining in the

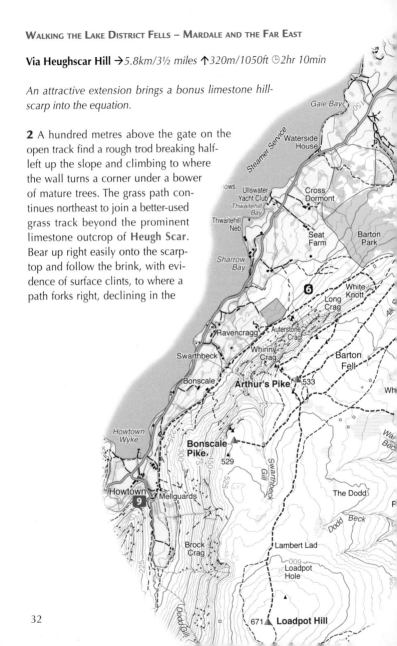

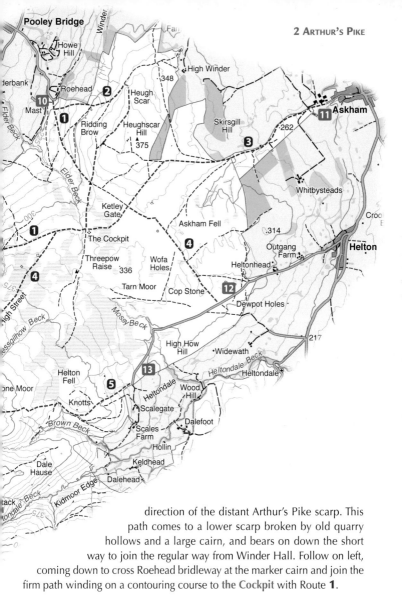

direction of the distant Arthur's Pike scarp. This
path comes to a lower scarp broken by old quarry
hollows and a large cairn, and bears on down the short
way to join the regular way from Winder Hall. Follow on left,
coming down to cross Roehead bridleway at the marker cairn and join the
firm path winding on a contouring course to **the Cockpit** with Route **1**.

Cairn circle on Moor Divock

Ascent from Askham 11

Via the Cockpit →*6.2km/4 miles* ↑*330m/1085ft* ⊕*2hr 25min*

Head southwest on clear tracks to the summit.

3 Walk southwest out of the village along the roadway, soon bearing right with the track, with a wall close on your right. Rise by a hipped stone barn and turn onto the green-way towards a gate onto the open common. Follow on with the close-cropped grass trod aiming for the tip of the distant shelter belt. A matter of 50 metres short of this, bear half-left with a declining green-way which leads down to a crossing of the Roehead–Helton bridleway. Go straight on across the marshy moor to join Route **1** at the Cockpit.

Ascent from Helton 12

Via the Cop Stone →*5km/3 miles* ↑*235m/770ft* ⊕*1hr 45min*

Wet boots are a price worth paying for this variant on the High Street approach from Helton.

4 A lovely green-turfed trail leads off from the open road, passing the enigmatic **Cop Stone**. The trail avoids sink holes and marshy ground until at a cross-ways it departs left, crossing a very marshy tract of moor to reach **the Cockpit**. Soon after the stone circle bear up left (southwest) on the historic bridleway of **High Street**, climbing at an easy gradient up **Barton Fell**. Take the right-hand fork to cross the infant **Aik Beck**, bending left towards the obvious summit, although paths seem to bypass it, and cut back north to reach the cairn.

Ascent from Helton Fell 13

Via Knotts →3.3km/2 miles ↑230m/755ft ⏱1hr 30min

The westward approach is the wildest but still well marked.

5 From the parking area on the fell road continue along the road until about 200 metres short of the gate into the enclosures leading to Scalegate and Scales Farm ('no through road' daubed on stone and private letter box). Follow the wall up (over marshy terrain), and as it bears left continue southwest, crossing over the low saddle of **Knotts** to run on right with a worn track to a ford bearing the lovely name of Jennie Brewster's Well. The regular passage of a shepherding quad bike ensures the old path is well marked as it heads up the grassy fell westward towards High Street (Route **4**) on **Whitestone Moor**. Head straight across – a strong sheep path invites, but dwindles to nothing when an intermediate cairned top comes into view. Aim to this and bear right on a tangible path to the summit.

Ascent from Fusedale 9

A really good fell circuit can be undertaken from Howtown by sweeping over Arthur's and Bonscale Pikes. Budget for another 3.5km for the return to and over Bonscale Pike or traverse to Pooley Bridge with Route 1 in reverse.

Via White Knott →5.5km/3½ miles ↑400m/1310ft ⏱2hr
6 Follow the popular bridleway as it passes through the gate at **Mellguards**. During the early part of its course the path runs beside a wall and crosses **Swarthbeck Gill** by a plank-bridge. (**Do not attempt** an ascent via the gorge

of Swarth Beck. There is one notable rock-wall that elevates the ascent into the realm of graded scrambling, so please keep well clear.) The continuing bridle-path is a delight and, although the summit is set back, the forward cairn is frequently visible. After a fenced tank and as the intake wall at the top of **Barton Park** draws near, find an old path veering right through the bracken. This swings up to round the north side of **White Knott** and leads onto the regular scarp-edge path.

On the near horizon you will see two cairns, and separate paths lead to each. The right-hand cairn is on the line leading to the viewpoint cairn, from where you head back up the fell southeast to reach the summit. The left-hand cairn is a sighter for the summit.

The summit

The summit with its modest cairn, is an ideal place to ponder the peace of the fells, but for a really good view stroll over to the northwesterly brink cairn above Whinny Crag. Pass a smaller cairn en route to the prime spot. The old beacon is suffering from being 'built too soon' and then exposed to the slings and arrows of a harsh climate and neglect.

The northwesterly viewpoint cairn overlooking Ullswater

Arthur's Pike scarp from above Roehead

Safe descents

Any path in the tangle of heather and rough moor grass that leads you NE (**1**, for Askham), or for that matter E (**5**, for the Helton fell road), will see you safe. The western scarp from Swarth Beck to White Knott has not one breach for sure descent.

Ridge route

Bonscale Pike → 1.3km/¾ mile ↓40m/130ft ↑35m/115ft ⏱25min
A clear path leads S then SW, angling easily into the upper valley of Swarthbeck Gill by the remains of a wash-fold. Stepping through the rushes, rise gently W to reach the cairn on the grassy summit.

Loadpot Hill → 2.7km/1¾ miles ↓25m/50ft ↑160m/525ft ⏱45min
Walk S to join a good path which duly unites with the Roman road on a gently swelling ridge. Some 100 metres after passing Lambert Lad (a standing stone set in the old track groove) bear left, climbing on the regular ridge path to reach the OS column on the plateau top.

3 BEDA FELL 509M/1670FT

Climb it from	The Hause **8**, Martindale **6** or Sandwick **7**
Character	Engaging ridge rising in the midst of Martindale
Fell-friendly route	1
Summit grid ref	NY 429 172
Link it with	Angletarn Pikes

Rising between the Howegrain Beck valley and secretive Boredale on a long spur ridge from Angletarn Pikes, Beda Fell lies in the heart of Martindale – and the impulse to climb it is hard to resist. This characterful peak is best comprehended from Brownthwaite Crag, from where its craggy eastern face is prominent, although Hallin Fell and Steel Knotts are equally good vantage points.

Filling the foreground as you look south from the summit, the Nab and its bounding dales, Rampsgill Beck and Bannerdale Beck are out of bounds. The Martindale Deer Forest is the breeding ground of the oldest native red deer herd in England – something we all should cherish and leave undisturbed.

Although the fell is a ridge climb pure and simple, it also offers several lateral connections for the explorer, with the tapered northern extension over Winter Crag a delight to tramp. Paths straddle this portion of the ridge in two places (3

↑ *Beda Fell from Hause Farm*

and 4), while where the fell merges with the main massif a bridle-path (5) slants up from Dalehead on course for Boredale Hause, giving scope for an entertaining round trip off the ridge by Boredale (6).

Ascent from the Hause 8

Via Winter Crag →2.7km/1¾ miles ↑330m/1085ft ⏱1hr 15min

The direct route up the north ridge

1 To minimise your time on tarmac, take the footpath immediately on the right before the road descends to Martindale, signed 'Doe Green'. This leads by a wall-stile and crosses a pasture above Hause Farm to a high wall-stile. After the next kissing-gate head downhill on the path to rejoin the road. Cross the bridge and on the rise come onto the left-hand bank following the wall up to the track. Go left, signed 'Mauldslack'. As the walled lane opens on the right, climb up by the wall to reach the low ridge-top. Turn left and climb south onto **Winter Crag**, a real treat although the bottom section of path can be hard to find when the bracken is high. A modest rock groove is the only challenge. Follow the ridge path to the highest ground.

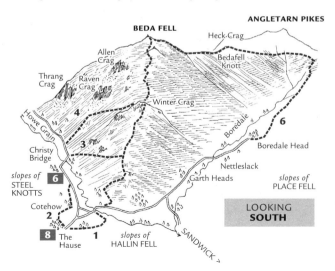

39

'New' church–old church link path →*0.9km/½ mile* ↑*15m/50ft* ⏱*20min*

A handsome alternative start, connecting to the open common beside the old church

2 Pass up by St Peter's Church, keeping the wall close right, rounding a bluff to a gate. Once the brief lane opens, keep left, coming by a seat to head over the access track to **Cotehow** (cottage). Pass on beside the wall to a gate and soon join the dale road advancing into the open meadow.

Ascent from Martindale 6

Join the north ridge either side of Winter Crag more directly by starting from the open common beside the ancient church of St Martin.

Via Winter Crag →*2.3km/1½ miles* ↑*325m/1065ft* ⏱*45min*
3 Follow the road south to cross **Christy Bridge** and bear off the road as you pass the farmstead. Ignore the slate sign 'bridle-path to Sandwick', and keep up and angle right above the wall with crags close above. The clear path leads up onto the ridge precisely at the metal seat, turning left to accompany the ridge and follow Route **2** over the crest of **Winter Crag**.

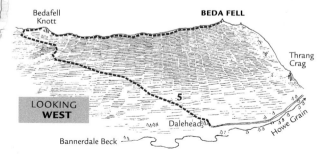

41

St Martin's Church backed by Winter Crag

Via Nickles →*1.8km/1 mile* ↑*320m/1050ft* ⏲*1hr*

4 A second option is to stay with the road, passing a roadside barn (Knicklethorns). As the wall is lost on the right, angle up the slope, with the path coming above a wall. Here switch up right to the ridge (above a knoll labelled **Nickles** on OS maps), with the only hindrance the bracken in summer.

Via Bedafell Knott →*3.5km/2¼ miles* ↑*350m/1150ft* ⏲*1hr 25min*

5 Cross **Christy Bridge** and follow the dale road by Henhow and Thrang Crag Farm to reach **Dalehead**. Here a deer conservation information panel draws attention to the paths to follow.

Walk on through the farmyard via the gates following the rising track, with the intake wall close left. The green path moves up from the wall as the last tree is passed and reaches a gate/stile in a fence above a higher walled enclosure. The drove-path forges on southwest up the flank of Beda Fell. Higher up the path detours round a small ruin – a fine place for a walkers' bothy – to reach the skyline. Turn right (northeast) following the delightful spine of the ridge over **Bedafell Knott** to reach the high point.

Ascent from Sandwick 7

Via Boredale Head →*7.8km/5 miles* ↑*470m/1540ft* ⏲*2hr 30min*

Tramp into Boredale to take in the full sweep of the fell from Boredale Hause.

6 Start by following the Boredale valley road for about three and a half kilometres. Short of the farm gate bend up the bank right with a waymarked permissive path that fords a gill directly above **Boredale Head** farm. The path contours above the intake wall to reconnect with the dale bridleway running on freely southwestward towards the dale head. As the path steepens look for the retaining bank of an old mine up to the right. The track, now rough underfoot, avoids a 'retired' zig-zag path and climbs through a natural cutting with inspection covers for the Hayeswater aqueduct. Reaching the broad grassy saddle of **Boredale Hause**, swing left to join the bridle-path from Patterdale. This fords **Freeze Beck** and runs on northeast high above a steep declivity to connect with the ridge path from Angletarn Pikes at a small cairn. Turn left – continuing northeast – glancing over the left shoulder of **Bedafell Knott** and heading along the roller-coaster ridge to the summit.

Alcove near the summit

The summit

Known as Beda Head, the summit knoll is a popular spot to pause right in the midst of the Martindale valleys, although the views are perhaps not as far-ranging as might be expected. This spot is perfect for anyone who values peace and quiet in a high place. A ragged cairn occupies the highest point.

Safe descents

Sizeable crags lie in wait down the northeastern slopes, so stick unwaveringly to the ridge path (N, **3** or SW, **6**) in poor weather. Winter Crag adds interest to the northern descent, without threatening real hazard, although even it can be avoided via a path that dips off the ridge, right, at the foot of the primary descent.

Beda Fell from Steel Knotts

Ridge route

Angletarn Pikes →*2.9km/1¾ miles* ↓*80m/265ft* ↑*135m/445ft* ⏱*45min*
The ridge path leads confidently SSW, level for a time but including a couple of notable rises, especially Bedafell Knott, after which it crosses the ridge-straddling bridle-path at a small cairn. Continue, watching for the chiselled profile of the western summit. Coming above Heck Cove follow a comparatively minor branch path right which beelines to the shapely summit ridge.

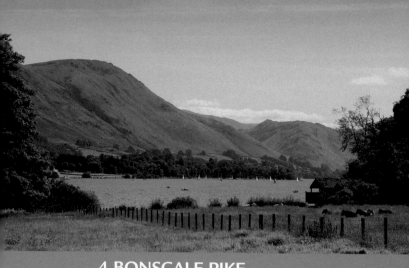

4 BONSCALE PIKE 529M/1736FT

Climb it from	Fusedale **9**
Character	A mirror image of Arthur's Pike with stunning views from the summit
Fell-friendly route	2
Summit grid ref	NY 453 201
Link it with	Arthur's Pike or Loadpot Hill

Viewed from Ullswater, and best of all from Hallin Fell, there is no doubt that Bonscale Pike is handsome and the summit views make it a climb for landscape connoisseurs. But it is a front, a facade without back or sides, a shoulder of Loadpot Hill separated from escarpment compatriot Arthur's Pike by one of the district's most forbidding ravines, Swarthbeck Gill, a foray into whose dark depths is not be recommended for even the most fervent of fellwanderers.

The Howtown Hotel beneath the slopes of the Pike is a bit of a Lakeland institution – a 17th-century farmhouse set in an idyllic spot and run as a hotel by the Baldry family for over 120 years. It has recently been enhanced from the viewpoint of day trippers with the addition of a public bar and charming tea room.

There are several lines of ascent, all of which stem from Howtown and are thus perfect as an accompaniment to a cruise on an Ullswater 'steamer', with every fare contributing to local conservation work, including repair and improvement of the footpaths.

Ascent from Fusedale 9

Three short climbs tackle the steep gradient of the western flank from different angles.

Via Mellguards →*1.9km/1¼ miles* ↑*360m/1180ft* ⊕*1hr*

1 From the four-way signpost leave the open road at once to cross the clapper-bridge spanning Fusedale Beck and rise within the walled lane to a gate entering the gravel drive to **Mellguards**, the prominent white house. Go through the gate by the house door and at once bear up right, following the intake wall to continue a short distance beyond where it bends right. Turn hard left in a rising groove leading onto a shoulder, and here find an

old drove-path steering back up to the right again. This path climbs above the gill and peters out on the grassy rise to the plateau. Turn left (due north) when you reach the ridge path to reach the summit.

Via the under-scarp
→*1.7km/1 mile*
↑*350m/1150ft* ⊕*1hr*

Three options present themselves at the end of this twist on Route 1.

2 Start with Route **1** but, from the second sharp bend north-northeast beyond the

Lower beacon with Sharrow Bay Hotel in the distance

wall-corner, continue to where
the fell shoulder broadens
further and passes a cairn
set on a boulder. Ignore

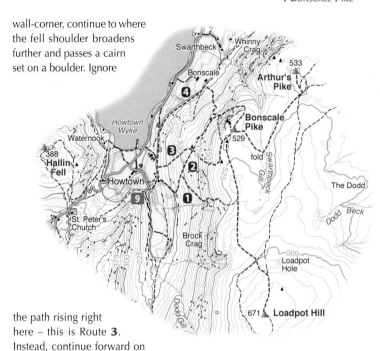

the path rising right
here – this is Route **3**.
Instead, continue forward on
a largely contouring line passing a second cairn among boulders to meet a
rising groove, a seldom-followed drove. Follow this by a small cairn.

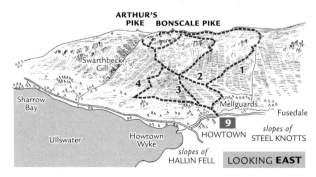

47

From here there are three ways to reach the summit. The first option is to bend right as a prominent headland become visible above and, keeping the boulder field to the left, climb onto this headland, now with a natural groove, onto the ridge. Turn left to reach the summit. The second option is to continue until both beacon pillars become visible and then turn right, this time following a wide grassy passage up between two crags to reach the lower beacon. The third option continues the furthest to pass the end cliff and follow round the ridge-end to find easy ground before swinging back right to the summit.

Via the shoulder route → *1.6km/1 mile* ↑*360m/1180ft* ⏱*1hr*

This route's one great virtue is the view back to the craggy Steel Knotts ridge and Hallin Fell above Howtown Wyke (the bay with the steamer jetty).

3 Start with Route **1**, but go through the gate beside **Mellguards** and follow the regular level bridleway beside the wall. Some 60 metres after passing the power-line pole step right, just before a green inspection cover. A popular path climbs directly (not a good way down because this initial bracken-clad bank is so steep). Two steepish sections prove it inferior to Route 1, as pigeon-hole erosion steps (bare level patches on grassy slopes from repeated footfall in the same places) are developing. Coming onto the grassy alp you reach a boulder with a cairn perched on top. Continue uphill with the scree slope to the left. The groove latterly zig-zags to reach the skyline, curving left by a cairn in the rushes to contour along the scarp edge to the summit.

Via the old drove → *2.2km/1½ miles* ↑*370m/1215ft* ⏱*1hr 10min*

Bonscale Pike from the Portland boat house, Waterfoot

A steep alternative, this route is invariably 'happened upon' in descent when the lateral path of Route 2 is missed.

4 Start with Route **1** but then follow the level bridleway from the **Mellguards** gate beside the intake wall to pass the base of a walled copse.

Some 20 metres before a ruined barn over the adjacent intake wall, with the crags seen high above, climb the steep fellside, finding the beginnings of the zig-zag drove which duly reaches Route **2** as the upper tier of crags comes close. Take any three of the routes available to the summit from here.

Swarthbeck ravine from Bennethead

The summit

The actual summit of this fell is uncertain. There are cairns on two knolls above the beacons, yet the ground continues to rise behind them. Most walkers will be intent on surveying Ullswater from the beacon cairns – and why not... it is an uplifting sight, and time should certainly be spent in unhurried admiration.

Safe descents

Avoid the immediate craggy ground beneath the summit. Follow the scarp-top path S (**2**) to where it heads down, thereby keeping to consistently grassy terrain. For all the steepness, you are assured of comfortable footing all the way down to Howtown Hotel and the steamer jetty.

Ridge routes

Arthur's Pike → *1.3km/¾ mile* ↓*35m/115ft* ↑*40m/130ft* ◷*20min*
A definite path leads E then SE to ford Swarthbeck Gill at an old wash-fold, then trends NNE to gain the summit cairn.

Loadpot Hill → *2km/1¼ miles* ↓*20m/65ft* ↑*165m/540ft* ◷*40min*
Follow the path SW and then S. This dips and rises onto a damp shoulder above Brock Crag, then slants SE, climbing to cross High Street and connect with the regular ridge path to the summit.

5 BRANSTREE 713M/2339FT

Climb it from	Mardale Head **19**, Mardale Banks **18**, Swindale **20**, Wet Sleddale **21** or Sadgill **31**
Character	A steep sentinel above the east side of Gatescarth Pass
Fell-friendly route	2
Summit grid ref	NY 487 103
Link it with	Selside Pike or Tarn Crag

Branstree is certainly steep when viewed from Haweswater perspectives, the actual summit, however, overshadowed by two stately cairns on Artlecrag Pike, an imposing block of vertically split slate a short distance to the northeast. From elsewhere it is less striking but, together with High Howes, a sizeable presence dividing the southern reaches of Haweswater from the upper end of watery Mosedale.

The only dwelling associated with the fell, Mosedale Cottage, is a treasure for seekers after simple lodgings in a wild setting. This former quarry-manager's and shepherds' abode has been restored by local enthusiasts from the Mountain Bothies Association and should be appreciated and respected. Above it looms a massive slate quarry, long derelict. With no railway or easy line of transport,

↑ *Branstree from Little Harter Fell*

stone hauling must always have been a major undertaking from this remote dale head.

Invariably the fell ascent is combined with Selside Pike, whether begun from Mardale Head (1 or 2), Swindale or Wet Sleddale (3–6) or Longsleddale (7 and 8).

Ascent from Mardale Head 19 or Mardale Banks 18

Via Hopegill Beck →*3.8km/2½ miles* ↑*485m/1590ft* ⏲*1hr 45min*

A steep and largely pathless approach to keep you on your toes

1 Walk along the road from the Mardale Head car park. Just before the road bridge spanning **Hopegill Beck** go through the hand-gate on the right to be confronted by a chaos of beck, boulders and trees. At once switch right to follow an obvious groove drove-path. This winds up, passing under the cheek of the **Hollow Stone**, a large tilted boulder, and progresses steadily, with the roar of the long mare's-tail cascades a constant accompaniment. When the bracken is up, getting close to the waterfalls is impossible. At other times you can do it but the gorge is too narrow for casual inspection. Higher up, as the slope eases, come by two ruins – the upper has the taller walls. The path becomes far less certain from this point on. After passing a small fold keep to the right of a great swathe of damp tussocks, with a large wash-fold close

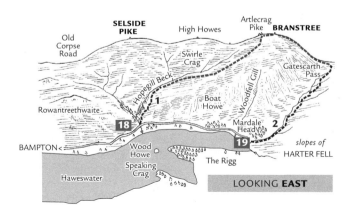

LOOKING **EAST**

to the beck confluence. There is no path, nor need of one, on the steady pull up the north ridge. Pause periodically to enjoy the view behind you. Two handsome cairns greet you on the **Artlecrag Pike** brow. The altogether less impressive summit lies further back (southwest), near the fence/wall junction.

Via Gatescarth Pass →2.7km/1¾ miles ↑460m/1510ft ⏱1hr 25min

Unlike most routes in the area this track has been engineered to cope as well as possible with occasional use by 4x4s.

2 From the three-way signpost follow the left-hand arm signed 'Public Byway Gatescarth Pass'. The track rises via a gate in harmony with **Gatescarth Beck** and with two stretches of multiple hairpins climbing to the brow. At your comfort, after the new path veers right and before the gate in the saddle-straddling fence, break off left to wade through the marshy flats and join the rising fence that climbs uneventfully to the summit plateau.

Ascent from Swindale 20 *off map N*

Via Mosedale →8.2km/5 miles ↑560m/1840ft ⏱2hr 45min

Start down marshy Mosedale on this long approach but escape up right over Howes before the worst of it!

Mosedale Cottage

3 Follow the road by Truss Gap to the road-end at **Swindale Head**. Continue within the gated drove-way, passing the stone barns by an irregular walled lane. After a gate/wall-stile cross the beck and follow the moraine track, soon coming along a narrow section between the great basin of **Dodd Bottom**, clearly once the location of a considerable tarn, and

Swindale Beck. The path swings up the rising moraine, revealing the drama of this wild sanctuary, with the contrasting ravines of **Forces Falls** (left) and **Hobgrumble** spilling almost straight down into Dodd

Swindale Head

Brown Howe

502

High Loup

Old Corpse Road

High Birkin Knott

3

The Knott

Wood Howe

18

Rowantreethwaite Gill

Selside End

Simon Stone

281

Hollow Stone

Mardale Common

Dodd Bottom

The Rigg

Swine Crag

Boat Howe

Selside Pike

655

Geordie Greathead Crag

Nabs Crag

Forces Falls

Mardale Head

19

Brant Street

Hopgill Beck

Swirle Crag

Captain Whelter Bog

Hobgrumble

Mosedale Beck

2

Dodder Gill

Artlecrag Pike

survey post

673

High Howes

Howes

5

410

713 ▲ **Branstree**

Mosedale Quarry (dis)

6

Gatesgarth Beck

Harter Fell

582

Gatesrth Pass

Selside Brow

Mosedale Cottage

Great Grain Gill

442

Mosedale

Adam Seat ▲ 666

Wren Gill

Brownhowe Bottom

8

Seavy Side

Brunt Tongue

Wrengill Quarry (dis)

423

Steel Rigg

Steel Pike

survey post

Tarn Crag ▲ 664

Harrop Pike

637

595

Raven Crag

7

River

Greycrag Tarn

53

Bottom and drawing walkers' attention. The old bridleway makes several sharp hairpin turns to negotiate the rough dale head slope. Above, the marshy ground is a

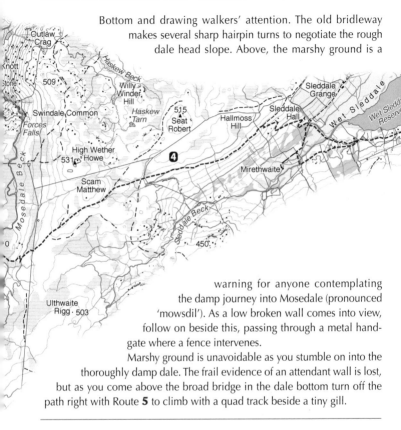

warning for anyone contemplating the damp journey into Mosedale (pronounced 'mowsdil'). As a low broken wall comes into view, follow on beside this, passing through a metal hand-gate where a fence intervenes.

Marshy ground is unavoidable as you stumble on into the thoroughly damp dale. The frail evidence of an attendant wall is lost, but as you come above the broad bridge in the dale bottom turn off the path right with Route **5** to climb with a quad track beside a tiny gill.

Ascent from Wet Sleddale 21

Via Sleddale Hall to Mosedale footbridge →*5.6km/3½ miles* ↑*230m/755ft* ⏲*2hr*

An ambitious and thoroughly rewarding approach into Mosedale, from which two lines of ultimate ascent enable you to loop over the summit for a back-tracking return

54

4 Follow the open track directly through gates. When you reach the head of the reservoir by a ruin there is a choice. The footpath heads on over the footbridge with matching handrails and veers right to cross a wall ladder-stile and a fence-stile to a crude set of stepping-stones over **Sleddale Beck**. After any rain the second stone will be submerged and therefore challenging to negotiate, as the water is deep. In which case the

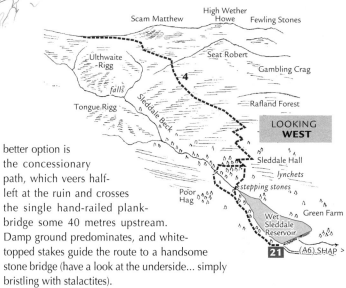

better option is the concessionary path, which veers half-left at the ruin and crosses the single hand-railed plank-bridge some 40 metres upstream. Damp ground predominates, and white-topped stakes guide the route to a handsome stone bridge (have a look at the underside... simply bristling with stalactites).

Ascend the pasture to a fence-stile and bear right, with the track winding up through the deer-fenced woodland. Coming to a barn and sheep pens, bear left with the open track which winds up to **Sleddale Hall**, and keep on the track as it continues hairpinning up the pasture to a gate. Now contouring on, the track advances well above the dale beck and the great cascades at its head. The next gate brings the track over the undulating shoulder of **Scam Matthew**, and after merging with a quad track it arrives at a gate overlooking Mosedale. Follow the zig-zag path down inevitably damp slopes to cross the broad plank-bridge spanning **Mosedale Beck**. Routes **5** and **6** spring from this point.

Wet Sleddale reservoir from above Sleddale Hall

Via High Howes →4km/3½ miles ↑340m/1115ft ⏱2hr 15min

The direct and largely pathless approach

5 Head straight across the valley, climbing to the right of a minor gill with crags up to the right. This grass path leads to a rocky crest with a cairn (at 544m). Ascend the Howes ridge southwest, weaving through the easy outcropping to find a tarn and a delightful rock-pool, while also enjoying fine views right down into the upland hollow of Hobgrumble Beck and through to Swindale Head. The ridge above is less enchanting, with a steady plod leading past a tiny memorial stone, 'Edward Dodds 1911', to reach the minor cairn on **High Howes** between Selside Pike and Branstree. At last a path appears – follow this west, slipping between a pair of tarns to encounter the Haweswater aqueduct survey post, a robust stone-built structure whose only purpose now is as a landmark. The path continues to cross the fence and clamber up to the two fine cairns on **Artlecrag Pike**. The summit lies a further 200 metres southwest.

BRANSTREE High Howes **SELSIDE PIKE** LOOKING **WEST**

Selside Brow 6 5 Geordie Greathead Crag Old Corpse Road

Howes Hobgrumble Gill Nabs Crag Swindale Head 3

Mosedale Cottage

slopes of TARN CRAG 4 *bridleway from Wet Sleddale* Forces Falls Swindale Beck

Via Mosedale Cottage →4.4km/2¾ miles ↑330m/1085ft ⏱1hr 50min

Longer but along tracks, this might make a more reliable return route.

6 From the **Mosedale Beck** bridge bear left and duly engage in a sequence of damp and pool-challenged sections of track which lead via gates to **Mosedale Cottage**. The ford of **Great Grain Gill** offers the biggest obstacle just short of the bothy. Above the bothy looms the spoil bank of a mighty slate quarry.

Passing on beyond the dwelling and the sheltering conifers, note a fork in the ways. The bridleway keeps low, slanting left through the wild corridor at the head of the dale to reach a gate. Turn right and ascend beside the fence or, alternatively, keep company with the rising quad track that comes onto a shoulder. The track is lost, with a sheep path your only guide, but you can follow this on a contouring course to reach the point where the rising fence meets a wall. Cross the fence and join the path to follow the wall to the fence-stile leading onto the summit.

Edward Dodds memorial on High Howes

Ascent from Sadgill 31 *off map S*

Two dramatic approaches from Longsleddale

Via Gatescarth Pass →*5km/3 miles* ↑*540m/1770ft* ⏱*2hr 15min*
7 Follow the drove-lane up the dramatic mountain corridor at the head of Longsleddale. Periodically exposed to wash-out damage, the lane passes close to the impressive **Buckbarrow Crag** before switching up, keeping close to a fine set of cascades which are hard to see from within the walled lane. Keep to the track via two gates, zig-zagging up the slope north to **Gatescarth Pass**. Go through the gate in the saddle and, to avoid the worst of the marsh, stride on a further 50 metres before veering right and duly reconnecting with the fence to ascend northeast to the summit.

Via Selside Brow →*5.3km/3¼ miles* ↑*530m/1740ft* ⏲*2hr 15min*

8 Follow Route **7** past **Buckbarrow Crag** and the cascades and then, after the first gate, walk over to a signpost, short of the sheep-pens. Follow this to head right over a ford and up the periodically marshy **Brownhowe Bottom** to the gate in the broad saddle. Do not go through, but instead walk up left beside the fence at the angle. The fence becomes a wall rising up **Selside Brow** to the stile at the top.

The summit

A circular concrete OS disc pinpoints the actual summit. A fence straddles the summit dome, running from Gatescarth Pass diagonally towards Selside Pike, while a wall leads towards the top from the southeast. A few stones make up the cairn but all else is grass. The best views are to be had from the western edge of the summit plateau, from where Harter Fell, Mardale Ill Bell and High Street are seen to perfection.

Cairn on Artlecrag Pike (photo: Maggie Allan)

Safe descents

The ridge fence leads SW (**7**) direct to Gatescarth Pass, a secure route for Mardale Head and Longsleddale. The wall from the fence/wall junction leads equally easily down SE (**8**) to the marshy hollow at the head of Mosedale, from where it is simple enough to reach Longsleddale by curving SW through Brownhowe Bottom to join the Gatescarth track. Mosedale (E, **5**) is an altogether damper experience, en route to Swindale, although Mosedale Cottage is a valuable refuge only a kilometre away.

Ridge routes

Selside Pike →2km/1¼ miles ↓115m/375ft ↑55m/185ft ⊕30min

Summit Ordnance Survey ring

Head NE to the pair of sturdy cairns marking Artlecrag Pike, and from there bear gradually right to accompany the ridge fence. You have two options: in mist stick resolutely beside the fence to the shelter-cairn on Selside Pike; on a fine day, step over the plain wire fence, pass the stone survey frame and splice through the attractive pair of tarns onto the grassy ridge of High Howes. Pass on from the summit cairn, with the evident path continuing NE via the peaty depression of Captain Whelter Bog and climbing to the turn in the fence on the summit.

Tarn Crag →2.6km/1½ miles ↓205m/675ft ↑155m/510ft ⊕45min

Head SE, cross the fence-stile and follow the wall down Selside Brow, latterly in the company of a fence, to cross the broad saddle rising over peat groughs, keeping the fence close left. Higher up cross a stile on a consistent path S to the summit.

6 BROCK CRAGS 561M/1841FT

Climb it from	Hartsop 3
Character	Knobbly shoulder high above Low Hartsop
Fell-friendly route	4
Summit grid ref	NY 417 137
Link it with	Angletarn Pikes or Rest Dodd

While some fells are gifted as fine subjects to look at, Brock Crags is far more a place to look from. For all its comparatively lowly height, the summit situation, above Hartsop, overlooking the confluence of Hayeswater and Pasture Becks and the broad Goldrill vale, is scenically superb. The southern slopes of the fell are dotted with thorn, while the western declivity, sheltered by Lingy Crag, is richly wooded.

The hamlet of Low Hartsop is invariably shortened to Hartsop in conversation, the farming settlement of High Hartsop, upstream from Brothers Water, having long been wiped from maps. The fell shares custody of exquisite Angle Tarn – and its three romantic islets and often-bustling birdlife – with the Pikes of that name, as well as the small herd of red deer that frequent the quieter slopes.

↑ *Brock Crags from Brothers Water (photo: Maggie Allan)*

Most walkers will content themselves with gaining the ridge by following the grassy groove up the southern flank of the fell, whichever way they start their expedition from Hartsop, but the more curious few will love the testing gradient of the wall that beetles straight up (5) or the adventurous climb up Angletarn Beck (1 or 2).

Ascent from Hartsop 3

Via Angletarn Beck →2.6km/1½ miles ↑430m/1410ft ⏱1hr 20min

No approach is more exciting than the intimate climb by Angletarn Beck.

1 Begin at the wooden signpost 30 metres west from the car park, and walk up a concrete roadway, via a gate, that provides access to the outside world for two elevated bungalows. Enjoy the views before dipping to a three-way fork. Keep ahead, guided by a yellow waymark, and pass Grey Rigg along a confined passage to a hand-gate. Here the path starts to decline on rocky ground and through a small ford of the ambitiously named **Eden Beck**. Go through a hand-gate and ford **Angletarn Beck** beneath an

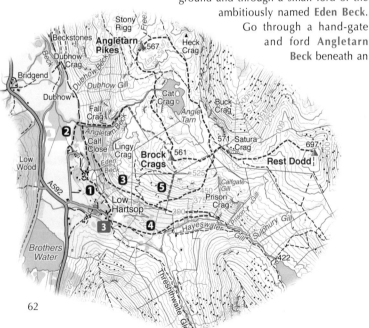

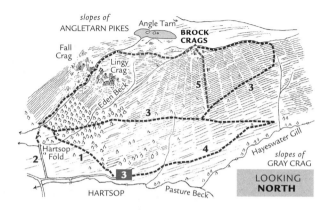

impressive set of leaping falls. (**2** Alternatively, avoid the early ascent by following the approach road to the car park back towards the main valley road and turning right just before at a white house, Langton Adventure Centre, along the byroad signed 'Hartsop Fold'. After the chalet park this becomes a confined path leading to a gate, ford and footbridge spanning Angletarn Beck.)

Turn right to walk up beside the beck. The ascent is obvious, although there are moments when a steady step is required as you work up the rocky flank, accompanied by a sequence of lovely cascades. **Fall Crag** eventually intervenes, and walkers are obliged to ford and progress with the wall close left. At a wall junction turn right

Fall Crag and Angletarn Beck

(southeast) and follow this wall over damp fell. Approaching the next wall junction, bear left to avoid marshy ground and pass through a narrow wall-gap (shepherding gate) and complete the ascent up the grassy bank.

Myers Head Mine wheel-pit remains (photo: Maggie Allan)

Via the southern slope →3.2km/2 miles ↑430m/1410ft ⏱1hr 30min

The popular ascent, via the groove on the southern flank of the fell, can be reached by two lines of approach. This way has one further variant, the steep direct climb beside the wall direct to the summit, which is surprisingly entertaining as well as good for the legs and lungs!

3 Start in common with Route **1** and after fording **Eden Beck** make a sharp turn right on a rising path. This is the course of the Hayeswater aqueduct, a loose gravel path rising through the rocky Calf Close wood. The path eases and comes along the open fellside as a green-way via a kissing-gate, now with a fence right, to reach the point where an old drove-path veers up the fellside northeastward. (**4** This point can also be reached from the opposite direction by following the dale track east from the car park, passing the sheep-pens by a gate. After the cattle grid, keep with the ribbon of tarmac as it rises with the wall left and passes through a gate en route to the waterworks building. Just short of the building make an acute left turn and follow a green-way that con-tours back along the fellside to come above the walled enclosures.)

Take the drove-path through a gap in a wall rising steeply up the fell to mount at a steady trajectory. The path comes onto the ridge-top, slipping through an old fence-line gate and over a broken wall to reach an old gate-way in a further wall. Go through and, with paths in three directions, turn left. The ridge path steps over the next wall, now with a wall right, then veers right over a low broken wall and advances through a damp peaty hollow, with two distinct pools, to reach the summit cairn.

Via south slope direct →2.5km/1½ miles ↑380m/1245ft ⏲1hr 10min

The sterner direct option

5 Follow Route **3** or **4** as far as the wall-gap at the start of the drove-path, and turn left to climb the grass slope, keeping the unsurprisingly intermittent wall close right. A bold volcanic buttress marks the end of the steep ground and offers a good spot to pause and admire the view back. As the wall drifts right, bear up half-left to pass a rock pool and reach the summit.

The summit

A most satisfying, if little-visited, viewpoint. A grassy seat beside a modest cairn is a place of peace and scenic pleasure, given a clement day. The fells around Dove and Deep Dales claim greatest attention, although the chiselled ridge of Gray Crag weighs in to the south, to captivate your camera.

Safe descents

The best option in poor weather is to follow the ridge path E (**3**) by the pool hollow. Cross a wall and a second wall to come to a shallow dip, where a path veers S, angling naturally down the slope SW. At the foot turn left with the green-way to join the waterworks' tarmac roadway, going sharp right with this down to Hartsop.

Ridge routes

Angletarn Pikes →2.2km/1½ miles ↓100m/330ft ↑105m/345ft ⏲40min
There are two options. The more direct heads N, passing through a wall-gap and skirting to the left of Cat Crag to come round to where the tarn outflow is forded at the broken wall-end. It rises to the regular path, slanting up left onto

Summit cairn (photo: Maggie Allan)

the rocky-ribbed summit – but this is not strictly the ridge route. The natural line is to go E, slipping through the pooled hollow and over and then alongside a broken wall. After stepping over a second lateral wall come down into a shallow hollow and bear left. This path leads onto the popular path trending NNW above the eastern shores of Angle Tarn. Take the right-hand fork level with the tarn's promontory, rising until you are level with Heck Crag's top, then swing left to reach the narrow rocky ridge of the summit over marshy ground.

Rest Dodd →*1.8km/1 miles* ↓*20m/65ft* ↑*155m/510ft* ⏲*40min*
Head E with the ridge path through the pooled hollow and over a broken wall. Keep with the line of the wall through a depression and rise to join the main ridge path from Angle Tarn at a gateway. Cross the bedrock top of Satura Crag and, as this dips, keep with the left-hand path mounting onto the grassy subsidiary ridge. At the crest the path swings SE, climbing to the brow. A peat step later and you are by the summit cairn.

7 CAUDALE MOOR 764M/2507FT

Climb it from	Hartsop **3**, Caudale Bridge **2**, Kirkstone Pass **1**, Woundale **36** or Town Head **37**
Character	Great confluence of ridges between Kirkstone Pass and Threshthwaite Mouth
Fell-friendly route	5
Summit grid ref	NY 419 100
Link it with	Hartsop Dodd or Thornthwaite Crag

Caudale Moor is one of a kind. Of its four biggest ridges only the one running north to Hartsop is sufficiently abrupt to have been annexed as a separate fell, Hartsop Dodd. To the west two mighty ridges embrace peaceful Woundale and historic Caudale with its high-sited quarry ruins to explore, while the east ridge separates wild Threshthwaite Glen, which fully merits its Scottish resonance, from a more open southern approach, up Trout Beck.

Take a few minutes out to peruse the dilapidated remnants of Caudale Quarry – ruined works sheds, a collapsed adit and much slate spoil tell their own tale of times past. The opening of this quarry coincided with the wholesale transition

↑ *Caudale Moor from Green Side*

from heather thatch to stone-tiled roofs on all levels of building and would have been initiated by the Dalemain Estate, at the northern end of Ullswater.

A multitude of soaring ridges and enticing dale-floor ascents of Caudale Moor compete for walkers' attention, with the Kirkstone Pass offering attractive elevated starts particularly from the Inn (5) but also from Woundale (6–9).

Ascent from Hartsop 3

Via Threshthwaite Cove →4.4km/2¾ miles ↑590m/1935ft ⏱2hr 15min

The natural line up this wild mountain glen

1 Exit the car park and bear immediately right, crossing Walker Bridge. Follow the gated track leading into the **Pasture Beck** valley. As you enter Threshthwaite Cove pitching is evident, most noticeably on the steep head-wall climb to **Threshthwaite Mouth**. Turn sharply up right, negotiating minor rocky steps to reach the plateau and the summit.

Via Hartsop Dodd →3.5km/2¼ miles ↑610m/2000ft ⏱2hr 20min

Climb abruptly over Hartsop Dodd to follow the continuing ridge direct to the summit.

2 Leave the car park and bear right crossing Walker Bridge. After the next gate/ladder-stile, where the track swings left, step off onto the pasture and rise with the wall close right to a stile at the wall junction. Continue with some worn and some pitched hairpins to the top of the wall. The path persists up the steep blunt ridge. In time the butt end of the ridge wall is encountered, leading to the stake marking the top of **Hartsop Dodd**. Follow the ridge wall south-southeast to the summit from here.

Ascent from Caudale Bridge 2

Via Caudale Beck →3km/2 miles ↑580m/1905ft ⏱2hr

Follow the old quarry path up the northwest spur.

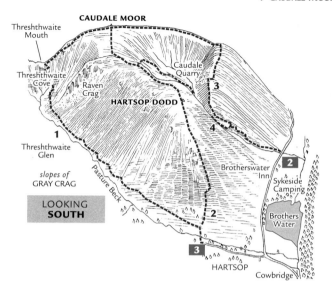

3 Walk up to the road bridge to find, up the bank above the gate, a wall-stile. Walk up on a retained path beside the wall to embark on the engineered zig-zag grooves, created for the laborious hauling of slate from the remarkable high-sited Caudale Quarry. Take the path slanting right, but be watchful to veer left again. (The path straight on leads to an adit and is not a place for walkers to gain the ridge safely.) The grooved haul-path has periodic water run-out points that seem to have functioned very well in keeping the path secure from over deepening. The climb to **Caudale Quarry** represents the main labour of the ascent as a whole. Take a few minutes out to peruse the quarry's dilapidated remnants. The ridge is soon reached only 40 metres to the right and is followed on an ever-lessening gradient up Rough Edge to the handsome cairn on John Bell's Banner. Aim east to join the wall, and find the summit cairn 30 metres northeast beyond the wall junction.

Via the Tongue →3.2km/2 miles ↑570m/1870ft ⏲2hr

A canny little option, useful in poor conditions as an easy line on and off the fell

69

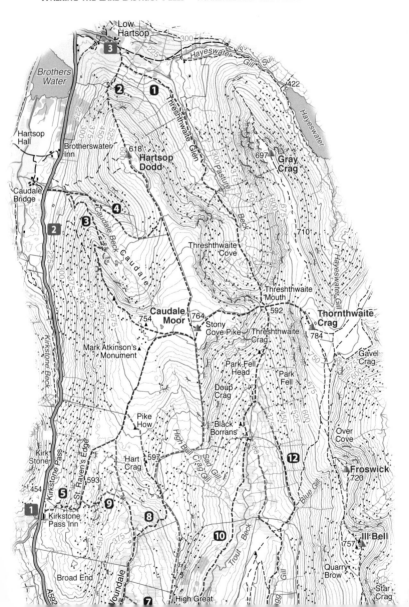

4 Start with Route **3**, but stay with **Caudale Beck** on a drove-path below the wall. Coming to a waters-meet step up right over the wall and hop over Caudale Beck to begin the old zig-zag groove path up the Tongue. Seldom followed by walkers, the way peters out, but simply keep on to reach a wall corner with integral sheep-creep. Keeping the wall to the right, ascend to find a grooved drove slanting half-left leading to the ridge wall, and here turn right to complete the ascent.

Ascent from Kirkstone Pass **1**

Via St Raven's Edge →3.2km/2 miles ↑350m/1150ft ⏱1hr 30min

This is very much a there-and-back route to the top, as circuits are just not possible.

5 The popular path from the large car park climbs via stiles to the ridge-top and the large cairn on **St Raven's Edge**. Keeping close company with the ridge wall head north, slipping through a depression at the head of **Woundale**. Stay with the wall – a sure guide to the summit – diverting only to note the cairn monument to Mark and William Atkinson on **John Bell's Banner**, towards the western edge just before the wall bears east.

Ascent from Woundale **36**

All these routes start half a kilometre east along the road from the starting point where the dale-floor track in Woundale leads off onto the southwest ridge of Caudale Moor.

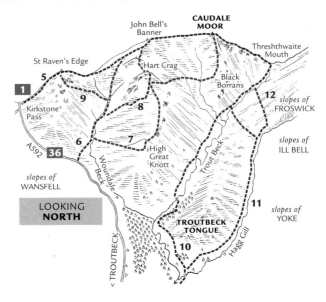

Direct →4km/2½ miles ↑460m/1510ft ⏱2hr

6 The gated track leads via a broad flagged bridge over **Woundale Beck**, with a classic sheep-wash fold. Heading up-dale by a glacial rigg, see a lone roof-less stone barn on the far bank, then reach a second wash-fold, unusually intact for its high situation. Keep on, holding a slight bias left with the feeder-gill, to reach the ridge wall and Route **5** on the way to John Bell's Banner.

Via Hart Crag →4.9km/3 miles ↑470m/1540ft ⏱2hr 20min

Stout stock fencing prevents lower access to the Hart Crag ridge.

7 To join the ridge as early as possible, set off with Route **6**, passing through a gate just past the crossing of **Woundale Beck** to wander up the damp fellside, with the ridge-straddling wall close right, to gain the ridge at **High Great Knott**. Turn left (north) to follow up the spine of the ridge. Cross a netting fence in the next cross-wall and then higher wooden rails at the next wall junction. From here accompany the ridge wall to meet a rising track.

(**8** You could also reach this point by staying with Route **6** a little longer, as far as the roofless barn, and then turning right on this quad-bike track.)

Weave through the ridge-top outcropping by an old wall, incorporating a bedrock peak, to reach a prominent cairn on the crest of **Hart Crag** itself. When the old wall falters in a marsh follow on with a dwindling path that climbs over **Pike How** to turn right and join the main path to the summit (Route **5**). Alternatively trend right before Hart Crag to stay with the wall down to ford **High Bull Crag** and **Sad Gills** and join company with the true south ridge. Follow the rising wall almost direct to the summit. There is no hint of a path, as there is no way up from the Trout Beck valley. More importantly, there is no way of crossing the wall at **Black Borrans** (whatever other guides might say).

Via St Raven's Edge →4.8km/3 miles ↑510m/1675ft ⏲2hr 15min

One more way up from Woundale remains...

9 Follow Route **6** as far as the higher wash-fold where an old quarry-way once struck up the left-hand slope – not visible until you are almost at the

Caudale Quarry remains (photo: Maggie Allan)

quarry. Make your way up to the roofless bothy that remains there below a shallow pecked-out cavern and rake-cutting. Climb directly up from here onto **St Raven's Edge** to join the regular path from Kirkstone Pass (Route **5**).

Ascent from Town Head **37** *off map S*

Via Trout Beck →*8.5km/5¼ miles* ↑*670m/2200ft* ⏲*3hr*

A journey in two parts, starting with a valley stroll but moving swiftly to the drama of the upper dale

10 Start by following Ing Lane through the meadows – this single-track road leads from Town Head to **Troutbeck Park** farm and is a popular stroll. Beyond the farm the walk takes on an altogether rougher, wilder complexion.

Pass by the old barn and round the back by the sheep-handling pens, guided by the footpath arrow onto a track rising by a gate. The path weaves on along an open woodland way to cross a broad slate bridge spanning **Trout Beck**. Follow it on up a decidedly damp dale, grazed by suckler cattle, and come to a fixed hurdle (rather than a gate). Climb over and continue with the path, negotiating the fringes of bracken and sedge marsh and passing an old sheep-pen complex to reach and go through a wooden gate in the upper-dale enclosure wall. Further damp ground leads by the first of several small cairns, and there is a moment where walkers on their way up go straight on, but walkers on their way down have created a more comfortable path to the right, closer to the beck. Take this latter route to the top of the upper rowan gorge with its lovely cascades.

The upper section of the path is less about the intimate and more about the rousing craggy heights above, as **Threshthwaite Crag** looms above and the trail slants up the grassy fringe of scree to the col of **Threshthwaite Mouth**. Here turn up the rock-steps, left, accompanying the ridge wall.

Via Hagg Gill →8.5km/5¼ miles ↑670m/2200ft ⏲3hr

A variant that coincides with the old Roman road and is better underfoot for longer

11 Alternatively, follow Route **10** from the road but fork right following a footpath sign off the road immediately after Hagg Bridge and before **Troutbeck Park** farm. Rise up the pasture, crossing a gill to reach and go through a kissing-gate. Bear right with the stony track, which enters the lovely glen of **Hagg Gill** through a sequence of gates and en route passes below two long-abandoned slate quarries. On the rise towards the third gate bear off left with a track to go through a sheep-handling pen by two gates to enter the **Trout Beck** valley pasture. Contour, keeping above the worst of the marsh to cross a ford just beyond a sheepfold complex and before the final enclosure wall. Go through the near gate to link with Route **10**. (**12** Or keep with the Roman road through the next gate, and as the adjacent field-wall drifts left follow suit on a narrow trod that contours into the dale-head pasture. Evidence of a path is quickly lost when the company of the wall is forsaken. Contour to reach the beck immediately above the rowan-filled gorge, ford and join the main path to the col just a little further on.)

The summit

A large cairn occupies the top, set away from the ridge wall. As befits the fell's name the summit has a certain plateau-like quality although the presence of ridge-top walls conveys the sense of shepherding, rather than a mountaineering environment. Further west a shallow hollow holds a tarn, missed by most walkers. The cairns above the north ridge and Mark Atkinson's cairn on John Bell's Banner are popular situations from which to enjoy fine views to north and west. Most walkers content themselves by sitting on the southern periphery, gazing towards the distant Windermere.

Safe descents

The walls come into their own when safety is an issue. Go W (**5**) for Kirkstone Pass and N (**2**) for Hartsop, and follow the wall down into the Caudale Beck valley (**4**) for easiest going. Avoid the wall heading due S, as this does not offer an escape, and the wall to Threshthwaite Mouth (E) has rock-steps just above the col that call for caution.

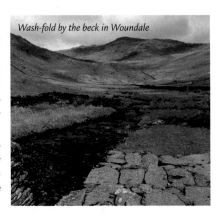

Wash-fold by the beck in Woundale

Ridge routes

Hartsop Dodd →*2.2km/1½ miles* ↓*175m/575ft* ↑*30m/100ft* ⏱*30min*
Follow the ridge wall N, keeping to the west side. This is a sure guide to the apparently lowly summit. But note that when you descend further to Hartsop or Caudale Bridge, consistently steep ground is encountered.

Thornthwaite Crag →*1.5km/1 mile* ↓*170m/560ft* ↑*190m/625ft* ⏱*40min*
Walk E, soon joining company with the ridge wall that eventually plummets to Threshthwaite Mouth, with several rather awkward rock-steps to handle – never as easy in descent. As it crosses the undulating col the wall climbs steep ground, accompanied by an appallingly loose trail. Protect both your knees and the trail itself by veering left as the rocky ground is reached. Cross the ridge wall and head NE, and once you have crossed the north-running wall, bear back right (pathless) onto the ridge, thereby keeping entirely to grass. Later, rejoin the broken ridge wall to reach the most handsome of beacon cairns.

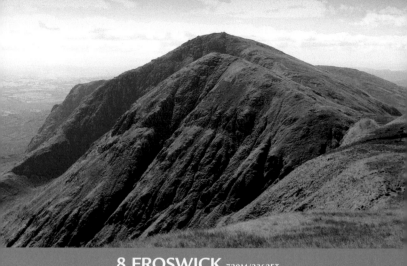

8 FROSWICK 720M/2362FT

Climb it from	Town Head **37**
Character	Shapely northern sibling of Ill Bell
Fell-friendly route	1
Summit grid ref	NY 435 085
Link it with	Ill Bell or Thornthwaite Crag
Part of	Kentmere Horseshoe

In height Froswick is the junior partner to Ill Bell – the two forming almost (but not quite) a matching pair – and together these conical fells have great visual appeal from far and wide. Unlike its higher twin, the fell has no line of ascent up its steep eastern flanks, rising above the head of Kentmere, but the Roman road up Scot Rake does offer a simple approach from (and more comfortable descent to) the west.

What the Roman militia thought of the climb from Hagg Gill can only be surmised. It seems an altogether unlikely line to take but excavations in 2006 before the rebuilding of the Kentmere Horseshoe paths by the National Park have confirmed it as the southern extension of the line of High Street – surely the most famous Roman road in Cumbria. This well-worn route was also once used

↑ *Froswick (with Ill Bell behind) from the northeast* 77

by packhorses bringing peat down to the Windermere area, its zig-zags much straightened over the intervening years by eager fell-baggers.

The fell is, however, much more generally climbed by walkers completing the Kentmere Horseshoe following the ridge path from Ill Bell to Thornthwaite Crag.

Ascent from Town Head 37

Via Scot Rake →6.7km/4¼ miles ↑600m/1970ft ⊕2hr 30min

1 Follow Ing Lane from Town Head as far as Hagg Bridge, just short of **Troutbeck Park** farm. Immediately after crossing the bridge bear right at the stile (long superfluous, as the fence has been missing for many years) and follow the footpath up the pasture along a minor gill to go through the kissing-gate and join the farm track. Go right, following the track via gates through the **Hagg Gill** valley. At the top, exit by the gate and step up on the grassy way with a wall close left and **Blue Gill** right. Where the wall contours off left, turn your mind more purposefully to the ascent. The grassy trod (known as **Scot Rake**) may be as old as the hills but it is a modest presence and has one small rock-step to negotiate. After curving through a shallow re-entrant, the path comes by loose stones, wash-out from a tiny gill. Directly above this leave the ancient 'road' and ascend the grassy slope to the col, joining forces with the well-tended ridge path climbing directly to the summit.

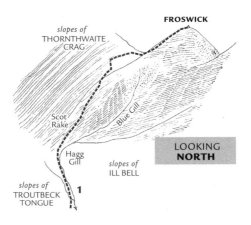

FROSWICK

slopes of
THORNTHWAITE
CRAG

Blue Gill

Scot
Rake

Hagg
Gill

slopes of
ILL BELL

LOOKING
NORTH

slopes of
TROUTBECK
TONGUE

1

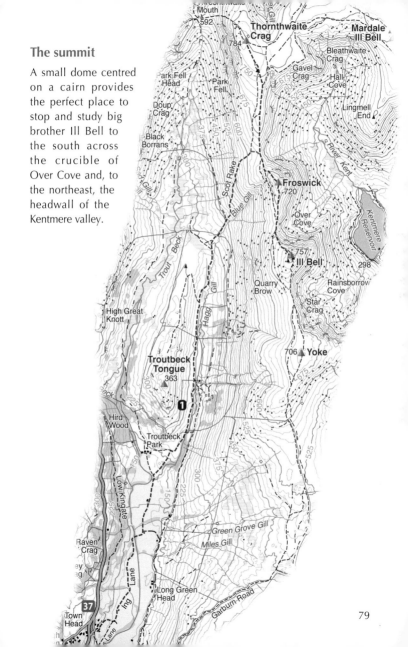

The summit

A small dome centred on a cairn provides the perfect place to stop and study big brother Ill Bell to the south across the crucible of Over Cove and, to the northeast, the headwall of the Kentmere valley.

Thornthwaite Crag
592
784

Mardale Ill Bell

Bleathwaite Crag

Gavel Crag

Hall Cove

Lingmell End

Park Fell Head

Park Fell

Doup Crag

Black Borrans

River Kent

Scot Rake

Blue Gill

Froswick
720

Over Cove

Kentmere Reservoir

Ill Bell
757

298

Troutbeck

Quarry Brow

Rainsborrow Cove

Star Crag

High Great Knott

Hagg Gill

Troutbeck Tongue
363

❶

706 ▲ **Yoke**

Hird Wood

Troutbeck Park

Low Kingate

Green Grove Gill

Miles Gill

Raven Crag

Ing Lane

Long Green Head

Garburn Road

37

Town Head

Summit cairn

Safe descents

The quickest route to valley level is by heading NW to the top of Scot Rake (**1**). Otherwise, head S as to Ill Bell and use the fell-runners' route from the saddle that contours along the upper western slopes onto Yoke and so down to the Garburn Pass for Troutbeck or Kentmere.

Ridge routes

Ill Bell →0.8km/½ mile ↓70m/230ft ↑105m/345ft ⊙30min

Head due S to the col, from where the one honest trail angles SE, with two optional paths above the prominent buttress. The path closest above the buttress gives the more handsome views into Over Cove.

The putative Roman road embarks on Scot Rake

Thornthwaite Crag →1.7km/1 mile ↓95m/310ft ↑160m/525ft ⊙45min

Keep tight to the ridge path leading NW down to the col, from where modern path work has secured a good firm trail, and climb N to a skyline cairn among a few rocks. From here easier ground is reached, trending NW to the beacon cairn.

9 GRAY CRAG 697M/2287FT

Climb it from	Hartsop 3
Character	Chiselled ridge running north from Thornthwaite Crag
Fell-friendly route	1
Summit grid ref	NY 427 117
Link it with	Thornthwaite Crag

Travellers heading south from Patterdale towards Brothers Water catch a fleeting glimpse of this ridge-end fell and sense a bulkiness belying its actual slender proportions. Rising purposely from Hayeswater Gill towards the iconic pillar of Thornthwaite Crag in the elevated company of High Street, it separates wild Threshthwaite Glen from shy, steep-sided Hayeswater, offering a grand start to a fell-round to east or west.

Walkers venturing to Hayeswater Gill bridge should note the stone ruins associated with the 19th-century Myers' Head Lead Mine down to the right. Once upon a time a nine-metre diameter waterwheel was set up by the side of the gill to work a Cornish pump for raising flood water out of the mine. The wheel pit survives with walls still standing to a height of 3.5 metres. Approaching

↑ Gray Crag from Brock Crags (photo: Maggie Allan)

the wheel pit from the north you can also spot a series of stone-built supports which helped direct water from Hayeswater Gill to power the wheel.

The common line up the Crag stems from either side of the Gill (1 or 2) – reaching an abrupt climb rewarded with great views – but you can also approach from Threshthwaite Glen (3) for a longer expedition.

Ascent from Hartsop 3

Via north ridge →*2.5km/1½ miles* ↑*510m/1675ft* ☺*1hr 30min*

An inevitably stiff start, but what a fine ridge to follow!

1 Set off from the car park along the bridleway signed 'Hayeswater', passing the large sheep corral. Leave the tarmac strip behind at a gate, and follow the open track down to cross the **Hayeswater Gill** bridge. The rough track rises by a gate, passing a rustic stone barn, and after a kissing-gate climbs easily on to where there is evidence of a walkers' path stepping off onto the near fellside (right). This path climbs the steep grass slope, angling left to avoid the skyline outcropping, with a spot of wash-out damage evident. The path rounds the crags to gain the north ridge proper. This narrow ridge, a fellwalker's delight, leads assuredly and handsomely onto the summit plateau.

2 As a variant to Route **1**, follow the metalled roadway from the cattle grid as it rises above **Wath Bridge** to come past the waterworks' building onto a path. This leads to a wall-stile directly over the inflow of **Calfgate Gill** into Hayeswater Gill – an interesting moment. Cross the footbridge, taking time to enjoy the tumbling waters. The path slants up to join the reservoir track (although you might be tempted to hold off joining it until you've had a look at the great waterfall down to the left). Follow the track towards Hayeswater dam, taking to the steep grassy slope at will some time after the point where a wall comes down to **Hayeswater Gill** from the northeast and the amazing cascades of **Sulphury Gill**. Climb pathless grassy slopes almost due west onto the ridge to meet Route **1** above the ridge-end outcropping.

Via Threshthwaite Glen →5.5km/3½ miles ↑570m/1870ft ⊙2hr 15min

Such a grand valley name suggests an impressive arena, and Threshthwaite certainly lives up to expectations.

3 Leave the car park and turn sharp right, signed 'Pasture Beck', by the gate to cross Walker Bridge. Keep company with the gated track, which leads into **Threshthwaite Glen**. The valley path winds up through a wall-gap and larger boulders at the quite distant base of **Raven Crag**, entering the enigmatic **Threshthwaite Cove**, where the walker is embraced in a wild mountain corrie. The path has received recent stone pitching attention, all the more necessary on the steep climb to **Threshthwaite Mouth**. Follow the

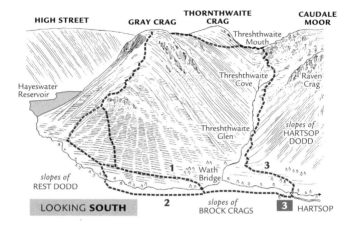

broken wall left towards **Thornthwaite Crag**, but as the slope steepens veer left, traversing the fellside to cross over a lateral wall and join the ridge path. This heads over the intermediate top and through the cross-ridge wall to reach the summit easily.

Gray Crag from the A592

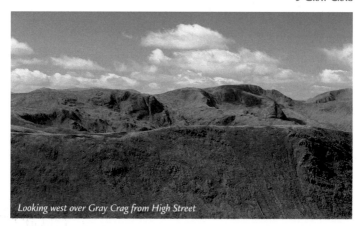
Looking west over Gray Crag from High Street

The summit

The summit cairn rests on a grassy patch. The best views are to be enjoyed cautiously from the nearby edges on either side of the ridge. Hayeswater is quite a subject from the eastern edge – notice the simply massive accumulation of debris on the far shore. It would seem to have collapsed from on high some hundreds of years ago, creating a gully chiselling out the Knott from the main mass of Rampsgill Head.

Safe descents

When heading N on the one ridge path (**1**) be mindful of the cliff at the ridge-end and take evasive action with either of the paths which skirt it on both sides. If in doubt head for Hayeswater dam, joining the access track down to Hartsop.

Ridge route

Thornthwaite Crag →2km/1¼ miles ↓50m/165ft ↑140m/460ft ⏲30min
The ridge path leads SSE, crossing two walls, the second wall coming quickly after a knoll some 14m higher than Gray Crag, from where the ridge eases up by the wall to the beacon cairn.

85

10 GRAYRIGG FOREST 494M/1621FT

Climb it from	Low Borrowbridge 29 or Grayrigg 30
Character	Easternmost Lake District fell overlooking the Lune gorge
Summit grid ref	SD 598 998
Part of	Westmorland Borrowdale Round

Travellers heading north on the M6 or West Coast Mainline will sense the arrival of the Lake District most assuredly as they squeeze through the Lune gorge approaching Tebay, the Howgill Fells in particular eye-catching in their billowing beauty. But tight left the great scarp of Grayrigg Forest is the first genuine fell within the recently extended National Park. As a further identifier, immediately below Grayrigg Pike a mast sits upon the prominent Dillicar Common.

This is a transitional world far removed from familiar Lakeland heights, the central fell mass attracting your gaze from afar. Red deer can be found shyly straying over these fells and the northern flanks falling into Borrowdale have native woodland and some picturesquely inspired Scots pines.

Ways lead up from three directions – from the east, from Hause Bridge up the shapely nose by Grayrigg Pike (1), from the north, by Birk Knott from Hause

↑ *Grayrigg Forest from Jeffrey's Mount*

Bridge (2) or Low Borrowbridge (3) and also from the west, by the communication masts from Grayrigg (4 and 5).

Ascent from Low Borrowbridge 29

For Routes 1 and 2, park at the scenic layby half a mile to the south of Low Borrowbridge. Do not try to walk between the two parking areas.

From Hause Bridge via Grayrigg Pike → *1.8km/1 mile* ↑*300m/985ft* ⏱*50min*

The grandest ascent in the tumultuous arena of the Lune Gorge, climbing between Great and Little Coums

1 Follow the verge a short distance to find a gate on the right at **Hause Bridge**. Bear up right with the track, quickly stepping off left up the bank to follow traces of a sunken drove-way. Ford the coum-draining gill and follow on up the obvious grassy ridge due south. There is a trace of a path which is rather lost as you set to work on the steep culminating section of the ridge with minor outcropping, targeting the twin-cairned top of **Grayrigg Pike** and its small wind-shelter.

   This point is reached in half an hour and what a thrilling place to stand! To get the best view of the Howgills follow the ridge a little further southeast to a small cairn from where the deep incursion of Carling Gill is clearly seen.

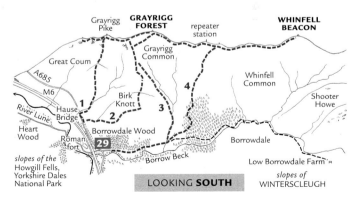

Do not attempt a descent in this direction. To claim the crown of Grayrigg Forest, turn and follow a thin path west to the site of a hand-gate (now filled by light sheep-barring netting which you can step over). The natural way due west to the attractive stone-built OS column has no apparent path.

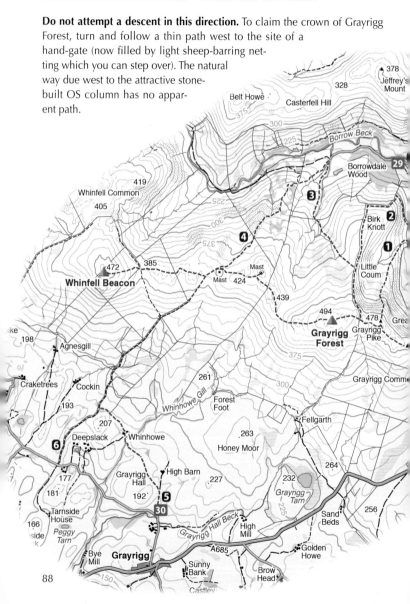

From Hause Bridge via Birk Knott →*2.4km/1½ miles* ↑*300m/985ft* ⏱*1hr*

A practical if novel line, useful for manufacturing a circuit

2 From the gate off the road bear right (north) with the rising cattle track and as you reach a gate angle up with the fence running under the east side of Birk Knott. When it meets a rising wall, turn sharp left to follow this wall steeply to begin with, later bending west and levelling out with views over **Borrowdale Wood**. At the wall junction either clamber over the low wall fill-in (former gap) or stay on the east side; the choice is yours.

Either way turn left (south) to climb over **Birk Knott**. The west-side route eventually picks up a quad track which leads to the OS column. That on the east side continues without hint of a path, skirting the scarp on its left, to a prominent cairn and then turns right with Route **1** to reach the summit.

Via Borrowdale Wood →*3km/2 miles* ↑*330m/1080ft* ⏱*1hr 10min*

A little more circuitous than the Hause Bridge ascents, but pleasant in the early stages up to the intake wall, then a simple plod

3 From the parking space go through the gate and follow the road along the foot of **Borrowdale Wood**, a lovely entrance to the valley. The road rises a little and comes to a low parapet bridge. Here branch off left. Spurn the track to follow the main gill flowing under the bridge. Keep to the

Heart Wood on Blease Fell seen across the Tebay gorge

The ridge wall above Great Coum

right-hand side, deftly avoiding bracken by keeping up to the right of the bank as the lightly wooded gill steepens a little. Coming to the intake wall cross a pipe set in the gill. Simply walk up with the gill to reach the ridge wall on **Birk Knott** and turn right with the quad track and Route **2**.

Via the bridleway →*4.3km/2¾ miles* ↑*360m/1180ft* ⊕*1hr 40min*

A reliable route in poor weather with a consistent track onto the ridge, traversing easily east to the summit

4 Follow Route **3** to the low parapet bridge and take a rough track departing half-left up to a gate. Here join a track rising through the spacious woodland. It quickly fades to a grassy track leading through a metal gate in a wall to complete the ascent to the **mast enclosure**. Turn left with the track towards the easternmost **mast** stepping off the track 30 metres short of the enclosure to follow a narrow trod to a wall-stile. The path continues a little past this point into a depression but is then lost on the mounting fellside, allowing you to plot your own course onto the felltop plateau and over to the OS column.

Ascent from Grayrigg 30

Quiet lanes lead all the way up onto the ridge-top... how sweet is that?

Via field-paths to the road onto the ridge →*5.2km/3¼ miles* ↑*390m/1280ft* ⊕*1hr 30min*

5 Follow the open concrete roadway north by the wall. After crossing a gill find a tractor track trending left across the pasture to and through a gate. Bear half-left passing to the left of an old quarried hollow and mature ash tree to find a wall-stile. Cross the next pasture to where a 'heck' (hanging fence) crosses a stony gill and clamber over the suitably lowered rails on the right under the bank to reach and cross a gated footbridge. Swing right to pass through the old farmyard at **Whinhowe**. Go through a gate and rise with the track to reach another gate and then keep forward aiming for a wall corner to the left. Cross the wall stile whose lower step is an old hurdle post with square holes. Skirt round a rushy patch and reach the open roadway. Turn right up the road with Route **6**.

Tarmac all the way to the ridge →*6km/3¾ miles* ↑*400m/1310ft* ⊕*1hr 45min*

6 From the parking verge, follow the open road that swings left from the stone bridge, dipping through the shallow valley wherein lie High and Low Deepslack Farms. Rise to a minor cross-ways to turn right through the gate and follow a lovely hedged lane with a fine view ahead of Whinfell Beacon. After a cattle-grid meet Route **5** and pass a mature copse with a clay-pigeon shooters' cabin to the right of the roadway. The open road crosses two further cattle grids, climbing steadily onto the ridge to arrive at the repeater station enclosure. Here turn right to fall into step with Route **4** to the summit.

Looking west from the OS column

The summit

The broad top of the fell is open pasture with a splendid stone-built OS column at its crown. A wonderful sweep of fell country is on display, most of which is not Lakeland at all. It's the Howgill Fells that command your attention. The Coniston and Langdale Fells, backed by the Scafells, are in the far distance and even Ill Bell almost 20km to the NW. The best place to stand is the scarp-top cairn

Grayrigg Pike

close to Grayrigg Pike from where both the Lune Gorge and the sleek-lined Howgills can be enjoyed in all their glory.

Safe descents

Backtrack W along the ridge to the repeater station and descend (SW, **6**) from there.

Ridge route

Whinfell Beacon → 3km/2 miles ↓ 150m/490ft ↑ 120m/390ft ⊕ 1hr 15min
Head W from the OS column, passing through a depression and then rising to a stile in the ridge-straddling wall. Pass the mast compound, following the track to the second repeater station compound. Follow the open road down the short way till the reflector posts end and bear off right to find a faint path that weaves along the damp ridge to a fence-stile in the cross-wall. Advance to a ladder-stile and climb direct to the top.

11 GREY CRAG 638M/2093FT

Climb it from	Sadgill **31**, Shap Summit **22**, Hollowgate **24**, Bannisdale Bridge **25** or Plough Lane **26**
Character	Meeting point of four long ridges sitting above Longsleddale
Fell-friendly route	2
Summit grid ref	NY 497 072
Link it with	Tarn Crag

Rooted in the majesty of upper Longsleddale, Grey Crag sends out four lonely ridges south and east towards the A6, once the eastern limit of the Lake District National Park. This is transitional territory. These ridges give scope for long days far from the crowds. Here you may experience a kind of soothing solitude, engaging with the wild, more likely to encounter red deer, red grouse and birds of prey than on the more populous fells.

Down to the southeast of the summit, Mere Crag, marking the top of Westmorland Borrowdale, is not 'mere' in the slightest. Most visitors will consider it quite impressive. A huge clean face of volcanic rock invites competent climbers, although even they need a rope, as the presence of two metal belay loop stakes above the crag attest.

↑ *Cairn on Long Crag, looking to a distant Grey Crag*

Not surprisingly most walkers claim this fell-top from Sadgill (1), in the thrilling arena at the head of Longsleddale, and including Tarn Crag in a compact rambling day or venturing on to claim Branstree and Selside Pike before backtracking down the historic Gatescarth Pass track and quarryman's lane. Less-trodden and more haunting approaches (2–6) lead up from the main road from Shap Summit to Plough Lane.

Ascent from Sadgill 31

Via Great Howe →2.4km/1½ miles ↑450m/1475ft ⏱1hr 20min

By far the shortest and most popular line of travel

1 From the lane end go through a field-gate into access land. Target the fence-gap at the top, climb the pasture bank (interspersed with outcropping) and then cross a gill to reach what turns out to be a stile. The path heads on up a stony gully onto a shelf. When you reach the next wall follow a waymark

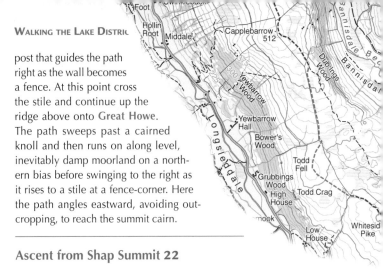

post that guides the path right as the wall becomes a fence. At this point cross the stile and continue up the ridge above onto **Great Howe**. The path sweeps past a cairned knoll and then runs on along level, inevitably damp moorland on a northern bias before swinging to the right as it rises to a stile at a fence-corner. Here the path angles eastward, avoiding outcropping, to reach the summit cairn.

Ascent from Shap Summit 22

Via Great Yarlside →6.9km/4¼ miles ↑340m/1115ft
⏱2hr 40min

The long layby on Shap summit provides a grand high-level springboard for the eastern approach to the adjacent summits of Grey and Tarn Crags.

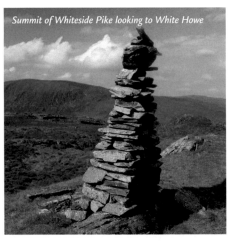

Summit of Whiteside Pike looking to White Howe

2 Carefully cross the padlocked gate and follow the track to the crossing with the old Shap Road. Head on in the company of the ridge wall onto **Whatshaw Common**, with scant evidence of a path. The wall and, briefly, fence provide a sure guide over typical upland herbage with the odd damp hollow, notably in the depression of **Wasdale Mouth**.

Ahead is a steady climb onto **Little Yarlside** on a quad track. Next take on the final real climb of this approach, onto **Great Yarlside**. Ignore the meandering course of the quad track and stick close to the wall. Pass through a gate and keep with the fence as a quad track merges on the right from Wasdale Pike. After a further loose-fitting gate reach the outcropped headland of **Harrop Pike**, with its old wall and striking cairn suggesting an ancient boundary point. Descend and, after a fence merges from the left, cross the adjacent fence and follow the clear path to and beyond the fence-corner, drifting south to the summit of Grey Crag.

Via High House Bank →8km/5 miles ↑480m/1575ft ⏱3hr

A comparatively low undulating ridge runs between the twin headwaters of Borrowdale, providing an absorbing 'lost in the fells' approach to the fell-top and the basis of a return route for a circular expedition with Route 4.

3 From Shap summit walk along the track to the cross-ways. Here go through the hand-gate on the left and follow the old road, which soon becomes a

Goat Scar across Longsleddale (photo: Maggie Allan)

broad green-way curving down to a gate. Beyond, the old highway curves left to a further gate leading into improved pasture. Follow the wall down to yet another gate into a short lane by Hause Foot. Cross Crookdale Bridge and advance beyond the line of leylandii, bearing off right short of the road-gate. The ascent proper begins by slanting up **Hazel Bank**. First pass under the power line and close by the pylon, then slip through the broken wall to continue up the steep rough pasture slope to find a quite obscure through-stone stile almost at the top, where the wall swings over the brow (with a netting top). The summit cairn on **High House Bank** is in view, but the slope ahead is tough tussocky grass, so slow progress will be made to this fine little crest.

Follow the ridge, periodically peering down on the farmsteads of **Borrowdale Head** and **High House**. Come to a gate in the ridge-straddling fence and bend gently west to join the regular quad track. This is your faithful guide almost all the way to Grey Crag. From the next gate the path swings up left to gain the crest of the enigmatically named **Robin Hood** with its beacon cairn. The next rise is to uncairned **Lord's Seat** from where continue west avoiding the outcropping above Crookdale and rising to the intermediate sky-line. Here you reach a fence running north to south. You can cross it at this point or go left to cross it at a fixed gate a little further south. Eroding peat drainage is the only obstacle on the early rise northeast that leads through small outcropping to the summit.

Ascent from Hollowgate 24 or Bannisdale Bridge 25

Via White Howe →*8.2km/5 miles* ↑*550m/1805ft* ⏱*3hr 20min*

The most natural circuit begins from Hollowgate Farm traversing the ridge above onto Fawcett Forest and returning along the Robin Hood ridge (Route 3).

4 Opposite the west entrance to the farm, go through the field-gate (currently padlocked, but not to inhibit walkers, so you can climb carefully over). A green track leads to a further gate. Beyond this bear sharp right and follow the rising fence (along the line of a buried gas pipeline). As the ridge-top gap is neared, trend left up the bank and follow the switchback ridge to a small cairn above a pool. There is no hint of a path on the undulating ridge, which has a few minor outcrops that are easily avoided on the rise to the spine of Fawcett Forest. (**5** Another start can be made off the old Shap highway. Find a quiet looping back-road by Low Jock Scar and a bridleway signed off this above **Thorn Cottage**. The old Shap road, now a green track, rises to a gate. From here leave the old way and follow the farm track left, passing through a further gate in a fence. As this fades bear up right to avoid the dense bracken, onto the ridge. Here a curious shed stands beside a gate. Go through the gate and, keeping the ridge fence close left, traverse the dip slope of **Lamb Pasture**, coming down to a gate. Ahead the continuing path falters after crossing a gill. Climb naturally onto the fell.)

As you set off along the ridge a path re-emerges. Reach the cairn on this nameless top of Fawcett Forest. The path declines, crosses a wall-stile and clambers onto the more substantial cairned top of **White Howe**. (Note a spur path that leads to a cairn commanding a superb bird's-eye view down on the quiet upper quarter of Bannisdale Head.) The main thread of the ridge path bends north and accompanies the wall, and, after an awkward step up, clambers over a ladder-stile. From here a lateral rock rib with three casual cairns gives a line to follow left before the route traverses the marshy ground northwest, eventually assisted by a quad track, onto the dry turf at the very head of Bannisdale. Walking from here north to a fence/broken wall on the brow, cross and descend on the remains of the wall, slipping through a damp hollow at the head of **Brow Gill**. Go through a metal gate close under **Mere Crag** whose striking volcanic face marks the top of Borrowdale. The ridge fence slips easily up past the crag, and as the ground levels go over the fixed gate and traverse the peaty origins of Stockdale Beck, weaving up through the minor outcropping to the summit cairn.

Ascent from Plough Lane 26 *off map S*

Via Whiteside Pike →*9.5km/6 miles* ↑*615m/2020ft* ⏱*3hr 45min*

A long and winding route makes its way, sometimes pathlessly, north to the summit.

6 Follow the branching road as to Mosergh Farm. Short of the buildings an unsurfaced lane is signed right (north). Follow this up to a handling pen with galvanised gates, the main gate oddly padlocked. Enter access land through

Summit cairn

the side hand-gate. The green track is quickly forsaken as you angle half-right into the Light Water valley, your sights firmly fixed on **Whiteside Pike**. There is little hint of a path but a small plaque reflects the importance the peak has within the local parishes, and the cairn certainly does it justice. A path is now apparent wending northwest down the heather moor and through a shallow valley to find a new wall-stile close to the wall junction. As you enter pasture the path is again lost. Bend left to take in the top of **Todd Fell** and a remarkable view into Longsleddale.

Angle down northeast to a ladder-stile into a marsh and keep left, now following the fence up to join a track and go through a gate in a lateral fence. The ridge path sweeps on, not strictly with the fence as it crosses **Capplebarrow**. Further north, after coming close by the fence, you reach a water obstacle. The ground beside the fence is very marshy, and to the right of this water lingers as a permanent tarn, so keep right and skirt it as well as you can. When you return to the fence there is further excitement to be had in walking on a quaking bog. **Swinklebank Crag** has a cairn over the broken fence and a fine view to boot. Step back and continue with the fence left over **Ancrow Brow** and then follow a broken wall to gain the brow at the very head of Bannisdale. Here fall into step with Route **5** to reach the final summit.

The summit

A small plateau of the most minor outcropping centres upon a cairn, while more significant rock exists to the south and west.

Safe descents

The path heading WSW (**1**) is your faithful guide to a safe dale-bottom harbour at Sadgill in upper Longsleddale. After crossing a fence-stile, this path curves S along the damp ridge to Great Howe, never failing as a path.

Ridge route

Tarn Crag →*1.4km/1 mile* ↓*40m/130ft* ↑*65m/215ft* ⏱*30min*
Head N to come to the projecting corner of a fence. Keep the fence close right on peaty ground, even though this makes the path less obvious for a short distance. Your attention will be more gripped by the possibility of damp feet as the basin to the north of Greycrag Tarn is crossed, although it is firmer than first impressions may suggest. Coming up the bank, the path duly veers away from the fence to reach the cairn and, close by, the Haweswater survey pillar.

12 HALLIN FELL 388M/1273FT

Climb it from	The Hause **8**, Sandwick **7** or Fusedale **9**
Character	The Howtown fell for all the family
Fell-friendly route	1
Summit grid ref	NY 433 198

Sitting pretty above the lake, Hallin Fell makes the perfect introduction to the scenic pleasures of Ullswater and, perhaps more importantly, a fine initiation into the delights of fellwalking itself. Parents should bring their children – and their parents for that matter. This is a fell for all seasons and allcomers – but choose your footwear carefully... the steep grass can be slippery!

If you've never stood on a Lakeland fell-top before, then Hallin Fell will show you how wonderful an experience it can be. The setting is sumptuous, steep and rugged, with a sylvan petticoat fringing the shore, and you can make a visit to the summit the cherry on the cake of an expedition on an Ullswater 'steamer'. Turn a tourist excursion into a modest but memorable mountain day!

Among the range of options, you can girdle the fell at low level (5) or part-way up on the south side (2), follow the throng from the Hause (1), or wend more

↑ *Hallin Fell from Cat Crag*

peaceably up the north and west slopes (3 and 4). Everything about this fell is pleasurable – it's a gem. Cherish it.

Ascent from the Hause 8

Direct →0.7km/½ mile ↑150m/490ft ⏱25min

1 Step across the open road from **St Peter's Church**. Ascend unhindered to the summit. The normal practice is to continue in a natural exaggerated loop, descending N from the landmark cairn and curving right to visit a lower cairn overlooking the Howtown Wyke landing stage before tilting back down to the Hause. Several casual variant paths exist within this area, beating back the bracken in season.

Via the west ridge →1.6km/1 mile ↑190m/625ft ⏱45min

A scenically blessed and quiet way up

2 Follow the footpath heading west off the roadside verge. This leads by three wall-stiles above the refurbished Hause Farm. Coming onto a bank, turn uphill with the path to join a lateral path drifting left above the intake wall. As this path moves downhill watch for a path angling gently up right. This comes above a badger sett and curves right more steeply, then turns left under rocks with a bield. When you reach a rock rib, bear right to reach the plainer slope and gain the summit rocks.

Ascent from Sandwick 7

No challenges here, just buckets of charm

Via the west ridge →*1.6km/1 mile* ↑*240m/785ft* ⏱*50min*
3 The hugely popular shoreline path leads east from the hamlet of Sandwick through gates. (You could also get to the start from the Hause by starting on Route **2** but keeping low at the first turn towards the fell to reach the lane via Bridge End.) Arrive at Sandwick Bay and continue along the lakeside path. After going through the kissing-gate in the wood break up right and follow the wall steeply to a hand-gate out of the woodland. Continue up with the rising wall to meet Route **2** and bend back left up the fell.

Via the northeast ridge →*2.5km/1½ miles* ↑*235m/770ft* ⏱*50min*
4 Start with Route **3** but keep to the rough woodland way through **Hallinhag Wood**. Above **Kailpot Bay** cross behind the great ice-smoothed headland adorned with Scots pines and go through a kissing-gate and along the shore rounding **Geordie's Crag**. As the path comes above a tree-bowered wall watch for a path turning sharply up the fell. Turn to task and follow this direct to the summit.

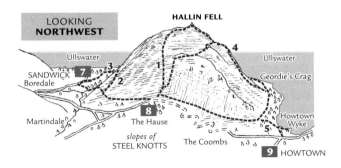

104

Kailpot Crag

Ascent from Fusedale 9

Girdle route →*4km/2½ miles* ↑*190m/625ft* ⊙*1hr 30min*

A great little walk for travellers on the steamer, or guests at Howtown Hotel, who are not inclined to climb to the summit

5 Embark on the orbiting path around the fell, with paths converging close to **Waternook** and rising to steps and a kissing-gate. Go left, keeping to the higher path and traversing the rough east slope of the fell up to **the Hause** to join Route **2**. Continue down by the wall into **Hallinhag Wood** to join the woodland way right and make your way slowly back round to your start point.

The summit

The magnificent square-built beacon illustrated in Wainwright's guide has suffered over the intervening 60 years, but, not withstanding the disruption to its upper tier, it still stands as a mighty landmark. It makes a worthy objective, perched proud as punch upon a bare rock plinth. The view down the lower reach of Ullswater will hold your attention, watching 'the toings and froings' of the steamers.

The handsomely rebuilt summit cairn

Safe descents

Follow the regular grassy trail SE to the Hause (**1**) for the surest ground.

Pasture and woodland above Sandwick

13 HARTER FELL 778M/2553FT

Climb it from	Mardale Head **19**, Hallow Bank **34** or Sadgill **31**
Character	Paternal craggy head of Mardale standing between Nan Bield and Gatescarth
Fell-friendly route	2
Summit grid ref	NY 460 093
Link it with	Kentmere Pike or Mardale Ill Bell
Part of	Martindale Skyline

While much attention hereabouts is drawn to Riggindale and its adjacent ridges, there is no doubting the head of Mardale. This drowned dale comes to an abrupt and impressive halt on Harter Fell, also the termination of the long northward-snaking ridge that divides Longsleddale from Kentmere. Either side of its great craggy presence are two popular passes. Gatescarth, the eastern saddle, carries a track into Longsleddale at times available for 4x4 drivers to test their vehicles to the limit. The high western col, Nan Bield Pass, holds a historic pedestrian route over to Kentmere.

   Much good work has been done on both of these popular routes. The frenzy of hairpins leading up to Nan Bield Pass have all been the subject of essential pitching work and the trail from Gatescarth Beck to the summit of the fell is one

↑ Harter Fell rising above Small Water from Mardale Ill Bell (photo: Maggie Allan)   107

of many in the Park re-constructed from inverted subsoil to secure a durable surface along a defined single route to minimise wider erosion.

These are the main lines of ascent (1 and 2). Approaches from the two valleys to the south tend to come via these lateral passes (3 from Kentmere and 6 from Longsleddale), although some walkers may make grassy plods from the Ull Stone on the Kentmere side (4) and via Wren Gill on the east side (5).

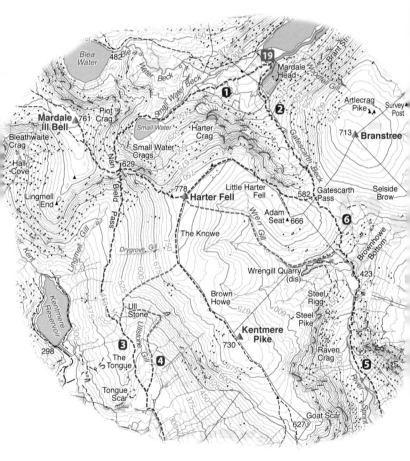

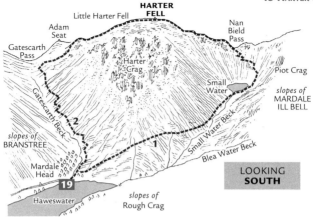

Ascent from Mardale Head 19

Via Nan Bield Pass →*3.2km/2 miles* ↑*525m/1720ft* ⏲*1hr 20min*

A really good fell climb – constantly ascending, constantly scenic

1 From the car park go through the kissing-gate and rise to the wall corner where three paths diverge. Take the middle route signed 'Public bridleway Nan Bield Pass Kentmere'. The heavily worn path leads via successive gates up through the moraine to come close to the fine cascades coming down from **Small Water**. Cross at the outflow and swing round the west side of the tarn, coming by a trio of stone shelters. The alcove 'seat' at the top is another partial shelter from the southerly draughts (as a 'bield' should be). Turn up left (east) and weave your way to the plateau. A line of cairns guides you to the summit cairn, just short of the ridge fence.

Via Gatescarth Pass →*3.5km/2¼ miles* ↑*535m/1755ft* ⏲*1hr 40min*

Not exactly a mirror of the Nan Bield route, but a natural return for a simple round trip and solid going throughout

2 From the three-way signpost follow the left-hand arm signed 'Public Byway Gatescarth Pass'. The track rises through a gate beside **Gatescarth Beck**, and, in two multiple-hairpin sections, climbs to the brow. Here the constructed trail swings right from the byway, 120 metres short of the gate in the saddle-straddling fence, and takes all but the most inquisitive of walkers with it making the cairn on **Adam Seat**, with its H/L-inscribed estate boundary stone of 1924, a seldom-visited side show. Continuing beside the fence pass a further pair of cairns, this time entangled with old metal stakes, to reach the summit.

Ascent from Hallow Bank 34 *off map S*

Via Nan Bield Pass →*7km/4½ miles* ↑*645m/2115ft* ⏱*2hr 45min*

Take the ancient bridleway to the pass and the west ridge.

Nan Bield Pass 'seat'

3 Follow either the road or bridleway through the hamlet of Hallow Bank, coming down the gated roadway to Overend. Beside the white-washed farmhouse diverge right, guided by the old slate sign 'To Mardale'. The bridleway leads by gates to a footbridge spanning **Ullstone Gill** and, after the final gate, curves up the bank onto the ridge of **the Tongue**, beating back the dense bracken. The normal line stays with the bridleway – look out for engraved bedrock underfoot – before the path steps up onto Smallthwaite Knott and contours well above **Kentmere Reservoir**, in its final stages tackling acute hairpins, to reach the col of **Nan Bield Pass**. From the bield wind-break bear up right with Route **1** to the plateau.

Via Ullstone Gill →*5.3km/3¼ miles* ↑*590m/1935ft* ⏱*2hr 30min*

A more direct route to the summit gets up close and personal with this dramatic gill.

4 Follow Route **3** looking out for a second slate waymarker stone (after the one at Overend) off to the right, part-way up the rising path from the gate

Ill Bell range from the Knowe (photo: Maggie Allan)

above the Ullstone Gill footbridge. It can be obscured by bracken in season. This is both the original line of the age-old bridleway and the haul-route of slate from the old quarry seen high on the west slope of Kentmere Pike. It requires a stiff clamber by a broken wall and much spoil. Standing in the lower portion you can look up to see a waterfall at the very top – and a wall above that to prevent sheep (and descending walkers) from inadvertently tumbling in! The lateral connection to the **Ull Stone** is awkward going but without hazard.

Alternatively, stick with the bridleway and Route **3** until the Ull Stone is more obviously accessible above. At that point, forsake the regular path for sheep trods to reach this unusually large, tilted, glacially-positioned rock. Climb on above, keeping first left, then right, to avoid all hint of outcropping. The objective is the ridge fence on **the Knowe** and a grassy trail left (north) to the summit.

Ascent from Sadgill 31 *off map S*

The walled lane up the upper corridor of Longsleddale from Sadgill gives a fine lead in, with great crags gathering impressively on either hand.

Via Wrengill Quarry →5.4km/3½ miles ↑600m/1970ft ⏲2hr 40min

5 Walk up the lane from Sadgill. After the pitched incline go through a gate and cross the stone bridge, the path following on as an open track. After a kissing-gate (where the broad gate is padlocked) the path begins the ascent beyond the fold. At the third hairpin bear off left on a short track to a padlocked galvanised gate. Head west above the wall which bars off the stony confusion of **Wrengill Quarry**. Reach an old water pipe and its race that once tapped an outflow of Wren Gill to power a quarry pump. Ford **Wren Gill** (you may take a little time to find a crossing point when the gill is in spate) and follow the dwindling gill to its high-pastured and rough source and on to the skyline and a stile in the ridge fence close to the summit cairn.

Via Gatescarth Pass

→6km/3¾ miles

↑615m/2020ft ⏲2hr 15min

6 Set off with Route 5, but stay with the zig-zagging track to **Gatescarth Pass**, climbing from **Brownhowe Bottom** to the fence in the broad saddle. Go through the gate and after 150 metres turn left upon the made path which leads up the scarp edge, via **Little Harter Fell**, assuredly to the summit.

Looking over Piot Crag to High Street

The summit

Metal fence stakes left lying about have been gathered by passing walkers and amassed on the summit cairn in an untidy heap. However, there is a tidy view from this wonderful high plateau – packed with drama in the foreground and excitement in the long range. The replacement fence does little to detract from the extensive views east towards the Pennines and Howgills. Most attention will be focused west over the neighbouring Ill Bell and High Street range, with eyes peeled to see many a favourite fell and even Blencathra making an appearance over the Straits of Riggindale.

Safe descents

For Mardale and Longsleddale follow the ridge fence and continuing trail E (**6**) to Gatescarth Pass. This avoids rocky ground entirely. Heading S with the fence along the spine of the ridge takes you over Kentmere Pike and Shipman Knotts, where an easy line avoiding rock can be followed for Hallow Bank, carved out by the local shepherd on his quad.

Ridge routes

Kentmere Pike → *1.8km/1 mile* ↓*80m/265ft* ↑*35m/115ft* ⊕*25min*
The ridge fence is a sure guide S. After a gentle dip in the ridge a wall is encountered, leading quickly to the summit, with the OS column sited over a stile in the wall.

Mardale Ill Bell → *1.7km/1 mile* ↓*145m/475ft* ↑*130m/425ft* ⊕*35min*
Head W with a couple of cairns aligned to the lip of the plateau, from where a consistent path weaves down the stepped ridge to Nan Bield Pass. The continuing path veers up left from the stone alcove, enjoying fine views of Ill Bell before slanting NW, with some recent stone pitching, onto the domed top.

14 HARTSOP DODD 618M/2028FT

Climb it from	Hartsop **3** or Caudale Bridge **2**
Character	Steep northern spur of Caudale Moor above Low Hartsop
Fell-friendly route	4
Summit grid ref	NY 411 119
Link it with	Caudale Moor

Hartsop Dodd is the blunt end of Caudale Moor's long north ridge – a striking presence above Brothers Water and a marvellous viewpoint well meriting the stiff climb from either Hartsop or Caudale Bridge. It rises fraternally over the Brotherswater Inn and Sykeside camp site to peer into the hidden delights of crag-backed Dovedale.

At one time there were two nucleated farmsteads associated with Brothers Water – that situated higher up the side of the dale was High Hartsop, hence High Hartsop Dodd (which is, in fact, lower than Hartsop Dodd by 99m/325ft), and the present community was Low Hartsop, normally now simply referred to as Hartsop. Naturally the more sheltered setting was more conducive to survival and High Hartsop is now long gone.

↑ *Hartsop Dodd from the outflow of Brothers Water*

The only sensible approaches are up the north ridge (1) or from the east (2–4). Keen eyes will spot a long-forsaken shepherds' path on the east flank of the fell – forsaken for good reason, being mightily steep.

Ascent from Hartsop 3

Via north ridge → *1.6km/1 mile* ↑*435m/1425ft* ⏱*1hr 15min*

Steep but straight to the point

1 Leave the car park and bear right crossing Walker Bridge. After the next gate/ladder-stile, where the track swings left, step off onto the pasture and rise

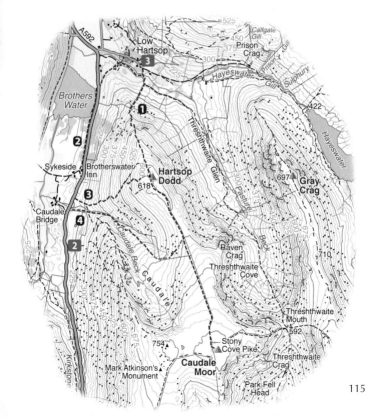

with the wall close right to a stile at the wall junction. Continue with some worn and some pitched hairpins to the top of the wall. The path persists up the steep blunt ridge. In time the butt end of the ridge wall is encountered, leading to the summit.

Valley connection via Brothers Water →*2km/1¼ miles* ↑*40m/130ft* ⏱*25min*

An appealing connection with Caudale Bridge, useful for a round trip

2 After crossing Walker Bridge bear sharp right, following the beck downstream by gates and passing by the cottage row and farmsteading into a walled lane that narrows to a gate. Drop to the road and cross over, passing through the gap (once a hand-gate) to wend beside the serene **Brothers Water**. The woodland fringe adds charm to the intimate outlook across the lake. The path rises and runs on field-side of the ensuing bounding road to the road entrance to Sykeside. Follow this by the cattle grid and bear up through the car park of the **Brotherswater Inn** to join the road towards Caudale Bridge.

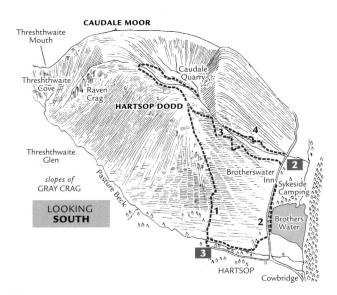

Looking down on Hartsop (photo: Maggie Allan)

Ascent from Caudale Bridge 2

Direct →*1.2km/¾ mile* ↑*420m/1380ft* ☉*1hr*

Follow the shepherds (and their charges) straight up the fell.

3 From the layby walk up the road to the bridge (or you may be lucky enough to find a parking space here) and then over it to a footpath sign and hand-gate. Enter the fell pasture, rising towards the beck and a ruin. Short of the ruin, near a broken wall, climb directly with a predominantly sheep-worn path. Pass up to the right of a thorn bush and reach a more consistent path, which progresses steadily in determined zig-zags up the steep grassy west slope of the fell. The path is never more than a shallow groove giving a real sense of following in shepherds' footsteps. As it reaches the grassy brow of the fell the path dissolves. Stroll across to the summit.

Via Caudale Beck →*2.5km/1½ miles* ↑*430m/1410ft* ☉*1hr 25min*

The ideal line of descent in misty conditions

4 From the layby walk up the road to the bridge and cross the wall-stile just before it, to the right. Follow the embanked path beside the wall, but keep with the beck as you join the popular path to Caudale Moor's northwest ridge. The adjacent wall is lost for a time as the beck constricts. At a beck confluence step up over the wall and skip over the beck, now rising with a definite zig-zag groove up the Tongue. Higher up the groove is less evident on the approach to a wall corner (with space for sheep to pass through). Go over, keeping the wall right until a distinct grooved path slants left gaining ground to the ridge. Here join company with the regular ridge route beside the wall turning up left to the summit.

The summit

Summit wall and cairn

The precise summit is marked by a weathered hardwood stake set into the broken ridge wall. Most visitors pay it little heed and contemplate the fruits of the climb beside the large cairn 'borrowed' from the ridge wall and set on the grassy platform a few paces to the west. The best of the view is indeed to the west, with the grand craggy backdrop of Dovedale centre stage.

Safe descents

The path N to Hartsop (**1**) is short and steep, but unfailing in its destiny. If gentler ground is sought, walk SSE (**4**) beside the ridge wall and bear off with the old drove that angles SW down by a broken wall at its corner. At the trace of a hog-hole step over and rediscover the drove descending the Tongue to the confluence with Caudale Beck. Soon after, find dale-bottom sanctuary on the Kirkstone road just above the Brotherswater Inn.

Ridge route

Caudale Moor →*2.2km/1½ miles* ↓*30m/100ft* ↑*175m/575ft* ⏲*40min*
About as uncomplicated as can be conceived. Just follow the ridge wall S.

15 HIGH RAISE 802M/2631FT

Climb it from	Martindale **6**, Burnbanks **17** or Mardale Head **19**
Character	Superior summit just off the High Street ridgeway
Fell-friendly route	2
Summit grid ref	NY 448 135
Link it with	Kidsty Pike, Rampsgill Head or Wether Hill
Part of	Martindale Skyline

To reach the summit of remote High Raise – in its solitary setting far from road access – is an achievement in itself. The second highest summit in the High Street range is a worthy objective offering generous views from the Pennines to the Coniston fells and a necessary feature of any thorough exploration of the fells of the Far East.

At its eastern foot, on Castle Crag, sit the remains of an Iron Age fort. Here a natural rampart fronted by a wall is surmounted by a shattered wall more than 2000 years old, with space for dwellings tightly limited. The tiny native kinship would have resorted to this waterless place only at times of extreme peril and for very short periods of time.

↑ *Whelter Crags, High Raise*

Probably most frequently bagged on the fine skyline trek from Martindale (1), the fell can also be reached from either end of Haweswater, climbing over the Long Grain ridge (2), penetrating the wilds of Measand Beck (looking out for red deer on Skreel Side) (3) or coming along the shore or up from Mardale Head to the great amphitheatre of Whelter Crags (4 or 5).

Ascent from Martindale 6 *off map N*

Via Keasgill Head →*6km/3¾ miles* ↑*640m/2100ft* ⏱*2hr 30min*

A common route to the top, part of the Martindale horseshoe, and uplifting throughout

1 From the verge follow the footpath rising directly behind the Old Church – regular use keeps the bracken at bay. Pass through a wall-gap (hand-gate missing) onto the ridge, coming over the rocky shoulder of **Brownthwaite Crag**. The path negotiates some pretty damp ground as it curves into the head of the **Fusedale Beck** valley, fording a gill beside two ruined shepherds' bothies. Curving right beyond **Gowk Hill**, embark on a steady pull across the western slopes of Wether Hill. Some of the way follows a groove, coming

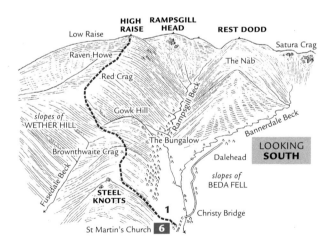

Winter aspect up the Longgrain Beck valley

up by **Mere Beck**. High up take the less-walked route by slipping across the dry upper section of the gill to go through the gateway in the rising wall and follow on with the fence, with minimal evidence of a path. Pass on by the undistinguished top of **Red Crag** and its peaty pool, **Redcrag Tarn**, to go through a hand-gate where the fence moves across to unite with a consistent ridge wall. Head on over **Raven Howe**, arriving at a stile where a fence breaks right from the wall-end. The stony summit is shortly gained off to the left from the Roman road.

Ascent from Burnbanks 17 *off map E*

Three routes to help you plan a circuit: the clear ridge route (Route 1), the wild and watery, unfrequented valley option (2) or the shoreline path (3) familiar to Coast to Coasters

Via Measand End →*7.3km/4½ miles* ↑*620m/2035ft* ⏱*2hr 45min*
2 From the car park walk up the roadway by the chalet bungalows, switching right by two hand-gates out of the woodland belt. Turn west, accompanying a good track with progressively better views across the great 'lake'. A large deer-exclusion gate/fence brings the trail into a newly-planted enclosure

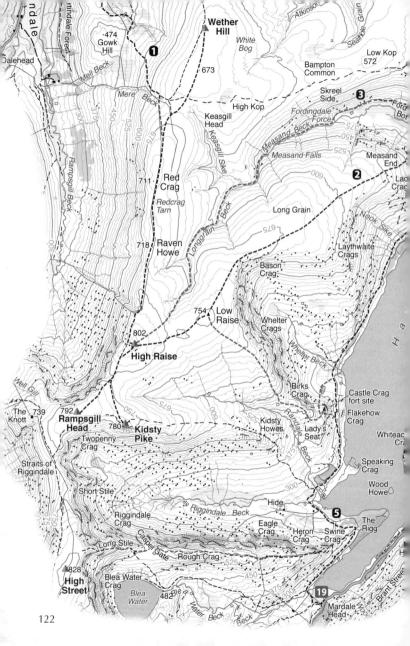

Wether
Hill

White
Bog

673

474
Gowk
Hill

❶

Dalehead

Low Kop
572

Bampton
Common

High Kop

Skreel
Side

❸

Ford
Bot

Keasgill
Head

Measand Falls

Fordingdale
Force

Measand
End

Lac
Crag

Red
Crag

711

Long Grain

❷

Redcrag
Tarn

Nook Sike

Raven
Howe

718

Laythwaite
Crags

Bason
Crag

754

Low
Raise

Whelter
Crags

802

High Raise

Whelter Beck

Birks
Crag

Castle Crag
fort site

Rampsgill
Head

792

Kidsty
Howes

Flakehow
Crag

The
Knott

739

780

Kidsty
Pike

Lady's
Seat

Whiteac
Cra

Twopenny
Crag

Randale Beck

Straits of
Riggindale

Speaking
Crag

Short Stile

Wood
Howe

Riggindale
Crag

Hide

❺

Riggindale Beck

Eagle
Crag

Heron
Crag

Swine
Crag

The
Rigg

Long Stile

Casper Gate

Rough Crag

828

High
Street

Blea Water
Crag

Blea
Water

482

❶❾

Mardale
Head

Brant Street

122

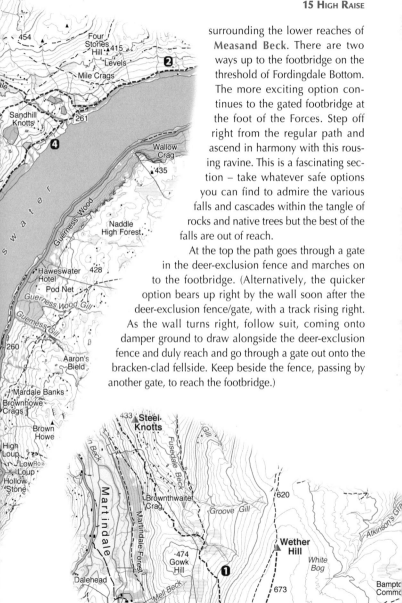

surrounding the lower reaches of **Measand Beck**. There are two ways up to the footbridge on the threshold of Fordingdale Bottom. The more exciting option continues to the gated footbridge at the foot of the Forces. Step off right from the regular path and ascend in harmony with this rousing ravine. This is a fascinating section – take whatever safe options you can find to admire the various falls and cascades within the tangle of rocks and native trees but the best of the falls are out of reach.

At the top the path goes through a gate in the deer-exclusion fence and marches on to the footbridge. (Alternatively, the quicker option bears up right by the wall soon after the deer-exclusion fence/gate, with a track rising right. As the wall turns right, follow suit, coming onto damper ground to draw alongside the deer-exclusion fence and duly reach and go through a gate out onto the bracken-clad fellside. Keep beside the fence, passing by another gate, to reach the footbridge.)

Two routes break from this spot. Standing on the west side of the Measand Beck footbridge the primary option heads southwest, but be sure to hold to the slightly right-hand option as bracken intervenes. The regular way, used by quad bikes, is more direct than the old drove shown on maps. This weaves up **Measand End** past a rock and then grassy groove onto the broad pasture above **Lad Crags**. The slope eases amid terrain interspersed with eroded groughs. As the higher plateau is reached, pass a slender peat hag. The quad track marches along the expansive **Long Grain** ridge towards **Low Raise**.

Take the opportunity to visit the edge, eventually to view the great combe beneath Whelter Crags, with Bason Crag in the foreground. The ancient stones comprising Low Raise have been reworked into a substantial cairn, and the remnant stone heap into a wind-shelter. The ridge path turns southwest to reach the summit.

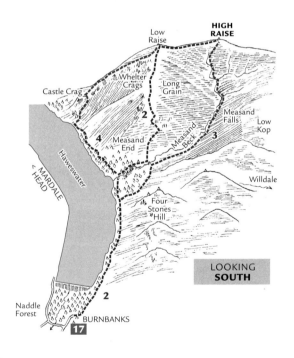

The ridgeway approach from Rampsgill Head

Via Measand Falls →*8km/5 miles* ↑*645m/2115ft* ⏲*3hr 30min*

3 Alternatively from the east side of the top footbridge follow the path running level along the base of the fell at the edge of the great basin of **Fordingdale Bottom**, clearly once a shallow tarn. This sheep trod becomes less evident as it comes above the large sheepfold complex, the layout suggestive of a sheep-wash, a Bampton Common gathering point. Come above **Fordingdale Force**, now on rocky ground, to draw closer to the gorge. The fellsides on either side of the beck are steep, but should pose no problem. Some way up the gorge a substantial waterfall comes into view. Keep up to overcome the awkward approach, then move down to inspect the 8m-high **Measand Falls**. The valley has a few more rough moments above this point, but nothing to hamper the determined gill-wanderer. Keep to the left-hand watercourse at the fork, holding to **Longgrain Beck**, and follow this southwest. Ultimately rise on tough but easier-angled moorland, targeting the stony summit.

Via Whelter Crags →8.5km/5¼ miles ↑720m/2360ft ⏱3hr 30min

4 Start with Route **2**, and continue along the clear lakeshore path. There is one scree-fringed section en route to a small footbridge spanning **Whelter Beck**, with its holly-laced ravine beneath. Step up right some 50 metres after the footbridge and skirt to the right of the small walled conifer copse to climb the broad gully between crags, the more prominent left-hand cliff being **Castle Crag**. There is some trace of the zig-zag path higher up, although it is apparent only outside the bracken season. Make a move left at the top to visit the **Castle Crag fort site**.

Backtrack to weave your way up onto **Lady's Seat** and then the ridge above **Birks Crag** and find a path that ventures to a ruined bothy and fold. Turn then to task and climb the minor outcropping of the broad ridge bounding **Whelter Crags**. Expect no path on this seldom-climbed ridge. Reach the top of Low Raise with some relief – it's a tough old climb. The reward is a stout cairn and the lowest of wind-shelters built from the loose tumulus relic. A clear path, reinforced by quad-bike use, leads on southwest to the main summit.

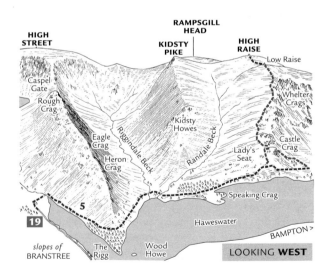

126

Fairfield and Great Gable

Ascent from Mardale Head 19

Via Castle Crag →*5.8km/3½ miles* ↑*625m/2050ft* ⏲*2hr 30min*

The direct route but still full of scenic interest

5 Leave the car park via the kissing-gate. As the wall turns right under the
bower of an oak, follow suit, following the sign 'Fellside path to Bampton'.
The path duly runs on via a hand-gate and three footbridges, the last a broad
walk over Mardale Beck. Go right, slipping over the ridge-end, sheltered
to the right by the conifers of **the Rigg**, and trend easily down left into the
valley of Riggindale. The path leads over successive footbridges – spanning
Riggindale Beck, and then **Randale Beck**. Hold faith with the trail, passing
below a conifer plantation, and with a wall right much of the way until the
trail rises by thorn bushes onto the shoulder of **Flakehow Crag**, a handsome
elevated viewpoint. Here there are two options to get to the top of the first
headland. Either turn directly left, climbing to the top of the hill-fort via
the steep slope left of **Castle Crag**. A scree-top path leads onto a grass and
heather bank – although steep, it is within normal tolerances and very direct.
Alternatively, descend with the continuing path until some 50 metres short of
Whelter Beck footbridge, then turn up left, joining forces with Route **4**.

The summit

The stony summit is unique in the High Street range and lends the place a special quality, as well as providing foreground for a photograph. The views are generous in all directions. The Pennines form a consistent skyline on the eastern arc, while the Helvellyn range dominates the western view, with several major fells, including from Coniston Old Man to Blencathra, well in evidence.

Safe descents

You are inevitably a long way from habitation in Mardale. To reach the road end, follow the ridge route S to Kidsty Pike, joining the well-made path heading E down by Kidsty Howes. There are some tricky moments as you emerge on steep ground leading into Rigindale. Hartsop is the nearest settlement, reached by following the skyline route S then W over Rampsgill Head to join the regular path glancing down by the Knott into the Hayeswater Gill valley. If you follow a ridge path you will find safe haven, eventually.

Ridge routes

Kidsty Pike →0.9km/½ mile ↓50m/165ft ↑25m/80ft ⊕20min
Join the Roman road which slips over the west side of the summit, descend SSW, and from the depression take the left fork, curving round the head of Randale direct to the summit.

Rampsgill Head →1km/½ mile ↓50m/165ft ↑40m/130ft ⊕25min
From the depression SSW of the summit take the right-hand path, coming naturally onto the brow to find the summit cairn beyond the impressive craggy edge.

Wether Hill →3.5km/2¼ miles ↓160m/525ft ↑30m/100ft ⊕1hr
(This route was surveyed by the Romans, so you can expect directness.) Follow the ridge path N, crossing a stile where a fence meets a wall. Keep with the wall, and where this ends go through a hand-gate then accompany the fence as it passes Redcrag Tarn and veers half-right to cross the broken wall and run on through the shallow depression at Keasgill Head. Here two paths are evident, both leading on to the cairn at the far end of the broad damp ridge of Wether Hill.

16 HIGH STREET 828M/2717FT

Climb it from	Hartsop **3**, Mardale Head **19**, Kentmere **33** or Hallow Bank **34**
Character	Whale-backed summit of the Far Eastern range
Fell-friendly route	3
Summit grid ref	NY 441 110
Link it with	Mardale Ill Bell, Rampsgill Head or Thornthwaite Crag
Part of	Mardale Head Horseshoe

High Street is the high focal point of the Far Eastern range of fells, towering over Blea Water to the east, Hayeswater to the northwest and forming the northern tip of the triangular plateau to the south that blocks the head of Kentmere – and it has been a natural gathering place down the ages.

The Romans swept a high road over the fells here to connect their forts at Galava (Ambleside) and Brocavum (Brougham, near Penrith), first garrisoned by Syrian cavalry. Their 'high street' ran up abruptly from the Trout Beck valley, along Scot Rake towards the current beacon on Thornthwaite Crag, then along the western brink of this central fell to exit north on the Straits of Riggindale over Rampsgill Head. In more recent centuries shepherds from neighbouring

↑ *High Street from Twopenny Crag*

valleys met on the plateau to reclaim wayward sheep and enjoy sporting rivalry, including fell-pony races – hence the fell's alternative name, Racecourse Hill.

The classic ascent is over Rough Crag from Mardale Head (2) offering the opportunity for a fine circuit including either Kidsty Pike or Mardale Ill Bell. Longer approaches are also described here from Hartsop (1) or Kentmere (4).

Ascent from Hartsop 3

Creep up on the summit from the north via secluded Hayeswater.

Via the Knott →5.4km/3½ miles ↑700m/2300ft ⏱2hr 45min

1 Follow the valley track east via Wath Bridge, ascending to Hayeswater dam. Bear left with three possible lines up the flank of the Knott. Take the most natural (far left) one heading north to come up by the wall and join the popular path from Angle Tarn, part of the Coast to Coast Walk and well-travelled. Climb a peaty rise with some pitching. Higher a loose gravel trail leads through a wall-gap and round the northern side of **the Knott**. Swing south on the level beside the wall and come down through the narrow section of the ridge known as the **Straits of Rigindale**. Keep the wall close right, ignoring the passage through what was the course of the Roman road. Come onto the minor cairned top of **Short Stile** for a special view into Riggindale.

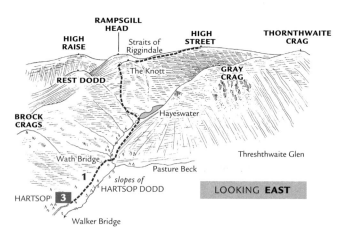

Long Stile and Rough Crag from the Straits of Riggindale

Continue through the pooled depression and rise to the summit (or, in good conditions, hold by the pathless eastern edge to prolong your enjoyment of Riggindale until the cairn is met at the top of the **Long Stile** ridge, and then head back west to the wall and the summit).

Ascent from Mardale Head **19**

A hint of Helvellyn and Striding Edge here in the blunt buttress ridge of Long Stile and the Rough Crag crest – but so much less travelled! Combine with Route 3 for a fascinating little loop.

Via Rough Crag ridge →4.7km/3 miles ↑620m/2035ft ⊕2hr 10min
2 Go through the kissing-gate, and, where three paths diverge under the bower of an oak, follow 'Fellside path to Bampton' right. This path was commonly taken by ornithologists venturing to the Riggindale viewing hide to strain their eyes for the now-lost Golden Eagle.

After crossing Mardale Beck on a broad bridge bear right and follow on beside the reservoir-bounding wall. Ignore the short-cut where the wall corners close – you do not need to contribute to further unsightly erosion. Continue to the shelter of the conifers on **the Rigg**, go through the gateway and

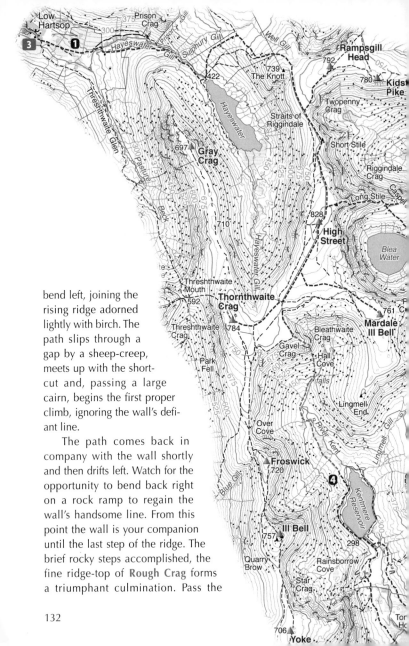

bend left, joining the rising ridge adorned lightly with birch. The path slips through a gap by a sheep-creep, meets up with the short-cut and, passing a large cairn, begins the first proper climb, ignoring the wall's defiant line.

The path comes back in company with the wall shortly and then drifts left. Watch for the opportunity to bend back right on a rock ramp to regain the wall's handsome line. From this point the wall is your companion until the last step of the ridge. The brief rocky steps accomplished, the fine ridge-top of **Rough Crag** forms a triumphant culmination. Pass the crest-topping cairn and walk down to pass to the right of the pool in the enigmatically named **Caspel Gate**. (Note that this is **not** a cross-over point on the ridge, as crags lurk on the east side.) The **Long Stile** spur ridge looms ahead, and the path copes confidently with its numerous stepped stages to reach the brink cairn. From here bear half-left to reach the summit.

Via Blea Water

→3.6km/2¼ miles
↑590m/1935ft ⏱2hr

3 Begin with Route **2**, but straight after the broad bridge spanning Mardale Beck bear left and follow the old way. After the first gate **Dudderwick Force** (waterfall) is down to your left. The path rises through a second gate, across from a fine fall in **Blea Water Beck**, with a sturdy juniper clinging to its upper lip. Beyond this point the path traverses marshy ground, although the line of an aqueduct pipe provides a drier alternative to the dam outflow of **Blea Water**. A path climbs the moraine directly from the concrete dam, angling up the slope to connect with the ridge path west of the **Caspel Gate** tarn as the rockier ground at the foot of **Long Stile** is met and you rejoin Route **2**.

Ancient ridgeway – Roman road?

133

Ascent from Kentmere 33 *off map S* or Hallow Bank 34 *off map S*

Via Hall Cove →*8km/5 miles* ↑*680m/2230ft* ⊕*3hr 45min*

Appreciate the true remoteness of this fell by tracing the upper course of the River Kent towards its source in Hall Cove, with a choice of two early valley approaches.

4 From Kentmere village, by either the road or green lanes, venture onto the private road to Hartrigg and continue on with the track to the **Kentmere Reservoir** dam. (The same spot can be reached from Hallow Bank by the gated dale-floor footpath via Overend and **Tongue House** (barn). From the barn cross to a ladder-stile to reach an area of slate spoil where once a quarrymen's bridge spanned the dale beck. Beyond, contour the banks to a point just beyond the man-made reservoir's outflow ravine. There cross a plankbridge and stepping-stones to cross the cobbled and stepped outflow channel itself by a gated bridge and reach the reservoir track.)

Keep to the path running along the western side of the reservoir, halfway along drifting down to avoid rocky ground. As the reservoir is passed so is clear evidence of a path through the damp dale-floor herbage well left

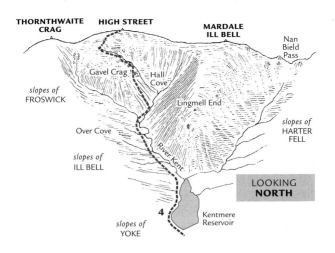

134

of the Kent, which for all its beck dimensions retains the name of 'river'. Coming near a wash-fold bear up left with the moraine ridge and trace along the top of this feature, beside the river.

Now take on the Gavel Crag ridge. At a noteworthy waterfall leave the beck and start to climb the steep fellside. Either drift half-left to avoid most of the rocky ground or tackle the ridge above. After the initial boulders it becomes a succession of small irregular outcrops, calling for canny

Eagle Crag below the Rough Crag ridge, as seen from Kidsty Pike

manoeuvres as you work your way, bit by bit, up the prow. Grass is found as the rocky shield is beaten and you climb onto the spine of the ridge to find the contouring path skirting the edge. Go right with this and, as the scree-streaked re-entrant that is the headstream of the Kent is reached, bear up north on the grassy moor to join the wall leading direct to the summit column.

The summit

While Roman road engineers took the pragmatic course along the western brink of the fell, the estate-defining wall traced the highest ground. This has greatly tumbled in the modern era but it is sufficient to ensure a welcome wind-break for rest and recuperation, a little distance either side of the OS column. To the south, a small holding pen is an unusual feature to find in such an elevated position. The summit is otherwise a bleak place but the view is mighty and generous. The Coniston and Langdale fell groups are well in evidence, as too is the angular form of Great Gable and, in a gap in the Helvellyn range, High Stile peeps through between Fairfield and Dollywaggon Pike. A special and little appreciated viewpoint is that over Blea Water from

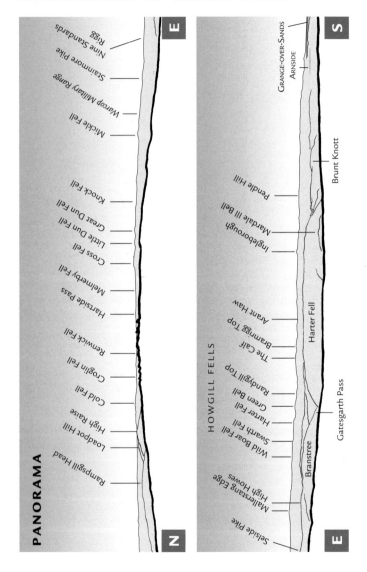

PANORAMA

N – E panorama:

Rampsgill Head, Loadpot Hill, High Raise, Cold Fell, Croglin Fell, Renwick Fell, Hartside Pass, Melmerby Fell, Cross Fell, Little Dun Fell, Great Dun Fell, Knock Fell, Mickle Fell, Warcop Military Range, Stainmore Pike, Nine Standards, Rigg

E – S panorama:

Seldide Pike, Mallerstang Edge, High Howes, Branstree, Wild Boar Fell, Swarth Fell, Harter Fell, Green Bell, Randygill Top, HOWGILL FELLS, The Calf, Bramrigg Top, Avant Haw, Harter Fell, Gatesgarth Pass, Ingleborough, Mardale Ill Bell, Pendle Hill, Brunt Knott, ARNSIDE, GRANGE-OVER-SANDS

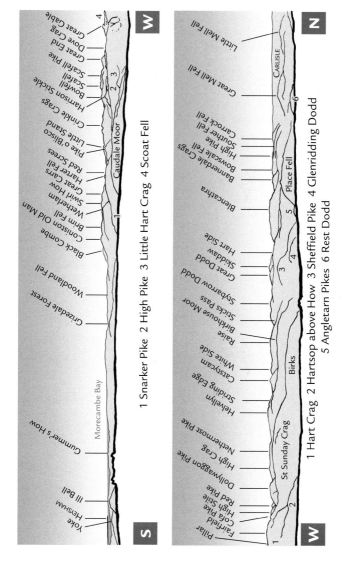

W

4 — Great Gable / Dove Crag / Great End / Scafell Pike / Scafell / Bowfell / Harrison Stickle / Cinkle Crags / Pike o'Blisco / Little Stand / Red Screes / Harter Fell / Great Carrs / Swirl How / Wetherlam / Brim Fell / Coniston Old Man / Black Combe / Caudale Moor / Woodland Fell / Grisedale Forest

S

Morecambe Bay / Gummer's How / Ill Bell / Yoke / HEYSHAM

1 Snarker Pike 2 High Pike 3 Little Hart Crag 4 Scoat Fell

N

Little Mell Fell / Great Mell Fell / CARLISLE / Carrock Fell / Souther Fell / High Pike / Bowscale Fell / Bannerdale Crags / Place Fell / Blencathra / Skiddaw / Great Dodd / Stybarrow Dodd / Sticks Pass / Birkhouse Moor / Raise / White Side / Catstycam / Striding Edge / Helvellyn / Nethermost Pike / High Crag / Dollywaggon Pike / Red Pike / High Stile / Cofa Pike / Fairfield / Pillar / Hart Side / Sheffield Pike / Glenridding Dodd / Angletarn Pikes / Rest Dodd / St Sunday Crag / Birks

W

1 Hart Crag 2 Hartsop above How 3 Sheffield Pike 4 Glenridding Dodd
5 Angletarn Pikes 6 Rest Dodd

137

the path to Mardale Ill Bell. Walk southeast – there is no path – until the slope starts to fall away to find several good vantage points.

Safe descents

Clearly the greatest dangers lie to the east, but a well-developed path system comes to walkers' aid in hostile conditions. For Mardale Head use the Mardale Ill Bell ridge path S then SE to Nan Bield Pass, thereby avoiding the steep ground of Long Stile. Although, if you can handle the rocks of Long Stile, the branch right from Caspel Gate to the outflow of Blea Water (**3**) makes a comparatively sheltered way down. For points west the solution is far easier to contemplate, with the way down to Hartsop found by following the ridge wall N (**1**) via the Straits of Riggindale and keeping by the wall and subsequent trail W down into the Hayeswater valley or Angle Tarn for Patterdale.

Ridge routes

Mardale Ill Bell → *1.7km/1 mile* ↓*80m/260ft* ↑*15m/50ft* ⏱*30min*
Walk S on the east side of the ridge wall to an engineered path. This trail leads S then SE on a gentle gradient down. As the new trail ends keep to the low ridge to reach the summit cairn.

Rampsgill Head → *2km/1¼ miles* ↓*130m/425ft* ↑*95m/310ft* ⏱*40min*
Those who relish following the Roman road should head W to encounter it short of the steep brink of the Hayeswater valley. Go N to slip through the ridge wall on the gentle rise in the Straits of Riggindale. Alternatively, you may enjoy keeping to the E side of the ridge wall from the OS column and visiting the cairn on top of Short Stile before rejoining the wall to the gap. As the path climbs from the gap bear off right at the fork coming over the top of Twopenny Crag. Keep to the edge, now travelling E, to find a path-fork which guides you directly to the summit cairn.

Thornthwaite Crag → *1.6km/1 mile* ↓*75m/245ft* ↑*30m/100ft* ⏱*25min*
Follow the ridge wall on the west side declining to where the broken wall breaks right. Continue with the wall right (20 metres) as far as the Roman road and then follow this, curving W to the beacon cairn.

17 ILL BELL 757M/2484FT

Climb it from	Kentmere **33** or Hallow Bank **34**
Character	Regal queen of a trio of summits above Kentmere
Fell-friendly route	1
Summit grid ref	NY 436 078
Link it with	Froswick or Yoke
Part of	Kentmere Horseshoe

One of the star attractions of the Far Eastern range of fells, Ill Bell is the central and highest member of the trio of distinctive and characterful hills lying between the Troutbeck and Kentmere valleys. Looming authoritatively over Froswick to the north and Yoke to the south, it shelters two craggy coves – Rainsborrow and Over Cove – on its eastern side, and sweeps up gracefully from the west – a fell to admire in any season.

Kentmere Reservoir nestles at its foot. The reservoir is not a natural lake but was built in 1848 to provide a controlled water supply to a gunpowder mill, a wood mill, a snuff mill and the James Cropper paper mill, now the sole owner. Above the reservoir rises the River Kent, a Special Area of Conservation which

↑ *Ill Bell (behind Froswick) from Kentmere Pike* 139

flows a short 20 miles down to Morecambe Bay through Kendal and has a reputation for rising and falling with dangerous rapidity.

Almost everyone climbs the fell by the perennially popular ridge path. The route described here is a fabulous off-beat, mildly scrambly alternative.

Ascent from Kentmere 33 *off map S* or Hallow Bank 34 *off map S*

Via northeast ridge →*6.4km/4 miles* ↑*660m/2165ft* ⏱*3hr*

The perfect climb, best on a warm summer's day and to be avoided in adverse conditions

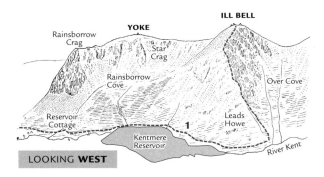

RAINSBORROW Crag — YOKE — ILL BELL — Star Crag — Rainsborrow Cove — Over Cove — Reservoir Cottage — Leads Howe — Kentmere Reservoir — River Kent — **1**

LOOKING WEST

1 From Kentmere village, by either the road or green lanes, venture onto the private road to Hartrigg and continue on with the track to the **Kentmere Reservoir** dam. (The same spot can be reached from Hallow Bank by the gated dale-floor footpath via Overend and **Tongue House** (barn). From the barn cross to a ladder-stile to reach an area of slate spoil where once a quarrymen's bridge spanned the dale beck. Beyond, contour the banks to a point just beyond the man-made reservoir's outflow ravine. There cross a plank-bridge and stepping-stones to cross the cobbled and stepped outflow channel itself by a gated bridge and reach the reservoir track.)

Follow on with the path above the western shore and keep to the lower path at a fork to curve under the breast of **Leads Howe**. As the reservoir ends, bear up left, easily finding the swelling northeast ridge. This steepens and minor outcropping, taken in bite-size chunks, entertains your hands and feet. Higher, the rocks are less of an issue and the summit is easily reached.

The summit

Nature and man have combined to achieve a place of great architectural merit. The vertically split slate bedrock underfoot is attractive in itself, but the greater harmony comes from the strategically sited cairns. The view is magnificent – particularly south to Windermere and, in the west, held between Wansfell and Red Screes, the fells from Black Combe to Pillar centred upon the Scafells.

PANORAMA

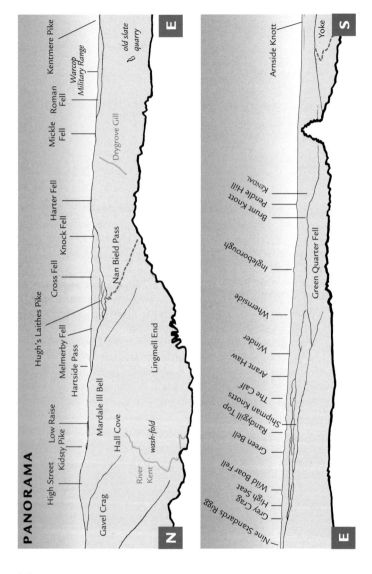

E

Kentmere Pike
Warcop Military Range
old slate quarry
Roman Fell
Mickle Fell
Drygrove Gill
Harter Fell
Knock Fell
Cross Fell
Nan Bield Pass
Hugh's Laithes Pike
Melmerby Fell
Hartside Pass
Lingmell End
Mardale Ill Bell
Low Raise
High Street
Kidsty Pike
Hall Cove
wash-fold
River Kent
Gavel Crag

N

S

Arnside Knott
Yoke
Burnt Knott
Pendle Hill
KENDAL
Ingleborough
Green Quarter Fell
Whernside
Winder
Arant Haw
The Calf
Shipman Knotts
Randygill Top
Green Bell
Wild Boar Fell
High Seat
Grey Crag
Nine Standards Rigg

E

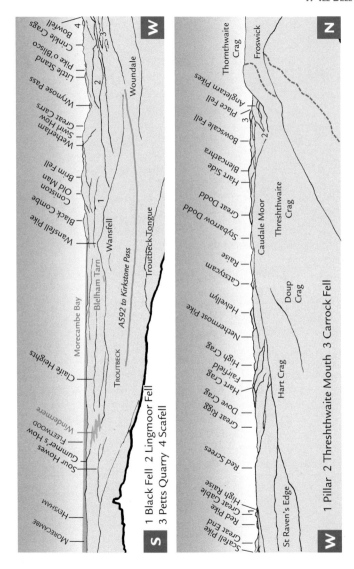

W

Bowfell
Crinkle Crags
Pike o'Blisco
Little Stand
Wrynose Pass
Great Cars
Swirl How
Wetherlam
Brim Fell
Conison Old Man
Black Combe
Wansfell Pike
Wansfell
Woundale
Troutbeck Tongue
A592 to Kirkstone Pass
Bletham Tarn
TROUTBECK
Morecambe Bay
Claife Heights
Windermere
FLEETWOOD
Gummer's How
Sour Howes
HEYSHAM
MORECAMBE

S

1 Black Fell 2 Lingmoor Fell
3 Petts Quarry 4 Scafell

N

Froswick
Thornthwaite Crag
Angletarn Pikes
Place Fell
Bowscale Fell
Blencathra
Hart Side
Great Dodd
Stybarrow Dodd
Caudale Moor
Threshthwaite Crag
Raise
Catstycam
Helvellyn
Nethermost Pike
Doup Crag
High Crag
Fairfield
Hart Crag
Hart Crag
Dove Crag
Great Rigg
Red Screes
Red Pike
Great Gable
Great End
Scafell Pike
Scafell
High Raise
St Raven's Edge

W

1 Pillar 2 Threshthwaite Mouth 3 Carrock Fell

Trio of cairns on the summit

Safe descents

The ridge path S gives all the security you need over Yoke to reach the Garburn Pass for Troutbeck and Kentmere.

Ridge routes

Froswick →*0.8km/½ mile* ↓*105m/345ft* ↑*70m/230ft* ⊕*25min*
Stick religiously to the tried, tested and well-repaired path leading NW from either side of the north cairn outcrop.

Yoke →*1km/½ mile* ↓*100m/330ft* ↑*50m/165ft* ⊕*20min*
Due S the ridge path runs along the brink of Rainsborrow Cove, with a minor rise to reach the cairn on the summit rock dais.

18 KENTMERE PIKE 730M/2395FT

Climb it from	Hallow Bank **34** or Sadgill **31**
Character	Eastern crown of Kentmere and western shield of the wild upper passage of Longsleddale
Fell-friendly route	2
Summit grid ref	NY 466 078
Link it with	Harter Fell or Shipman Knotts
Part of	Kentmere Horseshoe

Despite the name, in fellwalking terms the finest qualities of Kentmere Pike belong utterly to Longsleddale rather than its westerly neighbour. The great ridge that forms the high divide between upper Kentmere and Longsleddale has two notable summits, Harter Fell and Kentmere Pike, and the latter in turn has two dependant summits, Goat Scar and Shipman Knotts. Unassailable from the east, Goat Scar shields the main mass of the fell from Sadgill, diverting would-be summiteers up through Brownhowe Bottom.

In their path lies Wrengill Quarry – a scene of discordance and dereliction. Thunderous waters have caused major wash-outs, with slate spoil banks adding to the visual clamour. A massive quarried ravine sits to the south and an equally

↑ *Goat Scar and Kentmere Pike from Galeforth Brow*

impressive retaining wall to the north below a grassy platform, where further ruined workshops stand. Remnant mine rails protrude from just below the cave.

Many walkers do tackle the fell from Hallow Bank on the Kentmere side (1) but the more interesting approaches lead up from Longsleddale (2–4) and there's always the option to fashion and circuit to include both of these secluded valleys.

Ascent from Hallow Bank 34

A straightforward ascent offering insights into the upper Kentmere valley

Via Withered Howe →4.8km/3 miles ↑470m/1540ft ⏱2hr

1 Follow the road into the hamlet of Hallow Bank. Keep right below Brockstones to take the green track up from the garage by **Beald Head** to a gate onto a fell path. A consistent path, sometimes in a stony groove by trees and bushes, ensures a steady plod up to and through a gateless wall-gap, from where the top of the bastion outcrop of **Withered Howe** reveals a delightful view of the upper Kentmere valley. From here, rushes cause the path to keep reasonably close order with the rising wall, but it does bend north and northeast before the wall falters, slanting over a gill-head to reach a ladder-stile. From here take a direct line on a regular path to the ridge wall and follow it left to the summit.

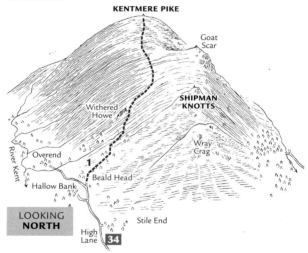

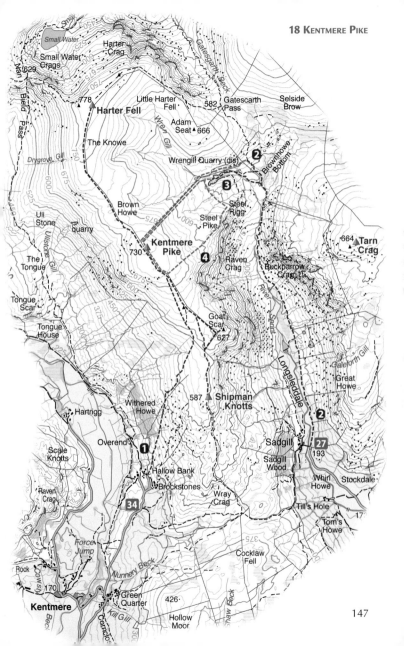

Ascent from Sadgill 31

There are three ways to the top from Brownhowe Bottom all starting with the drama of the wild dale head of Longsleddale. From here Route 2 is the simplest and safest while Route 4 heads up a rocky spur for maximum thrills.

Via Wren Gill →5km/3 miles ↑550m/1805ft ⏱2hr 15min

2 Walk north from the bridge within the rocky walled lane. The lane runs close under **Buckbarrow Crag** and then switches sharply right and left with cobbling – a stony surface that has been cruelly challenged by 4x4 vehicles. At this point the **River Sprint** thunders down a series of fine water shoots at Cleft Ghyll, from which walkers are denied easy access, although you could hop over the metal railings to have a look. From the gate at the top and bridge at the foot of Brownhowe Bottom you have three options.

Stay with the bridle-track via a kissing-gate/gate (where the broad gate is padlocked) and begin the ascent beyond the fold. At the third hairpin bear off left on a short track to a padlocked galvanised gate. Head west above the wall which bars off the stony confusion of **Wrengill Quarry**. Reach an old water pipe and race that once tapped an outflow of Wren Gill to power a quarry pump. Ford **Wren Gill** (you may have to take a little time to find a crossing point when the gill is in spate) and continue southwest, climbing beside the wall. Cross the fence, where a gate once stood, at the junction with the wall and step onto the open ridge path. Go left and soon reach the summit.

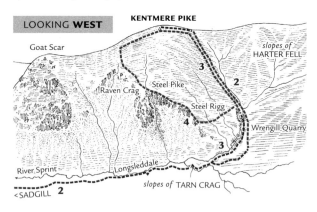

148

Hartrigg from the path above Hallow Bank

Via Wrengill Quarry →4.8km/3 miles ↑550m/1805ft ⊕2hr 20min

3 Start with Route **2** but at the three-way decision point follow the track into a walled pen and then turn off left immediately through a wooden gate and walk towards the slatey banks of the **River Sprint**. Keep up right on a thin path as the ravine becomes more constricted, coming over a tunnel arch. Pass a level area with the vestige of an old workshop and rusting scoop to ascend an incline. Keep to the right side, advancing to visit the remarkable waterfall beyond the two pillars that once carried an overhead track. **Take care:** footing is awkward, and the cavern beneath your feet forbidding. View the impressive arrival of **Wren Gill** as it tumbles into a hole akin to a limestone sink, disappearing through a chaos of boulders and seemingly blocking bedrock wall to emerge into the adjacent quarried canyon. Step back and complete your industrial journey beside Wren Gill. Ford the gill with care as it bends right to carry on in company with the wall/fence rising southwest – a long unremitting climb – and at the top keep left to stand precisely beside the OS column.

Via Steel Pike →5.6km/3½ miles ↑580m/1905ft ⊕2hr 30min

4 Alternatively, follow Route **3** as far as the top of the quarry, cross the main gill with care (you may have to search for a crossing point) and there skirt

149

left, keeping above the topmost canyon and traversing the slope, stepping over two minor gills, to clamber onto the edge of **Steel Rigg**. Hold the edge, coming beside a broken wall climbing out of the main valley. The view down Longsleddale is fabulous from here. As the wall ends find a metal fence post and follow the line of remnant posts to the ridge wall. Then complete the ascent by turning right beside the wall.

The summit

The ridge path sweeps past a stone cairn, but the actual summit is marked by a retired triangulation column. The pillar stands on the east side of the wall but a wall-stile has been provided (the view from the west side being the better one). Canny walkers stand on the top of the wall-stile and get the best of both worlds! Ill

Ridge wall reflected in a pool a short way south of the summit

Bell and Froswick inevitably draw the eyes across upper Kentmere. Beyond, familiar heights crowd to the west, although Scafell Pike is hiding precisely behind Ill Bell's summit.

Safe descents

For Kentmere or Sadgill keep tight to the ridge over Shipman Knotts and use the quad-bike track to get down the final slopes and avoid the rocks. The quickest route to a valley is on the N side of the wall/fence, descending NE (**2**) to ford Wren Gill and subsequently join the Gatescarth Pass track into upper Longsleddale.

Ridge routes

Harter Fell → *1.8km/1 mile* ↓*35m/115ft* ↑*80m/265ft* ⊙*30min*
The path accompanies a fence, with intermittent sections of wall, holding to the spine of the ridge N over the Knowe to the summit cairn.

OS column and wall-stile

Shipman Knotts →*2km/1¼ miles* ↓*170m/560ft* ↑*25m/80ft* ⏱*30min*
There is a strict route and a scenic route. The former follows the wall and then
fence and angles SSE down to a ladder-stile, where a fence converges acutely
from the left. The scenic route makes for this point, but takes the time and
trouble to visit the top of Goat Scar en route by keeping beside the fence, with
some damp ground approaching the right-angled fence-corner. Here find a
stile and access to the crown of the headland. A cairn marks the spot for a
long contemplation. Hopping back over the stile, continue with the fence
close left to the ladder-stile on the more direct route. After the stile, the path
negotiates further damp ground and slips by a knoll – contender for the summit – to visit the cairn. This is not the actual summit, which lies out of bounds
on the east side of the uncrossable ridge wall.

19 KIDSTY PIKE 780M/2559FT

Climb it from	Mardale Head **19**
Character	Sharp scarp overlooking Riggindale
Fell-friendly route	1
Summit grid ref	NY 447 126
Link it with	High Raise or Rampsgill Head
Part of	Martindale Skyline

Easily visible from points east and fondly identified from afar, travellers on the A6 and even the M6 motorway know the distant peak of Kidsty Pike well and seldom miss the opportunity to pick it out and judge the weather by how well it can be seen. A procession of Coast to Coast walkers also mark their arrival in the Lake District proper with this clear summit despite the steepness of the slope for burdened backpackers. But in truth the fell is nothing more than the extended eastern spur ridge of Rampsgill Head.

It's hard to imagine now that once upon a time Kidsty Howes was seldom crossed. The path that slices through the crest today has come into being as a direct result of the short-cutting habit of Coast to Coasters, compounded by wash-out. As a result, the path between the summit and Kidsty Howes has been

↑ *Kidsty Pike from Twopenny Crag*

radically modified to accommodate its popularity and create an elegant, but durable, trail.

The southern slopes are uniformly steep making the way up from Riggindale the only plausible approach. It's a slow haul but the view is breathtaking too!

Ascent from Mardale Head 19

Via Kidsty Howes →*4.5km/2¾ miles* ↑*575m/1885ft* ⏱*2hr*

1 Go through the kissing-gate and where three paths diverge under the bower of an oak follow 'Fellside path to Bampton' to the right. This duly crosses Mardale Beck on a footbridge and naturally turns right, running on under the rough slopes of the **Rough Crag** ridge to slip over the spur of **the Rigg**, with its stand of conifers, and angle down into Riggindale. Through a copse the path crosses Bowderthwaite Bridge, and short of the **Randale Beck** footbridge

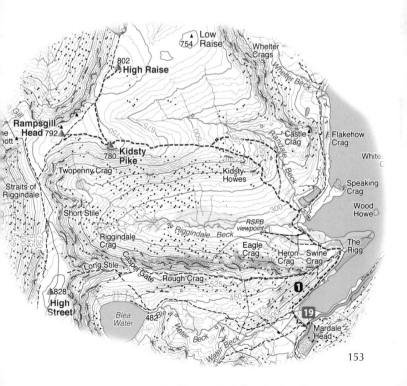

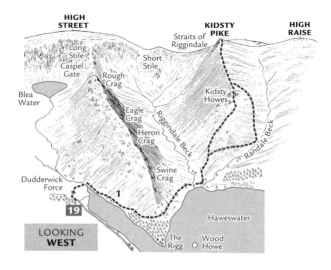

HIGH
STREET

KIDSTY
PIKE

HIGH
RAISE

Straits of
Riggindale

Long
Stile

Short
Stile

Caspel
Gate

Rough
Crag

Kidsty
Howes

Blea
Water

Eagle
Crag

Heron
Crag

Riggindale Beck

Randale Beck

Swine
Crag

Dudderwick
Force

1

19

LOOKING
WEST

Haweswater

The
Rigg

Wood
Howe

An arrow chiselled into stone by a surveyor in Randale Beck (looking to Branstree)

takes a turn up the damp slope to embark on the steady climb bound for **Kidsty Howes**. (A few hundred metres along the path, you could choose to follow the now-invisible line of the old shepherding path that used to lead more gently onto the northern slope of the ridge-end crest. Simply bear north until just above the beck and then bend left and west to pick up a path rising slowly to the ridge from the far side.) The popular path tackles the ridge which is less uncomfortable in ascent than in descent. Once on the grassy fell above, join the snaking trail to the top.

The summit

There is no doubting the summit – a cairn perched perilously on a small outcrop, from where the profound fall of the fell into Riggindale may take your the breath away, if the climb has not already claimed it! High Street is the centre of attention, but scan the skyline either side of Rampsgill Head to spot the Scafells, Pillar, Helvellyn and Blencathra.

High Street seen from the summit gully

Safe descents

In winter, when the bracken is down, avoid Kidsty Howes and instead drift far more easily into the Randale Beck valley, picking out the trace of the old path, which comes closer to the beck – but keep up in its latter stages, as there is a ravine. In summer, you are safer to trend ESE (**1**) on the more popular route.

Ridge routes

High Raise →*0.9km/½ mile* ↓*25m/80ft* ↑*50m/165ft* ⊕*20min*
An obvious path curves N across the headwaters of Randale. From the damp depression, where the Roman road is met, continue, rising to veer half-right onto the rocky top.

Rampsgill Head →*0.5km/¼ mile* ↓*10m/35ft* ↑*25m/80ft* ⊕*12min*
Follow the edge path W, and at the highest point break off right to reach the summit cairn within a mere few paces.

20 LOADPOT HILL 671M/2201FT

Climb it from	Roehead **10**, Askham **11**, Helton **12**, Helton Fell **13**, Cockle Hill **14**, Moorahill **16** or Fusedale **9**
Character	Northernmost summit of the High Street range
Fell-friendly route	4
Summit grid ref	NY 456 180
Link it with	Arthur's Pike, Bonscale Pike or Wether Hill

The most northerly component of the High Street range, Loadpot Hill is substantial if a trifle unexciting. While the western slopes fall sharply into Fusedale, to the east and north the fell declines moorland fashion. The deep hollow on the north side of the hill, identified as Loadpot Hole, is now considered to have Roman origins and to have been a source of road-stone for their genuinely 'High Street', which ran close by at this point, avoiding the summit plateau over the scenic western shoulder of the fell.

Where the Roman road realigns with the ridge on the south side of the summit plateau once stood Lowther House. The days when this was a shooting cabin are long departed, and only the bare outline remains, the remaining chimney stack having collapsed since Alfred Wainwright sketched it in the 1950s.

↑ *Loadpot Hill from Brock Crag*

Approaches can be made from all points north – longer expeditions from Roehead and Helton (1–4), shorter from Cockle Hill and Moorahill in the east (5–6) and shortest and steepest up from Howtown in the west (7–8)

Ascent from Roehead 10

A good leg-stretch along the Roman high road

Via the Cockpit →*7.2km/4½ miles* ↑*475m/1560ft* ⏱*2hr 30min*
1 Pass through the gate and follow the open track all the way up to the cairn almost on the brow. Bear off right on the firm dry path which leads to **the Cockpit** stone circle. Keep right with the main path, and shortly after the ford find a small cairn which marks the point of departure from the popular bridleway. Embark on the Roman road, climbing at an easy gradient up **Barton Fell**. The little top of **Arthur's Pike** may legitimately tempt you off right from the main path but otherwise your destiny stretches out ahead, seemingly ever more distant!

Notice the old way comes into a groove, which switches right immediately after the standing stone known as **Lambert Lad**. Avoid this and turn half-left off the Roman way to climb the final slopes of the fell ahead due

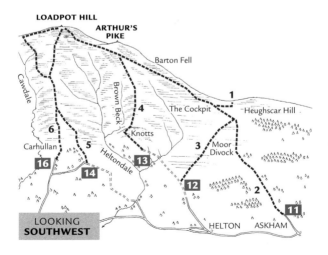

157

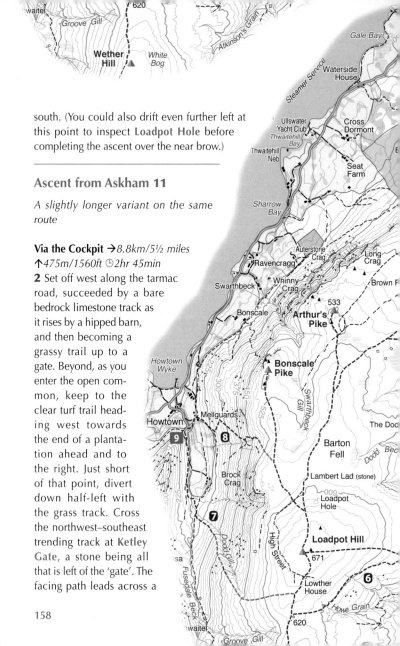

south. (You could also drift even further left at this point to inspect **Loadpot Hole** before completing the ascent over the near brow.)

Ascent from Askham 11

A slightly longer variant on the same route

Via the Cockpit →*8.8km/5½ miles*
↑*475m/1560ft* ⏱*2hr 45min*
2 Set off west along the tarmac road, succeeded by a bare bedrock limestone track as it rises by a hipped barn, and then becoming a grassy trail up to a gate. Beyond, as you enter the open common, keep to the clear turf trail heading west towards the end of a plantation ahead and to the right. Just short of that point, divert down half-left with the grass track. Cross the northwest–southeast trending track at **Ketley Gate**, a stone being all that is left of the 'gate'. The facing path leads across a

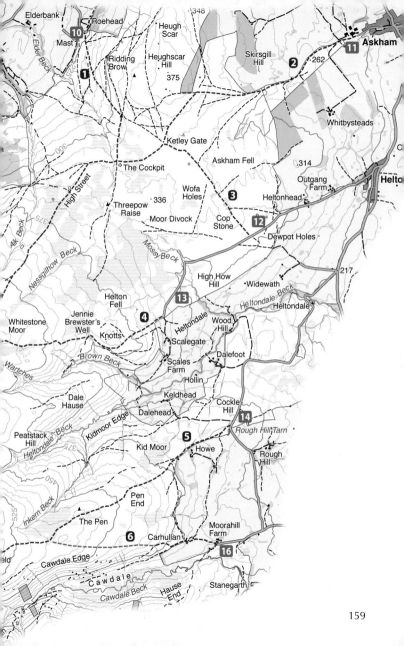

Elderbank
Roehead
10
Mast
Heugh
Scar
Heughscar
Hill
.375
.348
Skirsgill
Hill
Askham
11
2
.262
Ridding
Brow
1
Whitbysteads
Ketley Gate
Askham Fell
.314
Outgang
Farm
Helto
The Cockpit
Wofa
Holes
3
Heltonhead
Helton Fell
Cop
Stone
12
High Street
.336
Threepow
Raise
Moor Divock
Dewpot Holes
.217
Nessgilhow Beck
Mossy Beck
High How
Hill
Widewath
Heltondale
Heltondale Beck
Heltondale
Alk Beck
.375
13
Whitestone
Moor
Jennie
Brewster's
Well
4
Heltondale
Wood
Hill
Knotts
Scalegate
Dalefoot
Brown Beck
Scales
Farm
Hollin
Wartches
Dale
Hause
Keldhead
Cockle
Hill
Heltondale Beck
Dalehead
14
.375
Kidmoor Edge
Rough Hill Tarn
Peatstack
Hill
.450
5
Kid Moor
Howe
Rough
Hill
.525
Inkern Beck
Pen
End
The Pen
6
Carhullan
Moorahill
Farm
Cawdale Edge
16
eld
Cawdale
Cawdale Beck
Hause
End
Stanegarth

159

tract of decidedly damp moorland to reach the dry oasis of **the Cockpit**. Here join Route **1**.

Ascent from Helton 12

A third approach to the Cockpit, this time from the south across wetter territory

Via Moor Divock →*7.2km/4½ miles* ↑*375m/1230ft* ⏱*2hr 15min*
3 A lovely green turfed trail leads off the fell road, passing the enigmatic **Cop Stone**. The trail avoids sink holes and marshy ground until at a cross-ways it departs left, crossing a marshy tract of moor to reach **the Cockpit** stone circle. Here link up with Route **1**.

Ascent from Helton Fell 13

This variant largely dodges the marsh on the southern side.

Via Knotts →*5km/3 miles* ↑*370m/1215ft* ⏱*1hr 50min*
4 Ideally park 200 metres short of the gate accessing the enclosures leading to Scalegate and Scales Farm. The walk begins marshy underfoot following the wall up. As the wall bears left continue southwest, crossing over the low saddle of **Knotts** to run on to the right with a worn track to a ford – bearing the lovely name of **Jennie Brewster's Well**. The regular passage of a shepherding quad bike ensures the old path is well marked as it heads up the grassy fell westward to turn left with High Street and Route **1** on **Whitestone Moor** for the summit.

Ascent from Cockle Hill 14

A direct line tracks southwest to the summit.

Via the Pen →*4.3km/2¾ miles* ↑*355m/1165ft* ⏱*1hr 40min*
5 From the verge parking follow the left-hand track to **Howe** from the pool of **Rough Hill Tarn**. As the track turns in left keep up by the wall, and after a stone barn and tree shelter embark on the quad track up through the rushes, climbing steadily southwest onto **the Pen**. The solitary cairn lies off the line of

the regular path, which copes with the odd damp patch as it reaches the bield wall. From here bear up the fell west to reach the summit.

Ascent from Moorahill 16

A pathless, western course on a gentle gradient

Via Carhullan →5km/3 miles ↑360m/1180ft ⊕1hr 50min

6 Follow the walled lane from the gate and pass to the left of **Carhullan** farmhouse along a confined lane between barn walls. At some bedrock, the track steps up to reach a gate. Follow on with the wall left, but break up right onto the fellside, avoiding the bracken as best you can. The hint of an old path is quickly lost as a westward course is kept on an easy gradient. Follow this course duly to unite with the strong path from **the Pen**, which rises to pass beneath a bield wall. As a variant to the common walkers' way, bear off half-left after some 20 metres with the line of rushes defining an old drove-path on a southwest line. This route ventures to the head of Cawdale and the pool in the saddle between Wether and Loadpot Hills. At this point switch north with the regular ridge path, passing up by the minimal remnants of **Lowther House**.

Ascent from Fusedale 9

Two short climbs from the west not without their challenges

Via Dodd Gill →*3.2km/2 miles* ↑*500m/1640ft* ⏱*1hr 45min*

7 Follow the concrete farm-access roadway south. When you reach a cattle grid bear right with the footpath over the stone-flag bridge and run on above the beck, coming down to recross **Fusedale Beck** by a wooden footbridge. Bear right and cross the plank-bridge spanning **Dodd Gill**. Now embark on the climb left. There is an intermittent path higher up coping with some stony ground. Coming above the gill, cross the lateral line of a strong sheep path and continue pathless to join the ridge path in the intervening ground between the saddle and **Lowther House**. Turn left and pass up by the ruin, being sure to keep to the northward ridge path to gain the summit plateau.

Via Mellguards →*2.6km/1½ miles* ↑*500m/1640ft* ⏱*1hr 10min*

8 From the four-way signpost leave the open road at once to cross the clapper-bridge spanning **Fusedale Beck** and rise within the walled lane to a gate entering the gravel drive to **Mellguards**, the prominent white house. Go

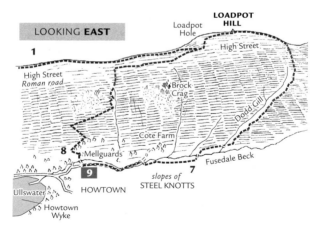

Skiddaw and Blencathra from the angle of the old Roman road northwest of the summit

through the gate by the house door and at once bear up right following the intake wall. Continue a short distance beyond where the wall angles right and then bend left in a rising groove leading onto a shoulder to find an old drove-path steering up right. This climbs above the gill and is lost as a path on the grassy rise to the plateau. Join the ridge-top path heading south-southeast and cross the Roman road to join the main path onto the summit plateau.

The summit

The focal point of the pasture plateau is an OS triangulation column. A small cairn lies 30 metres off the line of the regular flow of ridge walkers, to the east, composed of a handful of stones – some pure quartz – clustered around a Lowther/Dalemain estate boundary stone. The summit is not the best place to consider a view, there being no depth in any direction.

Safe descents

Distance is more the issue than craggy hazard. Join the Roman road N (**1**) heading down to Moor Divock for Pooley Bridge, Askham or Helton. Head E (**6**) for Bampton via Carhullan. The quickest route to a valley road at Howtown is W (**7**), but the slopes running into Fusedale are very steep.

Ewes standing by the ruins of Lowther House

Ridge routes

Arthur's Pike →*2.7km/1¾ miles* ↓*160m/525ft* ↑*25m/50ft* ⏱*40min*
Head N with the regular ridge path, descending to join the Roman road. After a little over 1.6km bear off, in effect keeping N direct to the summit.

Bonscale Pike →*2km/1¼ miles* ↓*165m/540ft* ↑*20m/65ft* ⏱*30min*
Start N, but at the first fork veer NW on a path that crosses the Roman road and follows on down onto the broad undulating ridge. Make a point of visiting the pair of beacon cairns known as Bonscale Tower, close under the summit cairn, to revel in a fine view of Ullswater.

Wether Hill →*1.4km/¾ mile* ↓*55m/180ft* ↑*55m/175ft* ⏱*30min*
Keep S with the evident ridge path. This passes down by the site of Lowther House to a depression with its glistening pool, then mounts the easy-angled peaty slope to the summit cairn.

21 MARDALE ILL BELL 761M/2497FT

Climb it from	Mardale Head **19**, Hallow Bank **34** or Kentmere **33**
Character	Craggy southeastern arm of High Street above Nan Bield Pass
Fell-friendly route	1
Summit grid ref	NY 448 101
Link it with	Harter Fell, High Street or Thornthwaite Crag
Part of	Mardale Head Horseshoe and Kentmere Horseshoe

Sitting to the southeast of the High Street massif, the northern slope of Mardale Ill Bell is defended by dark crags that hold snow and ice in winter. The stubby northeastern ridge similarly defended defines two steep corrie basins and their jewel tarns, known as the Mardale Waters – Blea and Small Water. To the south Lingmell End, a steep, less craggy arm projects into the upper Kentmere valley. Off to the east further crags flank the high connection with Harter Fell, over which the Nan Bield Pass, an ancient pedestrian passage, threads from north to south.

Little about the fell's profile can be considered bell-shaped, but 'ill' suggests that it was considered Mardale's treacherous height, and little wonder with all

↑ *Lingmell End from Kentmere Reservoir dam*   165

those crags. Perhaps as the dales folk of Mardale adapted the name Branstree from High Street, they borrowed from Kentmere's eye-catching Ill Bell to name another shapely summit.

The ascents from Mardale Head are the most logical and the best, but the long march from the south via Nan Bield (4) provides a useful means of shortcutting the Kentmere Horseshoe, while the stiff climb from Kentmere Reservoir up Lingmell End (5) will appeal to an intrepid minority.

Ascent from Mardale Head 19

Via Nan Bield Pass →*3.4km/2 miles* ↑*510m/1675ft* ⏲*1hr 30min*

A most enjoyable walk, with cascades, crags and a classic corrie tarn on the way up to the pass and a well-secured path beyond

1 From the car park go through the kissing-gate and up to the wall corner where three paths diverge. Take the middle route, signed 'Public bridleway Nan Bield Pass Kentmere'. The heavily worn path leads up through the moraine, through several gates, to come close to a sequence of beautiful cascades in the gill issuing from Small Water.

Looking over Nan Bield to Harter Fell

Cross at the outflow and swing round to the west side of the tarn, coming by a trio of stone shelters. The path has received essential pitching repair all the way to Nan Bield Pass, where the walled alcove forms a partial block to southerly draughts in this tight notch in the ridge. Bear right, rounding a splintered headland and stepping up on further big boulder pitching on the final easy clamber that leads onto easier ground and to the summit.

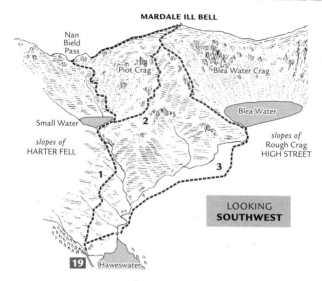

Via the east ridge →*2.6km/1½ miles* ↑*500m/1640ft* ⊙*1hr 40min*

Add a bit of extra drama with a pathless climb up and over Piot Crag.

2 Start out with Route **1** and turn off right just short of the Small Water shelters, climbing the increasingly steep grass slope to the right of **Piot Crag**. Above this, come to a tiny slate quarry, with the remnants of hut walls. Follow the grassy ridge above west as it eases onto the summit.

Via the north ridge →*3.2km/2 miles* ↑*520m/1705ft* ⊙*2hr*

Alternatively reach Piot Crag along the north ridge.

3 Walk through the gate and up to the three-way sign and there bear right to cross the Mardale Beck footbridge. Then turn left and follow a path that leads up by a gate and passes above the impressive tree-shaded Dudderwick Force to a further gate. Traipse up the sometimes damp moor well above **Blea Water Beck**, your destination the outflow of **Blea Water**. Ford the boulders beside

The hairpins rising from the south to Nan Bield Pass

the concrete dam and follow the grassy moraine ridge up to the rock arête. Tackle a minor rock-step – not as daunting as it appears from below – to get a foothold on the ridge. Join Route **2** to the summit.

Ascent from Hallow Bank 34

Via Nan Bield Pass →*6.3km/4 miles* ↑*605m/1985ft* ⏱*2hr 30min*

The old pedestrian route from Kentmere makes a satisfying expedition.

4 Follow either the road or bridleway through the hamlet of **Hallow Bank**, coming down the gated roadway to **Overend**. Beside the white-washed farmhouse diverge right, guided by the old slate sign 'To Mardale'.

The bridleway leads by gates to a footbridge spanning **Ullstone Gill** and, after the gate, curves up the bank onto the ridge of **the Tongue**, easily beating back the dense bracken in season. Keen eyes will spot engraved bedrock underfoot before the path steps up onto Smallthwaite Knott and contours well above Kentmere Reservoir, eventually tackling the acute hairpins to reach the notch of **Nan Bield Pass**. From the wind-break bear up left, curving round a rocky headland and then up large-boulder pitching onto the crown of the fell.

Ascent from Kentmere 33 *off map S* or Hallow Bank 34

Via Lingmell End → *7.3km/4½ miles* ↑*610m/2000ft* ⏱*2hr 45min*

The adventurer's route for those full of animal vigour

5 From Kentmere village, by either the road or green lanes, venture onto the private road to Hartrigg and continue on with the track to just short of the **Kentmere Reservoir** dam. Cross the footbridge, right, over the overflow channel and bend left to come onto the dam, trending right. (The same spot can be reached from Hallow Bank by the gated dale-floor footpath via Overend and **Tongue House** (barn). From the barn cross to a ladder-stile to reach an area of slate spoil where once a quarrymen's bridge spanned the dale beck. Beyond, contour the banks to the dam.)

Follow on with the ditch bank on the east side of the reservoir. Where **Lingmell Gill** enters, step over the wall and ford the gill. Climb up beside the gill until a clear line can be detected up the steep fellside of **Lingmell End** – the only grassy way onto this ridge from any angle. After some serious effort, reach a cairn and take a well-earned breather. The ridge north is open pasture, encouraging free-flowing strides to the summit.

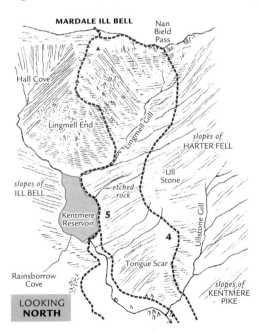

The summit

A tumbled cairn rests upon the lava shards of a mini Giant's Causeway outcrop. The view is not one to write home about, but the best of it is to be found from the edges, notably the northern brink above Blea Water. Spot the tantalising tops of Bowfell, Scafell and Scafell Pike just breaking the skyline immediately south of Thornthwaite Crag's beacon.

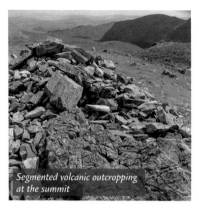
Segmented volcanic outcropping at the summit

Safe descents

The straightforward recourse is SE then E to Nan Bield Pass, from where Mardale Head (N, **1**) and Kentmere (S, **4**) are reached on much-travelled footpaths.

Ridge routes

Harter Fell →*1.7km/1 mile* ↓*130m/425ft* ↑*145m/475ft* ⏲*45min*
Follow the ridge path S then E – this has been given boulder pitching in places. Come down to the tight pass with its walled bield. Continue E by several stepped stages onto the plateau. A brink cairn directs you to the primary summit cairn just short of the ridge fence.

High Street →*1.7km/1 mile* ↓*15m/50ft* ↑*80m/260ft* ⏲*35min*
Travel easily W, and from the shallow dip pick up an engineered trail. This snakes up and across the grassy prairie, off the direct line, and delays your turn up to the ridge wall leading to the summit.

Thornthwaite Crag →*1.8km/1 mile* ↓*60m/195ft* ↑*40m/130ft* ⏲*40min*
Leave the summit SW to join the strong path that runs along the edge high above Hall Cove. Where this forks, keep W to pass the wall-end and join the Roman road heading SW to the beacon cairn.

22 PLACE FELL 657M/2155FT

Climb it from	Patterdale 5 or Sandwick 7
Character	Peerless viewpoint for the Helvellyn range commanding the upper reaches of Ullswater
Fell-friendly route	6
Summit grid ref	NY 405 169
Link it with	Angletarn Pikes
Part of	Martindale Skyline

Mountains are comprehended as much by their context as by their absolute scale, and Place Fell has all the individuality and charm to be a magnet to fellwalkers notwithstanding its small stature. View it from across Ullswater – its broad, shaggy, craggy, variegated slopes beautifully reflected in the lake – and it has a sense of spaciousness. The main mass of the fell, defined by secretive Boredale, forms a bulwark to a fabulous summit crest, its crowning glory for some. Others favour it for its shoreline path between Sandwick and Patterdale.

Across the lake at Aira Point sits the old manor house of the village of Watermillock, now an Outward Bound centre. In mid-Victorian times the owner

↑ *Place Fell across the head of Boredale*

of the house sought to create a picturesque view across the lake, duly 'enhancing' the cascades of Scalehow Force with a few sticks of dynamite!

Most walkers tackle the fell in isolation from the rest of the fell group in a short anti-clockwise circuit from Patterdale, climbing via Boredale Hause (1) and descending via Low Moss (2) into the Scalehow Beck valley. Yet there is also the lakeside path (3) to consider along with several great little adventures to be had in approaching from the north and east (4–8).

Ascent from Patterdale 5

The classic short circuit from Patterdale climbs up on Route 1 and down on Route 2 but it's just as satisfying tackled the other way round.

Via Boredale Hause →*3km/2 miles* ↑*500m/1640ft* ☺*1hr 20min*
1 Pass through the narrows between the village shop and the White Lion and turn left with the cul-de-sac road via **Goldrill Bridge**. Coming by cottages the road swings up left and comes to a gate, with a slate sign directing right through an adjacent gate for 'Boredale Hause'. The path duly turns right up the fellside – indeed there are two groove paths rising one above the other with a similar goal. The upper path is the one to take. Come up to the small ruin, marked on maps 'Chapel in the Hause' – perhaps once a bad weather sanctuary. The popular path bears left from the broad saddle of **Boredale Hause**, winding up the southern slope onto the knoll of **Round How**, where the slope eases. Walk on to climb the final rock ridge.

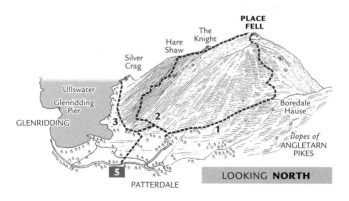

173

Via Hare Shaw →3.5km/2¼ miles ↑525m/1720ft ⏱1hr 50min

Often used as a descent after climbing the fell from Boredale Hause, this route also provides a splendid little expedition working up through the juniper to reach the Knight.

2 Follow Route **1** over **Goldrill Bridge** and after the gate at the road end turn left onto the green-way leading northwest – or, alternatively, walk a little way north along the main road to find a track leading right to **Side Farm**, from where turn left then quickly right to join the same green-way. Where this lovely bridleway comes onto a roche moutonnée rib turn up half-right, and the early green trail becomes more a stony trod, climbing through the juniper thicket. Gaining the brow at **Hare Shaw** the path switches right (southeast) rising up the groove beside **the Knight**, its boiler-plated slopes a shining armour. The cairn of this subsidiary peak demands a visit by the northern arête or from the south off the regular path. The route continues, passing a second laterally sited cairn en route to the summit.

Looking down on Boredale Hause towards Brothers Water

Ullswater Path

Patterdale to Sandwick →6.5km/4 miles ↑290m/950ft ⏱2hr 30min

The popular path for returning to – or setting out from – Patterdale, sometimes used in conjunction with the lake steamer and now part of the Ullswater Way.

3 Walk a little way north along the main road to find a track leading right to **Side Farm**, after which turn left to begin your lakeshore perambulation. Navigation is of the falling 'off a log' kind, and does not need spelling out. However, it is far more strenuous than might be expected, and there are sections where slippery rock and tree roots can greatly hamper your confident stride. Worth noting is that there are lower and higher path options just before **Silver Bay**. The more elevated inevitably has the better views well above the trees, and includes a mini 'pass' beside the **Silver Crag** headland, where a pool is passed and steps lead down by dense juniper to connect with the lower path.

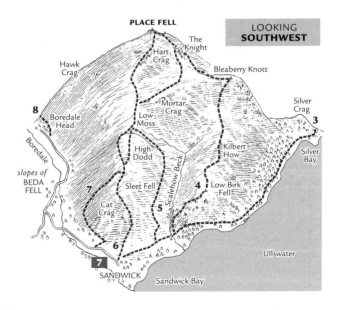

Rock headland below Kilbert How

Ascent from Sandwick 7

Via Birk Fell →*4.3km/2¾ miles* ↑*525m/1720ft* ⊕*2hr 15min*

An unfrequented wild ridge-top route, best tackled out of bracken season, with a magnificent westward outlook towards the Helvellyn range

4 Leave the open road above the hamlet of Sandwick, signposted 'Patterdale'. Accompany the wall-side path, pass a bank-barn and ford the gill. From here keep with the regular path, which descends to cross a wooden footbridge over **Scalehow Beck**. Stay with the regular path as it zigs right and continues up beside the wall. However, before it reaches the top, break away left into the bracken on a sheep trod that rises beside the ravine. When you get level with the great slab bear up right, weaving through the outcropping. Matters improve as the ridge proper is joined, leading to the prominent cairn on **Low Birk Fell**. The landmark wall-cairn appears untouched by time.

A ridge-top path of sheep-track proportions leads southwest over the bracken hollows and knobbles of **Kilbert How**. The ridge makes a big step up over the headland of Smeathwaite as the path heads up the southern slope to come onto the ridge proper. (The cairn indicated here on OS maps no longer exists.) A second prominent rise in the ridge off-set right, **Bleaberry Knott**, has a cairn and a wonderful view. A small rock-step leads down to the marshy plateau of splendidly-named Bottom Heads. Pass a small slate working to join forces with Route **2** at **Hare Shaw**.

Via Scalehow Beck →3.8km/2½ miles ↑490m/1610ft ⏱2hr

5 Set out with Route **4**, but, after the gill-ford, bear up half-left onto a turf drove-way. Rather than track the beck closely, keep up to the top of the adjacent enclosure to climb over **High Dodd**, gliding up the valley to meet the popular lower path short of the old slate quarry. Continue to **Low Moss** and the large sheepfold to turn right with the regular ridge route climbing southwest over **Hart Crag** to the summit.

Via High Dodd and the Knight →4km/2½ miles ↑520m/1705ft ⏱2hr

Another lovely ridge route, a little further from the lake but on clear paths

6 Start briefly with Route **4** but at the top of the very first rise bear off half-left, climbing to pass a metal seat, and continue to follow the path climbing the ridge. Passing a scenically sited ridge-end cairn, cross over the old wall and hold to the spine of the ridge, passing a further cairned top to meet up with the path climbing the Boredale slope (Route **7**). Continue up the ridge, detouring to take in **High Dodd** if you wish. The path eases southwest down to **Low Moss** to pass the sheepfold. Beyond this point, you can again follow the common way over Hart Crag or take a more exploratory course. For the latter, bear off right beyond the fold within a grassy groove that mounts west above **Mortar Crag**, with a further minor slate working above the path to the left. The path threads up a shallow passage, with the headland of **the Knight** up to the right, and soon joins the route from **Hare Shaw** trending south and passing below a second, slightly less prominent headland cairn to reach the summit.

Via Low Moss →4km/2½ miles ↑540m/1770ft ⏱2hr 15min

7 Walk back up the lane from Sandwick to near the access to Bridge End to pick up a green path drifting west to a path confluence. Turn acutely left to contour and come above the intake wall. Drifting down beneath **Cat Crag**,

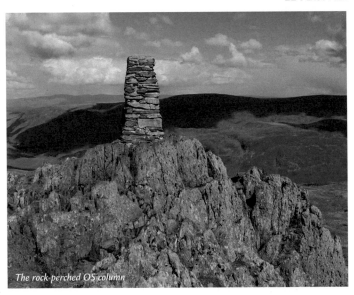

The rock-perched OS column

the path then moves away from the wall on a steady climb along the eastern flank of **Sleet Fell**, soon joined by a path climbing out of Boredale from Garth Head. Reaching the brow, the path hairpins as it joins Route **6**.

Via Boredale Head →6.4km/4 miles ↑550m/1805ft ⏱2hr 40min

A surreptitious valley approach to the hause of the same name

8 Walk up the Boredale valley road for about four kilometres. Coming close to Boredale Head Farm, turn up the bank right on a permissive path. This fords a gill directly above the farmstead and contours above the intake wall to join the dale bridleway running on freely southwest towards the dale head. Redgate Gill has recently taken a hit with wash-out, covering the green-way with stones. The track, now rough underfoot, climbs through a natural cutting with inspection covers for the Hayeswater aqueduct. Venturing on into the broad grassy saddle of **Boredale Hause**, switch up to the right towards the summit with Route **1**.

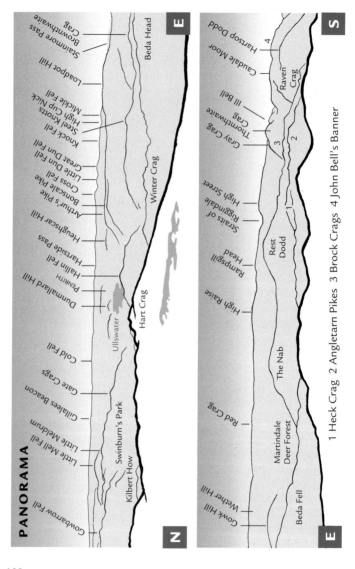

PANORAMA

Top panorama (E to N):

Brownthwaite Crag, Stainmore Pass, Loadpool Hill, Beda Head, Mickle Fell, High Cup Nick, Steel Knotts, Knock Fell, Great Dun Fell, Little Dun Fell, Cross Fell, Winter Crag, Bonscale Pike, Arthur's Pike, Heughscar Hill, Hartside Pass, Hallin Fell, PENRITH, Dunmallard Hill, Hart Crag, Ullswater, Cold Fell, Gate Crags, Gillalees Beacon, Little Meldrum, Little Mell Fell, Swinburn's Park, Kilbert How, Cowbarrow Fell

Bottom panorama (S to E):

Hartsop Dodd, Caudale Moor, Raven Crag, Ill Bell, Thornthwaite Crag, Gray Crag, High Street, Straits of Riggindale, Rampsgill Head, Rest Dodd, High Raise, The Nab, Red Crag, Martindale Deer Forest, Beda Fell, Wether Hill, Gowk Hill

1 Heck Crag 2 Angletarn Pikes 3 Brock Crags 4 John Bell's Banner

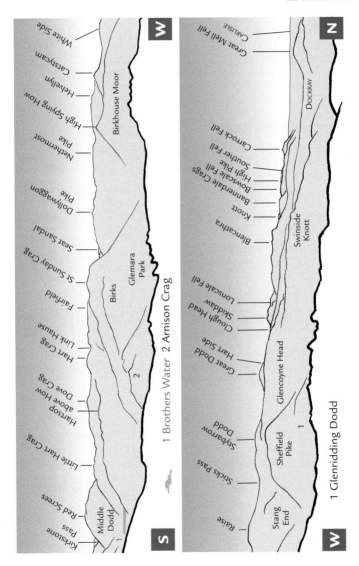

W

White Side — Catstycam — Helvellyn — High Spying How — Nethermost Pike — Dollywaggon Pike — Seat Sandal — St Sunday Crag — Fairfield — Link Hause — Hart Crag — Dove Crag — Hartsop above How — Little Hart Crag — Red Screes — Kirkstone Pass

Birkhouse Moor

Glemara Park

Birks

Middle Dodd

S

1 Brothers Water 2 Arnison Crag

N

Great Mell Fell — CARLISLE — Carrock Fell — Souther Fell — High Pike — Bowscale Fell — Bannerdale Crags — Knott — Blencathra — Lonscale Fell — Skiddaw — Clough Head — Hart Side — Great Dodd — Stybarrow Dodd — Sheffield Pike — Sticks Pass — Raise

DOCKRAY

Swinside Knott

Glencoyne Head

Stang End

W

1 Glenridding Dodd

181

The summit

This is one of the most satisfying summits in Lakeland. The OS column perches proud as punch on the rocky peak and the situation is spellbinding, enough to hold the most impatient walker for several magical moments, weather permitting. A conventional cairn rests on the

Pools just northeast of the summit

western crest on ground that gives the finest view over Patterdale and into the wild recesses of Grisedale. St Sunday Crag and the craggy eastern faces of Dollywaggon and Nethermost Pikes, and the ridges and faces of Helvellyn and the high rolling skyline of summits running north towards Blencathra, all captivate. Down to the south see the almost square sheet of Brothers Water, perhaps catching the sun's rays in the Hartsop vale below Kirkstone Pass.

Safe descents

Much of the fell is steep sided, so it is wise to stick to the tried and tested paths. In adverse conditions you are best advised to head S to Boredale Hause (**1**) for the swiftest, securest path to the valley.

Ridge route

Angletarn Pikes →2.7km/1¾ miles ↓270m/885ft ↑180m/590ft ⏱45min

Step down S following the regular path over Round How and winding quite steeply down the new trail to Boredale Hause. Straddle the saddle SE to briefly join a bridleway, watching for a small cairn indicating departure half-right on a path that slips through the upper course of Freeze Beck. Coming onto a brow veer right SW, avoiding the marsh, to step onto the rock ridge and ponder the lack of a cairn!

23 RAMPSGILL HEAD 792M/2598FT

Climb it from	Patterdale **5** or Hartsop **3**
Character	Head of the Rampsgill Beck valley on an ancient ridgeway
Fell-friendly route	1
Summit grid ref	NY 443 129
Link it with	High Raise, High Street, Kidsty Pike or Rest Dodd
Part of	Martindale Skyline

The summit of Rampsgill Head is a lynchpin location – the craggy head of the wild Rampsgill Beck valley and the crossover point of two trade routes, the centuries-old Roman High Street and the perennially popular modern-age Coast to Coast Walk. There are higher summits to north and south, but none that have quite such strategic importance.

The 'lost valley' of Rampsgill Beck has no casual access and, like adjacent Bannerdale, deserves respect as a quiet sanctuary for the indigenous red deer. A native herd has lived hereabouts for millennia. Lower down the dale a small woodland can be espied from the dale head and beyond this, spot the Bungalow, a startling red-roofed dwelling owned by the Dalemain Estate. It was built as

↑ *Rampsgill Head from Rest Dodd* 183

a hunting lodge in 1910 by the fifth Earl of Lonsdale in advance of a visit by the bombastic Kaiser Wilhelm II of Germany.

Two approaches are described here – one tracing the route of the Coast to Coast Walk from Patterdale (1) and another weaving its way up from Hartsop (2).

Ascent from Patterdale 5

Via Angle Tarn →*7km/4½ miles*
↑*725m/2380ft* ⏱*2hr 50min*

A fun and feature-filled section of the Coast to Coast route

1 Head south through the narrow street between the village shop and White Lion Hotel to bear left with the no through road leading over **Goldrill Beck**. This leads by a cluster of properties and bears left to reach gates. Guided by the slate sign 'Angle Tarn, Boredale Hause' go through and after 50 metres swing up right. Climb the steep bracken slope, keeping to the lower of the two adjacent paths to reach **Boredale Hause**. From here a part-pitched way leads through a gully and above the scarp, with a higher and a lower option as it passes under the main bastion of **Angletarn Pikes**. This leads round by the northern shore of **Angle Tarn** and on over the intermediary ridge above **Buck Crag** at the head of Bannerdale. Then,

184

after slipping through a gateway over the rocky top of **Satura Crag**, take the right-hand fork to contour across the southern slopes of **Rest Dodd** going through a gateway at the head of **Prison Gill**. After fording **Sulphury Gill** (high above its fine cascades) swing left round the shoulder of **the Knott**, detouring up to its summit if you wish before turning east to walk up to the summit of Rampsgill Head.

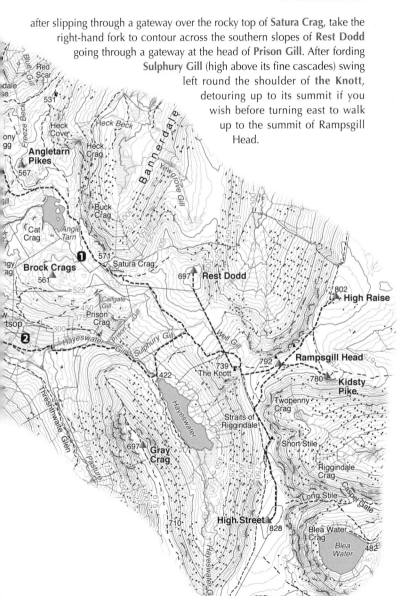

Ascent from Hartsop 3

Via the Knott →4km/2½ miles ↑610m/2000ft ⊕2hr 10min

Climb up to the ridge from secluded Hayeswater on easy paths.

2 Follow the valley track east via Wath Bridge, ascending to **Hayeswater** dam. Bear left with three possible lines up the flank of the Knott. Take the most natural (far left) one heading north to come up by the wall to join the popular path from Angle Tarn, part of the Coast to Coast Walk and well travelled. Climb a peaty rise with some pitching. Higher a loose gravel trail leads through a wall-gap and round the northern side of **the Knott**. Here join Route **1**.

The summit

The summit cairn is but one of several that adorn this fell-top, two having sprung up near the northern brink. This point allows the closer inspection of a projecting buttress which seldom features in climbing annals, but on occasion will have drawn intrepid rock stars to carry up a rope. The greater view is heaped with detail inevitably concentrated to the west, with the high horizon of Fairfield and Helvellyn breached only by Scoat Fell, Ullscarf and Pillar.

The projecting buttress of Tortoise Head and Tower Ridge, 50m below the northern brink

Safe descents

The regular thoroughfare W (**2**), descending promptly to the Hayeswater dam, gives a sure and safe line to a valley base, Hartsop.

Approaching the Straits of Riggindale

Ridge routes

High Raise →1km/½ mile ↓40m/130ft ↑50m/165ft ⏱20min
Travel NE through the depression and accompany the Roman road until it comes onto the crown, then veer half-right to the bouldery crest.

High Street 2km/1¼ miles ↓95m/310ft ↑130m/425ft ⏱35min
Head SW with the popular path that comes over Twopenny Crag into the narrow depression known as the Straits of Riggindale. Follow the wall, via the cairn on Short Stile, all the way up to the OS column.

Kidsty Pike →0.5km/¼ mile ↓25m/80ft ↑10m/35ft ⏱12min
A simple matter of walking E to the peak's outcrop-topping cairn.

Rest Dodd →1.8km/1 mile ↓200m/655ft ↑105m/345ft ⏱30min
Travel W to join the regular path which swings from N to W. When you come to the wall, keep its company in descent, stepping over Well Gill and passing through the damp depression, then climb to where the wall departs W. Here keep N to the cairn on the crown of the fell.

24 REST DODD 697M/2287FT

Climb it from	Hartsop **3**, Patterdale **5** or Martindale **6**
Character	Anchor point of the Nab and the Martindale Deer Reserve
Fell-friendly route	2
Summit grid ref	NY 433 136
Link it with	Angletarn Pikes, Brock Crags or Rampsgill Head
Part of	Martindale Skyline

The majority of ridge walkers tend to give Rest Dodd the slip using the connecting ridge above Satura Crag to avoid a big dip on their way to Rampsgill Head. Yet no honest circuit of the Martindale skyline would be complete without visiting the summit, if only to marvel at the grand craggy prospect of its neighbour to the east. The fell's north ridge is far from conventional. It swells into the great protruding nose of the Nab, which would be considered a separate fell in its own right were it not a protected deer reserve.

Wander around the top a little to get a sense of the setting – aloof in a private world high above the secretive Bannerdale and Rampsgill Beck valleys. On a sunny day there is every excuse to dawdle on the summit and listen to the skylarks, far removed from the regular procession of casual walkers. Access to

↑ *The Nab and Rest Dodd from Bannerdale*

the Nab is sensibly restricted to a there-and-back path from the parent fell but it is well worth doing for an even deeper sense of solitude.

Routes set off from Hartsop (1 and 2), Patterdale (3) and, best of all, from Martindale (4) and the excursion to the top of the Nab along the northern spur (5), shared only with the reclusive deer, is also described here.

189

Ascent from Hartsop 3

Via Satura Crag →4km/2½ miles ↑515m/1690ft ⏱1hr 45min

Switchback up to the Crag for the simplest and most direct approach.

1 Head up the valley track, but after crossing the cattle grid bear up with the tarmac roadway, aiming for the waterworks building. On reaching the road-end, switch acutely back on the green-way overlaying the Hayeswater aqueduct. As you pass above walled enclosures look out for a path that turns acutely right up the fellside. Take this as it leads through a wall gateway and rises in a groove to the head of **Calfgate Gill**. Slip over a broken wall and through a gateway, and bear right beside the wall to meet up with the ridge path from Angle Tarn. Step over the rocky top of **Satura Crag**, and as the path declines take the left-hand-fork path. This gains height on the swelling grassy ridge, rising right well before the wall (access line for the Nab). Climb irresistibly to the cairn on the northeastern brow of the fell, with the summit cairn only a short stroll and a peat step away.

Via Hayeswater →3.5km/2¼ miles ↑530m/1740ft ⏱2hr

A useful variant for making a round trip with Route 1

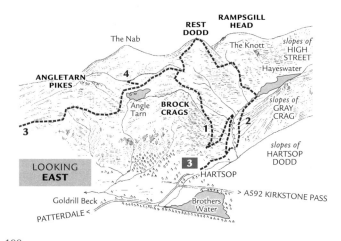

Notch in the ridge path from Angle Tarn looking to Fairfield

2 Follow the valley track east via Wath Bridge, ascending to **Hayeswater** dam. Bear left with three possible lines up the flank of the Knott. Take the most natural (far left) one heading north to come up by the wall and meet the popular path to Angle Tarn, part of the Coast to Coast Walk and well travelled, at the head of **Sulphury Gill**. Follow this left, then march up the steep fellside, avoiding peaty ground, to the wall angle at the top. From here continue to the summit cairn.

Ascent from Patterdale 5 *off map NW*

The longest approach is from Patterdale but there's plenty to entertain you en route.

Via Angle Tarn →*5.8km/3½ miles* ↑*590m/1935ft* ⏲*2hr 20min*
3 Head south through the narrow street between the village shop and White Lion Hotel to bear left with the no through road leading over **Goldrill Beck**. This leads by a cluster of properties and bears left to reach gates. Guided by the slate sign 'Angle Tarn, Boredale Hause' go through and after 50 metres swing up right. Climb the steep bracken slope, keeping to the lower of the two adjacent paths to reach **Boredale Hause**. From here a part-pitched way leads through a gully and above the scarp, with a higher and a lower option as it passes under the main bastion of **Angletarn Pikes**. This leads round by

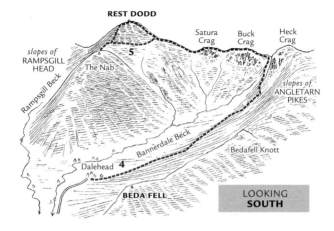

the northern shore of **Angle Tarn** and on over the intermediary ridge above **Buck Crag** at the head of Bannerdale to join Route **1**.

Ascent from Martindale **6** *off map N*

Via Heck Cove →*4.8km/3 miles* ↑*500m/1640ft* ⏲*2hr 30min*

A great fellwalking ascent in a wild setting

4 Walk 2.5km across and up Martindale from the church, along the road, to the road-end farm at Dalehead. Go right by the deer notice at the turning point, ford the gill and go through the hand-gate. Keep the intake wall close left on a level course. After a fence-gate the green-way leads on into **Bannerdale**, looking down upon a sycamore-shaded field barn and then a ruin incorporated in the adjacent wall. The path drifts slightly away from the wall as it approaches a gate (do not go through) and now embarks on an altogether more flimsy course, traversing the steep slope with patches of scree on a very narrow trod – **watch your footing**. In due course it draws into a skyline notch next to **Buck Crag** and joins the regular trail heading east. Coming through a narrow gateway the path weaves through bedrock exposures to begin the climb onto Rest Dodd. Be careful not to be lured by the tempting path right, running across the southern flank of the fell to the Straits of Riggindale. The ascending path veers from east to northeast onto the swelling grassy ridge and then swings southeast again at the fork with the Nab access path. Arrive at a small cairn on the summit lip from where a short hollow and peat-grough step bring you to the large summit cairn.

Spur Path to the Nab

From Rest Dodd (descent) → *1.6km/1 mile* ↑*120m/395ft* ⊕*35min*

5 The spur path sets off from a stile at the base of the Rest Dodd north ridge. This point can be reached either by descending from the summit of Rest Dodd due north, an uncomplicated path, or from off the high shoulder where a wall crosses the northwest ridge. Do not go through the open gateway (for working access only) but follow the wall on its southern side, dipping and then contouring, ignoring

Access stile to the spur path to the Nab

another wall gap and gateway partway along. Continue to the very end to find the stile, where the ground falls smartly away into the upper realms of the Rampsgill Beck valley. The summit is just over a kilometre from the stile and reached by crossing the intervening shallow depression, where eroding peat makes progress less pleasant in damp weather. One flat stone is all that is passed en route to the cairn, set upon a simple domed summit.

The summit

Grass predominates, with a small exposure of blanket peat a reminder of the damp climate. The large cairn is a fine viewpoint, inevitably restricted by the bulk of High Raise and Rampsgill Head to the east, but there is a fine view in the western arc from Red Screes round by Fairfield and the Helvellyn range overtopping the Angletarn Pikes ridge, where Heck Crag and Cove make a striking foreground to St Sunday Crag and Helvellyn.

Safe descents

To the W and S routes lead to safe dale havens, notably Hartsop by the Hayeswater Gill valley (**2**).

Ridge routes

Angletarn Pikes →*3km/2 miles*
↓*220m/720ft* ↑*90m/295ft* ⏱*1hr 15min*
A consistent path leads off the west brink of the summit dome and runs down to join the regular ridgeway on the skyline of Satura Crag. Pass through the wall-gap and skirt to the E of Angle Tarn, bearing off half-right as this swings to the north side. Reaching the brow, level with the knoll above Heck Crag, bear left (W), skirting the peaty ground to find a narrow trod leading SW onto the rock ridge.

Narrow trod running up under Heck Crag

Brock Crags →*1.8km/1 mile* ↓*155m/510ft* ↑*20m/65ft* ⏱*30min*
Leave the summit W, descending the ridge path which swings SW to a dip in the ridge to come over the bare rock crest of Satura Crag. Go through the gateway and bear left accompanying the wall SW, duly crossing the broken wall at its junction beyond a depression. Soon ushered right over the adjacent broken wall, negotiate a pooled hollow to reach the summit.

Rampsgill Head →*1.8km/1 mile* ↓*105m/345ft* ↑*200m/655ft* ⏱*50min*
Descend S, following the wall SSE down through a damp depression to climb by Well Gill. Where the heavily used path crosses, go left with this, rounding the north shoulder of the Knott. As this levels, take your own line to climb left onto the domed summit.

25 SALLOWS 516M/1693FT

Climb it from	Kentmere **33**, Ullthwaite Bridge **32**, Moor Howe **35** or Church Bridge **38**
Character	With Sour Howes one of a pair of pleasing little felltops south of the Garburn Pass
Fell-friendly route	1
Summit grid ref	NY 437 040
Link it with	Yoke

Most summit-baggers content themselves with a smash-and-grab raid of Sallows from the Garburn Pass, but this approach misses the point of the fell's situation. Sallows is a distinguished high point in its own right, commanding green vales, its countenance facing south. However, the best views are from the western brink of its southwesterly companion Sour Howes, gazing west across the Trout Beck valley beyond Wansfell Pike to the Langdale Pikes, backed by the serrated roof of England.

Bands of slate periodically outcrop in the area and were formerly exploited for local building purposes, notably at Applethwaite Quarry (a fascinating place to explore with due care) on the western flank of Sour Howes. The Brock Stone

↑ *Sallows from Green Quarter*

by contrast must have been carried to its present location at the latter stage of the last Ice Age and is perfect for agile boulderers.

Sallows and Sour Howes provide scope for lovely round-rambles in the foothills of Lakeland, linking an array of pleasant tracks from the low country between Kentmere and the Trout Beck valley.

Ascent from Kentmere 33

The busy Garburn Pass route (1) has been improved but is still heavy going. The meandering approach of Route 2 is much gentler, even pathless in parts, under foot. Combine the two for a good half-day circuit.

Via the Garburn Pass →*3.2km/2 miles* ↑*355m/1165ft*
⏱*1hr 25min*

1 Follow the village road north from the church to the Nook, opposite which the **Garburn Road** (restricted bridleway to Troutbeck) is signed up right. As you wend your way up make a point of looking down on **Kentmere Hall** farm with its pele tower (a rarity in Lakeland). Follow the track on through the gate and at once cross the stile left, marching up the blank damp fell onto the ridge and bending further left to find the summit.

Via Whiteside End →*4km/2½ miles* ↑*375m/1230ft*
⏱*1hr 40min*

2 Follow the metalled lane to **Kentmere Hall** farm, passing on past the farmyard and over the **Cowsty Beck** bridge, keeping with the gated track. Approaching the third gate swing up the pasture right, climbing to a stile to the right of a gate accessing the rough pasture of **Kentmere Park**, grazed by cattle and sheep. Here bend right (north) pathlessly via the low ridge, starting with the gill to your right and a wall to your left and aiming for the rocky peak of **Scour Rigg**. Skirting its base, swing up leftwards (west) with intermittent evidence of a quad track, then follow a grass path that passes a line of four old stone shooting butts as it climbs onto the summit ridge.

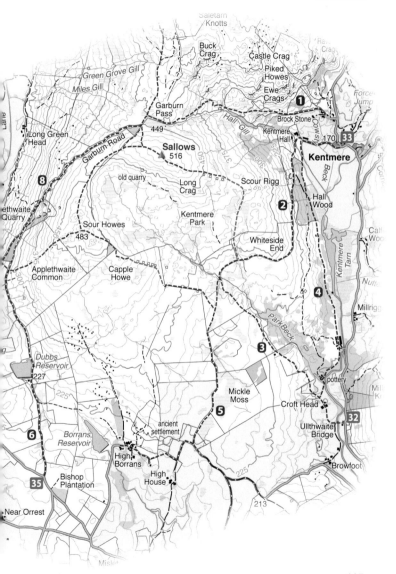

Saletarn Knotts

Green Grove Gill

Miles Gill

Buck Crag

Castle Crag

Piked Howes

Ewe Crags **1**

Forces Jump

Garburn Pass

Hall Gill

Brock Stone

Kentmere Hall

449

Kentmere

170 **33**

Long Green Head

Garburn Road

Sallows 516

Lane

Cowin

Long Crag

Scour Rigg

Hall Wood

2

old quarry

ethwaite Quarry

Sour Howes

483

Kentmere Park

Whiteside End

Applethwaite Common

Capple Howe

Calf Wood

Kentmere Tarn

4

Millrigg

Park Beck

3

Dubbs Reservoir

227

225

Mickle Moss

5

Croft Head

pottery

Mill

32

6

Borrans Reservoir

ancient settlement

Ullthwaite Bridge

35

Bishop Plantation

High Borrans

High House

Browfoot

Near Orrest

213

Misle

197

Ascent from Ullthwaite Bridge 32

Via Park Beck and Sour Howes →6km/3¾ miles ↑430m/1410ft ⊙2hr

Another fellwandering option to throw into the mix as you plan your day, this time taking in Sallows' close neighbour Sour Howes

3 Follow the metalled lane over **Ullthwaite Bridge**. This leads to and between Ullthwaite Fold and white-washed **Croft Head**, a traditional Westmorland farmhouse. Pass on through, via the gate, and follow the confined lane. Ignore the footpath signed right ('Kentmere Hall'). Stay with the main bridleway (also signed to Kentmere Hall). This drove-way winds up through bracken, passing a lone bothy to ford a gill. From here it runs on via stepping-stones and a ford spanning **Park Beck** to reach a gate at the junction with a second bridleway track. Don't go through the gate, but swing left over the stepping-stones, following the open track over a culverted gill. Turn south for a short while and then, when you get to a thorn bush on your left and the remains of a dead tree on your right, branch acutely right on a narrow trod, a former hunting track, which fords a gill at the site of a small bridge and comes to a wall corner. Go left round this and follow the wall up to a gate. Go through and swing right, drifting slightly away from the right-hand wall and aiming for a small outcrop on the near brow and the remains of a stone shooting butt.

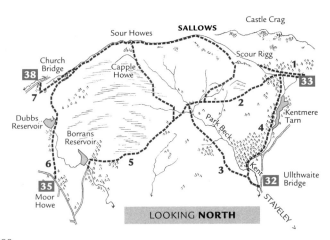

Garburn Road rising out of the Troutbeck valley (photo: Maggie Allan)

Head straight up the damp fell without a trace of a path past five butts to come by the right-hand wall on **Capple Howe**. Skirt a marshy pooled hollow to reach a stile to the right of a small conifer plantation. Follow the broken wall up beside the trees to a second stile and keep on with the open path onto the ribbed ridge that leads to the cairnless summit of **Sour Howes**. The continuing path dips and follows the ridge north, coming back into contact with the ridge wall to reach a stile. From here the ridge path climbs a little more to reach the bare summit.

Valley connection with Kentmere Hall →*3.4km/2 miles* ↑*90m/295ft* ⏱*1hr 10min*

A lovely dale path – particularly useful for a low-level return

4 Starting with Route **3**, this route branches right as a footpath beyond **Croft Head**, signed 'Kentmere Hall 1¼', first as a walled lane to a footbridge over **Park Beck**, close to its confluence with the **River Kent**, and then as a confined path to Kentmere Pottery, after which follow the access roadway to the works of Hollingworth & Vose. Follow the painted yellow figures on the tarmac through the environs of the factory to reach a gated green-way, largely

Kentmere Tarn

screened from the irregular shores of **Kentmere Tarn**, that continues all the way to **Kentmere Hall** farm – a handy connection with Route **2**.

Ascent from Moor Howe 35

Two southern approaches from the lovely high way between Troutbeck and Ings both begin with a little road walking before launching onto the open fells.

Via Borrans Lane →*7km/4½ miles* ↑*370m/1215ft* ⏱*2hr 40min*
5 From the end of Dubbs Lane, walk along the road just over half a kilometre southeast to the start of Borrans Lane, signed 'High Borrans'. This runs down and then up by the entrance to **High Borrans** (an outdoor centre run by North Tyneside Council), passing through the farmyard, over the cattle grid and along the twin-banded tarmac strip track as for Woodside. Before you reach it, where a green salting box stands by the roadway, go through the facing field-gate and join a bridleway beside a fence. This leads to a gate. Step over a gill and follow the track through two fields through another gate. Enter a fenced lane beside a wall, and where this ends go through a gate.

With the open bridleway from High House converging from the right beside a gathering of field-stones all shaded by a sycamore, turn left through the gate signed 'Kentmere Hall'. Rise up a further fence/wall lane, and at the next gate swing right to go through a further gate into a walled lane. Spurn the lane to turn immediately left through the adjacent gate upon a green track signed 'Kentmere' with a wall now to your left. After the next gate the track skirts the edge of an extensive marsh, **Mickle Moss**, sparsely colonised by spindly alder. (Three gates further, as you pass a thorn bush, you could opt to bend half-left following the narrow trod of Route **3**, should you wish to climb Sour Howes first.) Continue to the stepping-stones over **Park Beck** and go through the next gate, keeping to the track until immediately after the next gate. Here step up left with Route **2**, bound for Kentmere Park and Sallows direct.

Via Dubbs Lane →4.8km/3 miles ↑355m/1165ft ⏱2hr

6 Walk up Dubbs Lane, which is a byway open to all traffic (BOAT). The firm, basically level track provides a fine start to proceedings. Pass the actual 'dubb' (sheep washpool) only as the waterworks building of **Dubbs Reservoir** draws near. The track deteriorates as you pass the reservoir. March on until, with a conifer copse in sight, facing stiles are found crossing the line of the lane. Here climb the high ladder-stile. The path goes up by an

Rock-rib summit of Sour Howes

irregular rock ridge, giving entertainment to the climb en route to a stile. Head on with the path onto the wildly undulating pasture of **Sour Howes**, passing a tiny pool to reach the cairnless rock high point. From here, drift down left with Route **3** to Sallows' equally minimal summit.

Ascent from Church Bridge 38

Set out on Route 7 to take in Sour Howes and head back on Route 8 with big views to take your mind off the rough terrain.

Via Sour Howes →3.7km/2¼ miles ↑430m/1410ft ⏱1hr 25min

7 Cross the footbridge beside the main road and, following the footway a matter of metres, seek the narrow lane entry across the busy road. This marks the beginning of the **Garburn Road**, a rough-surfaced track for most of the way, but soon rounding an extremely well-pitched bend to turn northeast on a steady rise. Crossing the line of a bridleway, come up towards a conifer copse and find a stile right. Leave the lane and follow this footpath, which crosses Dubbs Lane by facing stiles and continues straight up the fell with Route **6**.

Via Garburn Pass →*4km/2½ miles* ↑*400m/1310ft* ⏱*1hr 35min*
8 The swiftest route to Sallows' summit follows Route **7** initially, but keeps with the Garburn Road on its steady climb, passing below the tree-decorated remnants of Applethwaite Quarry. Coming up to the gate at the top of the lane, climb the adjacent stile on your right and climb straight up the fellside to the summit.

The summit

A lateral rock spine of no more than ten metres in length defines the summit. The view is not the fell's greatest gift, being somewhat hampered by Sour Howes to the southwest, although keen eyes will be drawn towards the Langdales, and Yoke looms to the north. Elsewhere the view round the southern arc is far ranging – from the Howgills, via Ingleborough and Morecambe Bay to Black Combe.

Safe descents

Stride back NW down to the stile onto the Garburn Road for sure guidance in mist for Kentmere (E, **1**) and Troutbeck (SW, **8**).

Ridge route

Yoke (off map N) →*3km/2 miles* ↓*70m/230ft* ↑*260m/855ft* ⏱*1hr 10min*
Follow the ridge path NW but dip off NNW to the stile at the northern tip of the small plantation. Go right through the gate and follow the open track to the right-hand bend. Here step off onto the northward-running newly surfaced trail, which gives a sure guide up to a kissing-gate and beyond, with some valuable drained pitching on the one brief climb onto the plateau.

26 SELSIDE PIKE 655M/2149FT

Climb it from	Mardale Banks **18** or Swindale **20**
Character	Mass of wild fell commanding the head of Swindale
Fell-friendly route	2
Summit grid ref	NY 491 111
Link it with	Branstree

The guardian height of Swindale, Selside Pike looks broodily down on this unspoiled shy green strath, spared the fate of its two dammed neighbours, Mardale and Wet Sleddale and perhaps little changed from the days when horses plied the Old Corpse Road from the church at Mardale to the consecrated ground at Shap. The head of the dale, surrounded by crags, is a textbook demonstration of the effects of long-ago glaciation, and the farmhouse here has yet to be connected to the National Grid.

Perhaps this is the point to confess that some small changes in the local environment were in fact made by the author of this guide, over 40 years ago while walking the fells with Alfred and Betty Wainwright. We all felt that both Harper Hills and Hare Shaw were inappropriately unmarked and so I set about building the cairns you see today to rectify the situation.

↑ Selside Pike from Rough Crags

Selside Pike is often climbed from the Mardale Head road (1–2) in a round trip that includes Branstree, but there is no doubt that the best expedition (4–5) begins from Swindale, again starting by the Old Corpse Road, and concludes by Geordie Greathead, visiting the top of Hobgrumble Gill and wild-watered environs of Forces Falls.

Ascent from Mardale Banks 18

Via Hopegill Beck → *1.9km/1¼ miles* ↑*370m/1215ft* ⏱*1hr 20min*

Short sharp ascent beside a narrow ravine on intermittent paths

1 Walk down the road (south) a little and, immediately after crossing the Hopegill Beck road bridge, go through a hand-gate to be confronted by a chaos of cascades, boulders and tree growth. But the shepherds' way is at hand, so at once switch right to follow an obvious groove drove-path. This winds up to pass under the Hollow Stone, a large tilted boulder, and progresses steadily, with the roar of the ravine a constant accompaniment. When the bracken is thick, getting close to the waterfalls is impossible. At other times it still takes commitment and care as the ravine is narrow. Higher up, as the slope eases, come by two ruins. The path becomes far less certain from here on, and damp tussocks herald arrival at a large sheepfold with a fenced extension. Keep to the left, tracking **Hopegill Beck** and coming to a beck confluence. Clamber up the facing rigg and simply head east up the plain grassy west ridge of the Pike. Early evidence of a path is lost as the slope steepens, with little in the way of rock to deflect a beeline ascent to the fence-corner and summit.

Via the Old Corpse Road → *3km/2 miles* ↑*370m/1215ft* ⏱*1hr 40min*

The converging ravines of Hopegill Beck and Rowantreethwaite Gill are particularly scenic on the early zig-zagging rise but best kept at a distance for safety's sake.

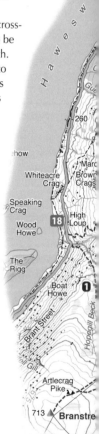

Burnbanks
Gill Dubs
17
213
Naddle Bridge
Woodnook Gill
Park Bridge
Naddle Farm
Scalebarrow Knott
339
Wallow Crag
Hugh's Laithes Pike
435
Guerness Wood
Naddle Beck
Naddle High Forest
Reservoir
419 Harper Hills
Low Goat Gill
3
20
Mere Sike
Swindale Foot
Haweswater Hotel
428
Pod Net
Rowley's Hill
Mullender's
Swindale
Langhe Pike
ness Wood Gill
Hare Shaw 503
Truss Gap
Trussgap Brow
Spear Gill
Gill
Aaron's Bield
Woof Crag
Black Crag Gill
Truss Gap
Waite Howes
Rowantree Crag
384
Banks
ve
4
Swindale Head
Swindale Beck
Gouther Crag
Ritchie Crag 529
Old Corpse Road
High Birkin Knott
5
Outlaw Crag
Glede Howe
2
Gouthercrag Gill
Wantreethwaite Gill
Selside End
The Knott
Simon Stone
509
Willy Winder Hill
Mardale Common
Dodd Bottom
Forces Falls
Swindale Common
Haskew Beck
Haskew Tarn
Selside Pike
655
Geordie Greathead Crag
Nabs Crag
Hobgrumble Gill
618
Captain Whelter Bog
High Wether Howe
531
Swirle Crag
Scam Matthew
673
High Howes
Howes
Moscow Beck
rvey Post
410
Mosedale Quarry (dis)

2 The **Old Corpse Road** comes up by the roofless ruins of sturdy stone peat-store bothies. The path eases onto the moor, and you can stride on until you reach a stake where a quad track crosses the old way a little over the marshy watershed. Here bear right and ascend the northeast ridge of **Selside End**. The quad track veers off half-left to a sheep-feeding box, but the ridge path continues, slipping through a peaty exposure and on to the summit.

Ascent from Swindale 20

Three rewarding lines of ascent either via Hare Shaw (Route 3) or from Swindale Head (Routes 4 and 5)

Via Hare Shaw →6.4km/4 miles ↑450m/1475ft ⏱2hr 20min

Avoid the road walk to Swindale Head with this meandering and often marshy route along the tops.

3 Step directly up from the parking space, the path forcing a line through the bracken immediately right of an invariably dry stony beck. (The bridleway is quirkily signed by the wall on the far side of the beck but this over-complicates matters and is best ignored.) The regular route slants easily across the slope rising onto the moor. Keep forward, escaping the bracken to cross just one really damp patch in reaching the main track close to the ridge wall (opposite the bridleway gate from Naddle Farm). Turn left and follow the track's undulating course to come up onto **Harper Hills**, visiting the prominent cairn up to the left. A thin path continues south from here, although you can rejoin the track. By either means descend to a gate, ford the gill and pass the fenced enclosures.

Ruin beside the Old Corpse Road above Mardale Banks

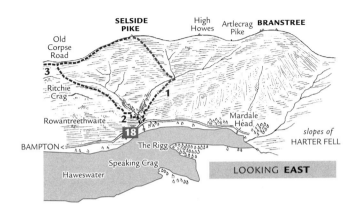

To trace the main skyline ridge, bend off the track left, avoiding the marshy hollow and bracken to climb the pathless slope onto the cairnless **Powley's Hill**. Evidence of a quad track leads to a cairn on a small fractured rock knoll. From here bend right to visit a cairn on a north-facing outcrop and then trend south again, passing a cairn on a rise and then the smaller cairn on the actual summit of **Hare Shaw**. A faint sheep trod leads south, navigating various further marshy expanses and at least two small fenced bogs. Cross the line of one quad track more on the ridge to come down onto a more consistent track to reach the 'pass' cross-ways with the **Old Corpse Road** at a cairn and stake. Continue south, climbing Selside End in harmony with Routes **2** and **4**, onto Selside Pike.

Via the Old Corpse Road →*5.2km/3¼ miles* ↑*440m/1445ft* ⏱*2hr*

The direct climb from the head of Swindale

4 Follow the tarmac road a couple of kilometres to its end at **Swindale Head**. After a gate beside the farmhouse a bridle-path sign 'Mardale' directs right up the tapering enclosure to a gate. A groove leads up to a hand-gate and over a ford, beneath a pleasing cascade. Walk up beside the wall, avoiding the dense gorse, to a somewhat stunted but nonetheless great umbrella of a sycamore.

207

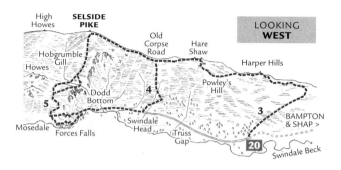

Immediately above this find a path veering left away from the wall. A cairn guides you onto the **Old Corpse Road**. This crosses a gill and makes onto the open fell with the possibility of a stake to guide you. The odd old cairn on the damp, gently angled fell slope leads to a distinct cross-way at a stake, where Routes **2** and **3** converge. Turn south to climb Selside End to the summit.

Via Dodd Bottom and Hobgrumble Gill →6.4km/4 miles ↑500m/1640ft ⊕2hr 30min

The gill name alone should be enough to tempt you to try this route but it's also a grand little climb with a couple of variants for the curious.

5 As with Route **4**, follow the tarmac road to its terminus and then follow the gated drove-way beyond **Swindale Head**, passing the stone barns by an irregular walled lane. After a gate/wall-stile cross the plank-bridge over the out-flowing beck from **Dodd Bottom** and follow the moraine track. Soon reach a narrow section between Swindale Beck and the great basin of Dodd Bottom, clearly once the receptacle of a tarn. The path swings up the rising moraine, sensing the drama of this wild sanctuary.

Many walkers come this way just to see the shy wonders of the Far Eastern range of fells, **Forces Falls**. So while you may be content to stick resolutely to the hairpin bends of the old bridle-path climbing up the rough dale head slope ahead into Mosedale, the better course is to explore the falls. To do so, climb with the path on the moraine after the beck turns sharply left and as you

Moraine dividing Swindale Beck from Dodd Bottom

come through a block of rushes bear off left on a faint trod, which leads over marshy ground to the foot of the cascades. (The sturdy footbridge installed in 1984 at the foot of the falls has been swept away so there is, for now, no easy means of viewing the falls from the east side.) Climb the bedrock banks to view higher instalments of this fabulous cataract, the sponge-like gathering ground of Mosedale ensuring a steady flow to give visual splendour to the falls at most seasons of the year.

It is not practical to explore the ravine from within, but a faint path makes its way up the rocky shoulder and gives scope to view the noisy gorge at various points, with the final mare's-tail fall and swirling pool, definitely the highlight, simply accessed. Above this naturally reconnect with the bridleway by the broken wall. Above, tackle marshy ground typical of Mosedale. As a low broken wall comes into view bend right with the quad track to weave a grassy line up the slope to meet the fence. Follow the fence west, dipping through the basin of **Hobgrumble Gill**. (For an attractive variant, as you come onto Nabs Moor drift right and come down along the brow of **Nabs Crag** to reach the impressive head of the Hobgrumble Gill ravine but **watch your footing**.) Continue on with the fence and climb unhindered to the summit.

The summit

The considerable wind-shelter rests a little distance from the precise summit but that will be little impediment in a storm. Close behind the shelter the ridge fence takes a right-angled turn – again useful for navigation in the said storm. The view is split between the Eden and the greater near mass of High Street, itself best viewed from the western edge of the plateau.

Top Falls, Forces Falls

Safe descents

Although the fence is a handy guide, the simplest recourse in atrocious weather is to head NE then N via Selside End. A clear path leads down to the pass traversed by the Old Corpse Road (moorland track). Go left for Mardale Head (**2**) and right for Swindale Head (**4**).

Ridge route

Branstree →2km/1¼ miles ↓55m/180ft ↑115m/375ft ⊕40min

The continuous ridge fence is a mist-defying navigation aid but it does not follow the highest ground all the way. Captain Whelter Bog is a minor bare peat moment in the first depression, at which point the strict ridge can be adhered to by crossing carefully. There is a thin path leading over the gentle dome of High Howes, some 18m higher than Selside Pike. This route enables you to pass a large pool and visit the survey post erected by the Haweswater engineers as alignment for their aqueduct down Longsleddale to Watchgate, bound for Mancunia (Greater Manchester). The two cairns on Artlecrag Pike provide the main foreground interest on the ridge connection, the vertically fractured bedrock underfoot reminiscent of Ill Bell.

27 SHIPMAN KNOTTS 587M/1926FT

Climb it from	Sadgill **31** or Hallow Bank **34**
Character	First step up from the Stile End pass above Sadgill
Fell-friendly route	2
Summit grid ref	NY 473 062
Link it with	Kentmere Pike

The gradual fall of high pasture from Harter Fell over Kentmere Pike and Goat Scar is briefly held in check upon the knobbled top of Shipman Knotts. A comparatively narrow statement of fell-hood, it forms a craggy partition dividing upper Longsleddale from Kentmere, a sturdy ridge wall snaking over its crest.

On either side of the fell are contrasting hamlets. The shaded bower of Sadgill is an enchanting place. Stand before the bridge and consider the scene: two traditional farmsteads set against the mighty backdrop of Goat Scar, representing the triumph of human endeavour pitted and sustained against a wild, unforgiving terrain and climate. Contrast the residential community of Hallow Bank on the Kentmere flank, basking (at least sometimes) in the afternoon sun.

Ways to the top are rather limited, too – confined to the south, from off the Stile End pass (1 or 2), and the west, by Withered Howe (3).

↑ Shipman Knotts – not the true summit, but the accessible one

Ascent from Sadgill 31

At the point of obvious transition from rolling moorland to craggy mountains, from Silurian to Borrowdale volcanic rock, sandwiched by a thin band of Coniston limestone, there runs an old inter-dale connecting track which is the obvious springboard for ascents from either side.

Via Sadgill Wood →3km/2 miles ↑390m/1280ft ⏱1hr 40min

1 Cross Sadgill Bridge and bear left to go through the gate right of the grand old Westmorland barn to enter a gated lane. As the rough-terrain track levels go through a gate and break right from the farm track, stepping through marshy ground to embark on the ascent proper, guided by the

212

Sadgill and Sadgill Wood (photo: Maggie Allan)

rising wall on your right. A rock-step adds interest (but would be unpleasant during a wet-weather descent). Above **Wray Crag** the ridge takes a breather, replaced by further marshy ground through the knolls. The climb is resumed beside the snaking wall to the not-quite summit cairn. (The true summit, on the east side of the ridge wall, is not accessible.)

Ascent from Hallow Bank 34

Via Stile End →2.3km/1½ miles ↑320m/1050ft ⏱1hr 15min

2 Turn east up the gated lane, passing the **Stile End** field barns. Go through a third gate and follow the open track round a curve. As a tree is passed on the right break onto a quad-bike green-way half-left through the early bracken and climb the southeast slope avoiding outcropping. Reach the ridge to join forces with the more-popular recreational route from the top of the Stile End Pass and Route **1**.

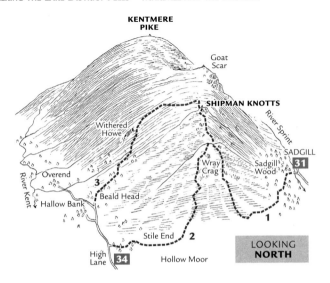

Via Withered Howe →*2.3km/1½ miles* ↑*330m/1085ft* ⏱*1hr 25min*

Short and sweeter than it sounds

3 Follow the road into the hamlet of Hallow Bank, keep right, and, below Brockstones, take the green track up from the garage by **Beald Head** to a gate onto a fell path. A consistent path, sometimes in a stony groove by trees and bushes, ensures a steady plod up to and through a gateless wall-gap, from where the top of the bastion outcrop of **Withered Howe** is soon gained. From here soft rushes cause the path to keep reasonably close to the rising wall. When it runs out continue up the fell (east) without the benefit of a path, curving onto the damp ridge unfettered, bound for the summit knoll.

The summit

The summit proper lies on the east side of the wall, but no provision has been made to allow walkers to visit it so it's best to leave it be. The view is just the same on this side of the wall. Yoke, Ill Bell and Froswick make the best composition for your camera. Distant fells are limited to a small cluster above the Garburn Pass, Black Combe, the Coniston fells, Pike o'Blisco and Crinkle Crags.

Safe descents

Follow the wall S onto the knolled shoulder and hold to the course of the quad-bike track down to the Stile End track (**2**). This angles off the SE shoulder, avoiding Wray Crag and certainly avoiding the plague of the wall-side path, which has two uncomfortable rock-step moments.

Ridge route

Kentmere Pike →*2km/1¼ miles* ↓*20m/65ft* ↑*165m/540ft* ⏱*40min*
Walk N, passing to the left of a knoll and coping with marshy ground before crossing a high ladder-stile. Bear right with the fence to visit the top of Goat Scar, greatly recommended, or follow on NW with hasty hikers, coming up by the fence, and later a wall, to reach the summit.

Sadgill Bridge with Goat Scar in the background

215

28 STEEL KNOTTS 433M/1421FT

Climb it from	Fusedale 9, The Hause 8 or Martindale 6
Character	Elegant ridge directly up from Howtown
Fell-friendly route	3
Summit grid ref	NY 440 181
Part of	Martindale Skyline

This little rocky ridge with its distinctive summit – and the even more distinctive name of Pikeawassa – may lack the stature of many a fell but it will endear itself to all who pay it attention. It forms the western sidewall of the quiet pastures of Fusedale while to its west lie the glories of Martindale in all its serenity, a landlocked world apart.

The old Church of St Martin, Martindale, dedicated to St Martin of Tours, has sat here since at least 1220, with the present building probably being built at the end of the 16th century. The yew tree at its northeastern corner is thought to be over 1300 years old. Services are still held here once a month over the summer.

The natural lines of ascent for Steel Knotts come up from both the new (3) and the old (4) churches, with a lovely bonus up the north ridge from Howtown (2) and one off-beat rear route out of Fusedale (1).

↑ *Steel Knotts from across the southern entrance to Fusedale*

Ascent from Fusedale 9

Via Fusedale →2.4km/1½ miles ↑260m/855ft ⏱1hr 15min

The nifty backdoor approach

1 Follow the concrete farm road S as for Cote Farm. Coming to a cattle grid, step over the footbridge right and follow the footpath that rises then declines to cross the footbridge over **Fusedale Beck**. The succeeding path angles right and crosses **Dodd Gill** on a smaller footbridge and heads up the valley. As this section ends, step off down to the right and ford the beck. Angle half-left, pathlessly, avoiding the bracken, to a ruckle of stones and then switch up right to find an earthy path through the upper band of bracken and reach the saddle close to the wall-stile. Turn right to complete the ascent unhindered.

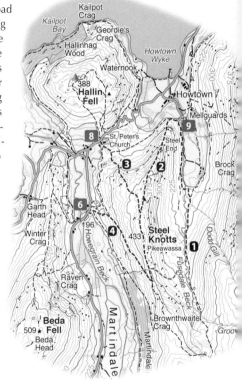

Via Steel End →1.5km/ 1 mile ↑255m/835ft ⏱1hr

A joy every step of the way

2 Follow the bridle-track rising from the verge parking at the cattle grid. The bridle-path comes up by the wall, passing an ash tree to reach a manhole cover and AV (auxiliary valve) marker. Break left onto **Steel End**, with a tangible path mounting through the bracken and up a gap in the ridge-end outcropping. Ascend the north ridge by a sequence of pleasant stepped stages.

Ullswater from Birkie Knott

Bracken continues until the higher ridge is gained and the path switchbacks, easily passing an intermediate cairn en route to the summit outcrop.

Ascent from the Hause 8

Via Birkie Knott → *1.2km/¾ mile* ↑*195m/640ft* ⏱*40min*

The blunt craggy ridge of Birkie Knott is a grand little challenge, best used as an ascent.

3 From St Peter's Church the bridleway heads southeast over the bracken-clad knoll to the left of Lanty Tarn. Depart the bridleway and set to work climbing the nose of the ridge ahead. As the slope abates, the path wends south onto a grassy ridge to the ridge path and Route **2** south of the prominent cairn.

Ascent from Martindale 6

Via the bridleway → *1.5km/1 mile* ↑*230m/755ft* ⏱*1hr*

In spring golden daffodils carpet the garth of this humble 16th-century kirk and a route leads straight up to the ridge.

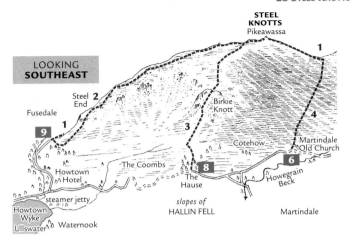

STEEL
KNOTTS
Pikeawassa

LOOKING
SOUTHEAST

Steel **2**
End

Fusedale

9 **1**

Howtown
Hotel

The Coombs

steamer jetty

Howtown
Wyke
Ullswater   Waternook

Birkie
Knott

3

Cotehow

8
The
Hause

slopes of
HALLIN FELL

Martindale
Old Church

4

6

Howegrain
Beck

Martindale

1

4 From the open verge beside the church walk up behind the ageing yew onto a bridleway that slants right up through the bracken and goes via a hand-gate in a downward wall onto the ridge. Cut back left to cross the ridge-wall stile after 100 metres and complete the climb up the open turf of the south ridge.

St Martin's Old Church

The summit

A striking blade of pale volcanic rock with the name Pikeawassa defines the summit. Even more striking is the view, particularly south into the secret world at the head of the Howegrain Beck valley, centred upon the Nab, intervening between the valleys of Rampsgill Beck and Bannerdale. More immediately Beda Fell is clearly seen to the southwest. The summit lies at the southern end of a lovely ridge, which is best explored in a south–north expedition to Steel End.

Safe descents

Head S to cross the wall-stile and, after 100 metres, switch right (**4**) for Martindale.

29 TARN CRAG 664M/2179FT

Climb it from	Sadgill **31**
Character	Great mass of fell at the very head of lonely Mosedale with Buckbarrow Crag looming over the upper reaches of Longsleddale.
Fell-friendly route	3
Summit grid ref	NY 488 079
Link it with	Branstree or Grey Crag

Likely to be climbed, much as George Mallory climbed Everest, 'because it is there', rather than for its own intrinsic beauty, Tarn Crag sits at the northeastern edge of everything Lakeland. Its steep west wall, centred upon the fierce buttresses of Buckbarrow Crag, lends majesty to the head of Longsleddale and gives the fell sufficient dignity to claim its rightful place in the company of Cumbrian mountains.

Near the summit is the remains of a surveying pillar. This unusual stone and concrete construction is cleft at the top to provide a sight line and was originally surrounded by a wooden frame, now decayed. This is one of four such pillars built during the construction of the Haweswater aqueduct in the 1930s. Below

↑ *Tarn Crag from Steel Pike*

Branstree and Tarn Crag is the first section of the pipeline – the longest in Britain at the time – carrying water from the reservoir to Manchester.

Only one route to the top is really any fun, that by Galeforth Brow (1). Other routes from Longsleddale are described here but not their sodden counterparts from Mosedale, saturated but drained of joy.

Ascent from Sadgill 31

Route 1 is the only really entertaining way up – with a little scope for improvisation – but Routes 2 and 3 share the opportunity to savour the drama of the head of Longsleddale.

Via Galeforth Brow →2.8km/1¾ miles ↑470m/1540ft ⏱1hr 45min

1 From the lane end go through a field-gate into access land. Target the fence-gap at the top, climb the pasture bank (interspersed with outcropping) and then cross a gill to reach what turns out to be a stile. The path heads on up a stony gully onto a shelf. When you reach the next wall follow a waymark post that guides the path right as the wall becomes a fence. At this point cross the stile and switch back north alongside the wall. Keep with this, although

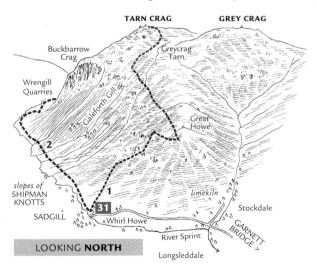

LOOKING **NORTH**

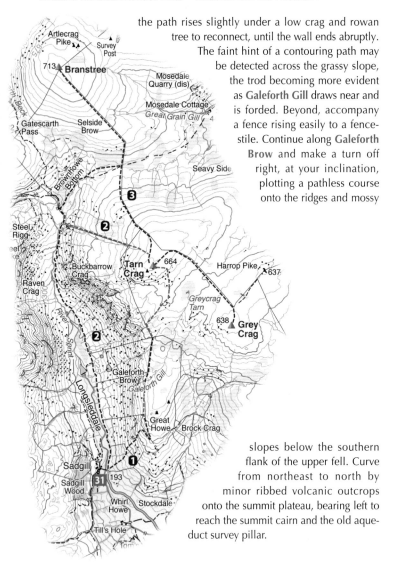

the path rises slightly under a low crag and rowan tree to reconnect, until the wall ends abruptly. The faint hint of a contouring path may be detected across the grassy slope, the trod becoming more evident as **Galeforth Gill** draws near and is forded. Beyond, accompany a fence rising easily to a fence-stile. Continue along **Galeforth Brow** and make a turn off right, at your inclination, plotting a pathless course onto the ridges and mossy

slopes below the southern flank of the upper fell. Curve from northeast to north by minor ribbed volcanic outcrops onto the summit plateau, bearing left to reach the summit cairn and the old aqueduct survey pillar.

Via the quarry lane-end

→ *3.9km/2½ miles*
↑ *490m/1610ft* ⏱ *2hr 10min*

2 Follow the drove and old quarry access lane north from Sadgill. As the broad valley floor squeezes down spot a new hand-gate on the right, inserted for the express use of rock climbers intent on Buckbarrow Crag. Keep within the lane, which becomes pitched as it steepens, with the lure of handsome waterfalls over the wall to the left in Cleft Ghyll. Come up to, and go through, a gate. Now turn to claim and climb your fell. Go right following the wall and then fence over the brow. Higher

River Sprint at Cleft Ghyll

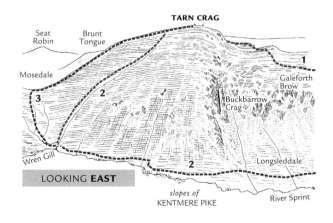

TARN CRAG

Seat Robin

Brunt Tongue

Mosedale

Galeforth Brow

1

3

2

Buckbarrow Crag

Wren Gill

Longsleddale

2

LOOKING **EAST**

slopes of KENTMERE PIKE

River Sprint

Haweswater survey pillar

up cross a lateral plain fence (no stile) to ease onto the ridge, joining the edge path leading right to the summit.

Via the north ridge →*5km/3 miles* ↑*485m/1590ft* ⏲*2hr 30min*
3 Follow the walled lane with Route **2** and stay with it beyond the track gate, and on rounding a bend come to a three-way signpost. Break right, signed 'Mosedale/Swindale', fording the beck draining **Brownhowe Bottom**. Keep to the more obvious path through damp ground, rising to a gate in the broad saddle, where Mosedale begins. Don't go through. Instead turn right and follow the regular path beside the fence, easily evading a few early peat groughs. Higher up cross a lateral fence-stile to reach the summit plateau, with one consistent path all the way to the cairn.

The summit

A small cairn sits on the highest point, the Haweswater engineers' survey pillar giving the southern brink a fascinating subject beside a rippling, reflective pool. Indeed, this southern scarp edge is a place to linger and reflect, taking a long perspective on Lakeland's bountiful fells, which may be said to have their beginnings here.

Safe descents

Walk N, taking the early pathless line down a shallow hollow NW to cross the plain fence (**2**). Follow on, descending on easy ground with a fence close left, and later a wall, to reach the gate at the top of the lane into Longsleddale.

Ridge routes

Branstree →*2.6km/1½ miles* ↓*155m/510ft* ↑*205m/675ft* ⏱*1hr*
Head N to join the fence as it descends via a stile into the damp depression. Pass the gate and follow the continuing fence up. It bends and is replaced by a wall on Selside Brow. The path on grass rises steadily to a fence-stile on the summit.

Grey Crag →*1.4km/¾ mile* ↓*65m/215ft* ↑*40m/130ft* ⏱*25min*
Track NE to join the ridge fence, with pools beyond. A sure and trusted companion, the fence comes down into a shallow basin of peat and soggy mosses. (For all its ankle-dipping, this route is much better than following a compass bearing direct from Tarn Crag to Grey Crag, which would put the hapless navigator into waist-deep and worse water crossing the bog of Greycrag Tarn.) Where the fence ends on a peaty waste bear S, with more clarity in the path, to the summit cairn.

Goat Scar from Great Howe (photo: Maggie Allan)

30 THORNTHWAITE CRAG 784M/2572FT

Climb it from	Hartsop **3**, Town Head **37** or Kentmere **33**
Character	Focal point of ridges and routes north of the Ill Bell range
Fell-friendly route	3
Summit grid ref	NY 432 100
Link it with	Caudale Moor, Froswick, Grey Crag, High Street or Mardale Ill Bell
Part of	Kentmere Horseshoe

With reasonable ridge routes to five fells available, it is easy to see Thornthwaite Crag's all-round appeal. And to top it all is the lure of the tall cairn on the summit, once of the most iconic in Lakeland. The Roman road glances just to the east of this site, although walkers, bikers and horse-riders generally make the detour to pay it homage.

This pillar is known as Thornthwaite Beacon, suggesting that a fire has been lit here over the years to relay messages or mark important events. It would have been seen from many points in the south of the district and perhaps from some to the north – a major landmark on the ancient highway.

↑ *Thornthwaite Crag from Caudale Moor*

The routes highlighted here rise up from Hartsop in the north and Troutbeck in the south. Beware that the path climbing east beside the wall from Threshthwaite Mouth (reached on Routes 1 and 4) is an abomination of loose stones. Avoid this horrible line of ascent by turning north on reaching the steepening slope, keeping below the rocks until matters improve. There is only a sheep trod on the grassy slope as the route comes over a lateral wall and works up onto the ridge from Gray Crag (and no path at all here), but the going is at least feasible and pleasant.

Ascent from Hartsop 3

Via Threshthwaite Mouth →4.4km/2¾ miles ↑620m/2035ft ⏱2hr 30min

Walking up Threshthwaite Glen you might well imagine yourself in some lonesome Highland setting blinkered by mighty Munros.

1 From the car park, cross **Walker Bridge** and follow the bridle-track, which leads through gates into the **Pasture Beck** valley. This winds on merrily at an easy gradient until it encounters rougher going via a wall-gap and passes up by great boulders. Much of the path from this point on has been repaired by Fix the Fells with the headwall trod a sequence of stone steps by way of a couple of gill crossings. Coming onto the saddle, cross the broken wall and turn left. This is **Threshthwaite Mouth**. Turn off the horrible stony ridge trail as the

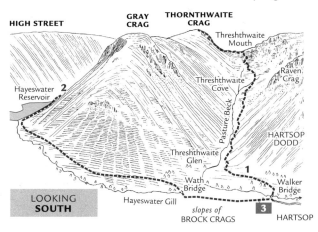

HIGH STREET   GRAY CRAG   THORNTHWAITE CRAG
Threshthwaite Mouth
Raven Crag
Hayeswater Reservoir **2**
Threshthwaite Cove
Pasture Beck
HARTSOP DODD
Threshthwaite Glen
Wath Bridge
Walker Bridge
1
LOOKING **SOUTH**
Hayeswater Gill
slopes of BROCK CRAGS
3
HARTSOP

scree and outcropping intervene and turn north, pathless, to skirt round to the ridge coming up from Gray Crag until the terrain improves. Walk up the ridge or wend back round to the original path from here to reach the handsome beacon cairn from the northwest.

Via Hayeswater →5km/3 miles ↑620m/2035ft ⏱2hr 45min

A valley route almost to the summit, the early stage by the track up the Hayeswater Gill valley a delight and the wild dale above rough underfoot and barren

2 Follow the regular track from the car park through gates, heading east and past the sheep pens. Avoid the inviting metalled waterworks road-way after the cattle grid. The track crosses **Wath Bridge** and ascends by gates and a mossy-roofed field barn to reach the reservoir. Hold to the near (western) shoreline. Follow a dwindling path, which is lost on a rising rigg as the lake ends. Thereafter, contour to find the easier ground until the boulders in the final phase at the source of **Hayeswater Gill** cannot be avoided. The blessed relief of the Roman road, for all its worn bed, comes as salvation. Turn right to reach the beacon within 200 metres.

Ascent from Town Head 37 *off map S*
Set out on the Roman road to High Street and beyond.

Via Scot Rake →7.3km/4½ miles ↑660m/2165ft ⏱3hr 15min

3 Follow Ing Lane from Town Head as far as Hagg Bridge, just short of **Troutbeck Park** farm. Immediately after crossing the bridge bear right at the stile (currently superfluous, as the fence is missing) and follow the footpath up the pasture along a minor gill to go through the kissing-gate and join the farm track. Go right, following the track via gates through the **Hagg Gill** valley. At the top, exit by the gate and step up on the grassy way with a wall close left and **Blue Gill** right. Where the wall contours off left, turn your mind more purposefully to the ascent. The grassy trod

Ill Bell range from the south slope

(known as **Scot Rake**) may be as old as the hills but it is a modest presence and has one small rock-step. Spurn the ridge path as long as you can and stay with this ancient route through the grassy pasture tending gently up to join the ridge.

Via Threshthwaite Mouth →*8.3km/5¼ miles*
↑*720m/2360ft* ⏲*3hr 45min*

A little-considered variant breaks from the Roman way.

4 Follow up from Troutbeck with Route **3** but, at the point where the path climbs away from the wall adjacent to Blue Gill, turn off left on a sheep path beside the wall, and continue in the same direction as the wall drifts down left. The trod is quickly lost, but the going is straightforward, if rush-bound in places. Ford the headstream of **Trout Beck** immediately above the upper section of a rowan-filled ravine, where a waterfall spills excitedly into the dark channel. On top of the facing rigg find a path, created by descending walkers. Follow this narrow path in the grass up the valley, soon to be joined, acutely from the left, by the popular ascent path. The odd hoary cairn confirms the path's course, never in doubt, coming under the scree slope beneath **Threshthwaite Crag** to reach the high threshold. At which point rise to the ridge and follow Route **1** to the summit.

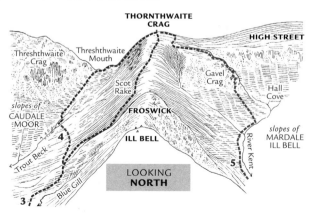

231

Looking north from Froswick with Herdwick ewe and lamb in the foreground

Ascent from Kentmere 33 *off map S* from Hallow Bank 34 *off map S*

Via Kentmere Reservoir →*7.3km/4½ miles* ↑*630m/2065ft* ⏲*3hr 10min*

Work your way carefully up, initially beside the diminishing River Kent, on this voyage of discovery.

5 From Kentmere village, by either the road or green lanes, venture onto the private road to Hartrigg and continue on with the track to the **Kentmere Reservoir** dam. (The same spot can be reached from Hallow Bank by the gated dale-floor footpath via Overend and **Tongue House** (barn). From the barn cross to a ladder-stile to reach an area of slate spoil where once a quarrymen's bridge spanned the dale beck. Beyond, contour the banks to a point just beyond the man-made reservoir's outflow ravine. There cross a plank-bridge and stepping-stones to cross the cobbled and stepped outflow channel itself by a gated bridge and reach the reservoir track.)

Keep to the path running along the western side of the reservoir, halfway along drifting down to avoid rocky ground. As the reservoir is passed so is clear evidence of a path through the damp dale-floor herbage well left of the

Kent, which for all its beck dimensions retains the name of 'river'. Coming near a wash-fold bear up left with the moraine ridge and trace along the top of this feature, beside the river.

Now take on the **Gavel Crag** ridge. At a noteworthy waterfall leave the beck and start to climb the steep fellside. Either drift half-left to avoid most of the rocky ground or tackle the ridge above. After the initial boulders it becomes a succession of small irregular outcrops, calling for canny manoeuvres as you work your way, bit by bit, up the prow. Grass is found as the rocky shield is beaten and you climb onto the spine of the ridge to find the contouring path skirting the edge. Here keep left (west) until a re-entrant gully intervenes and then bear right (north) onto the plateau. Join the Roman road to reach the summit.

The summit

Exposure to fierce winds and wild weather has inflicted damage to the crown of this monumental pile but the great cairn still stands upon its fractured rock footing, the perfect place to rest and partake of refreshment. The panorama is spacious and rewarding. The Helvellyn range serves up much of the fell fayre, but from Black

Thornthwaite Beacon

Combe to Pillar the roof of Lakeland is there to be seen, with Mickledore set directly above Stony Cove Pike. A fine stretch of the Roman road is visible sweeping north along the western edge of High Street, apparently springing from beneath your feet.

Safe descents

For travel S the Scot Rake path (**3**) is as safe as they come. The ridge N to Gray Crag is preferable to skipping down to Threshthwaite Mouth and into the Threshthwaite Glen. **Beware** the crag at the northern tip of the ridge (keep right to avoid it) when joining the Hayeswater access track for Hartsop.

Ridge routes

Caudale Moor → *1.5km/1 mile* ↓*190m/625ft* ↑*170m/560ft* ⊕*40min*
Leave the summit on the E side of the ridge wall and stick to the ridge path (ultimate destination Gray Crag). Watch for a lateral wall down to the left, aim down to it, cross it and come under the rough slope onto the ridge with its broken wall into Threshthwaite Mouth. Climb W from the notch, with several rock-steps to entertain (or irritate) depending on prevailing conditions. Coming over the rock obstacle onto the grassy fell maintain company with the wall until the cairn of Stony Cove Pike lures you half-left.

Froswick → *1.7km/1 mile* ↓*165m/540ft* ↑*95m/310ft* ⊕*45min*
Follow the regular path S to a cairn on the brink, from where a modern trail ensues, leading down the ridge and through the saddle, and climbing on the path angling SE to the summit cairn.

Gray Crag → *2km/1¼ miles* ↓*140m/460ft* ↑*50m/165ft* ⊕*30min*
Walk N along the spine of the ridge, with handsome views on both hands. After a cairn, slip over a broken wall straddling the ridge to reach the solitary summit cairn.

High Street → *1.6km/1 mile* ↓*30m/100ft* ↑*75m/245ft* ⊕*40min*
Follow the worn trail E, which swings around the head of the Hayeswater valley and crosses over a broken wall in trending NE. Watch for a path breaking half-right which leads direct to the summit column.

Mardale Ill Bell → *1.8km/1 mile* ↓*40m/130ft* ↑*60m/195ft* ⊕*30min*
Follow the Roman road until the broken wall. Here turn right (E), joining the edge path above Hall Cove, and veer off as the ground modestly rises onto the summit.

31 TROUTBECK TONGUE 363M/1191FT

Climb it from	Town Head **37**
Character	Lowly wedge of moorland beloved of Beatrix Potter
Fell-friendly route	1
Summit grid ref	NY 422 064

The smallest fell in this guide, Troutbeck Tongue, is proof that scale and size are not everything. Having no connection in any shape or form to another fell, it stands proud as punch in its own humble domain. This lowly wedge of rocky upland provides nascent walkers with all they need to gain their first foothold in fellwalking and, in combination with a stroll through the much-loved village of Troutbeck and its pastures, it is superb.

While the valley of Trout Beck may seem to be a traditional hay meadow when viewed from Ing Lane, it turns wild and inhospitable upstream of Troutbeck Park farm. To the east of the fell runs a quiet side-valley drained by Hagg Gill, where ran the Roman High Street. Beside it you can find old slate quarries with much discarded stone, presumably not up to requirements, and there's another small quarry to discover on the west side of the Tongue's summit ridge.

Approach from the south, along Ing Lane, and choose from three different routes up the steep east flank of the fell once you get there.

↑ *Troutbeck Tongue and the Hagg Gill valley from the foot of Blue Gill*   235

Ascent from Town Head 37

The direct line is a great ascent by any measure, ideal for new recruits to fellwalking, but can easily be extended into a circuit by bringing either Route 2 or Route 3 into play.

Via the south ridge →*3.6km/2¼ miles* ↑*240m/785ft* 🕒*1hr 45min*

1 (If you're starting from the village, stroll along the confined **Truss Lane** to enter Ing Lane below Town Head.) From the parking, walk back and down the roadway, passing a cluster of dwellings, into the valley. **Ing Lane** runs through the middle of the dale-floor pastures, cut and dried for hay and black-bag silage in the late summer months. After just over one and a half kilometres a gate brings you into the open meadows. Cross **Hagg Gill** and be guided by the footpath sign. Cross the pasture half-right, rising to a hand-gate in a wall to join a rough surfaced track going right (there is no way left contrary to the OS mapping).

Hagg Gill valley

The track comes round into the Hagg Gill valley and leads through a gate. Here step up left, not tidily, nor with clear signs of a path. A path comes into being once you are up beside the wall. Soon the path turns upwards, beating a way up the bracken slope onto the rocky spine of the south ridge. Cross a fence-stile and continue up the ridge by several turns to reach the summit cairn.

Via the north ridge →*5.7km/3½ miles* ↑*250m/820ft* ⏰*1hr 50min*
2 Walk across the meadows with Route **1**, but at the foot of the fell keep within the **Hagg Gill** valley on the bridle-track through two further gates, and as the wall on the right dips away turn up left onto the cut green-way. This

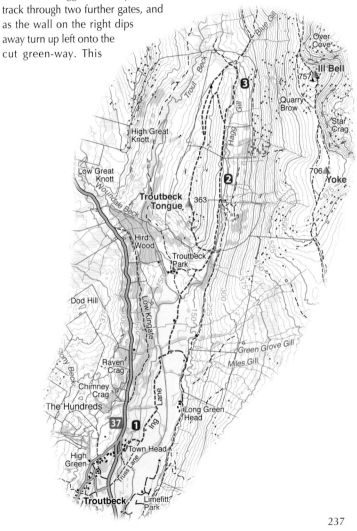

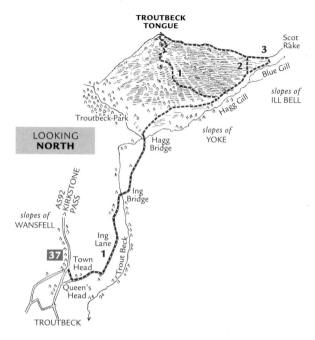

comes onto the ridge, at which point turn acutely left. Rough moor grass will slow your eager stride up to a wonky stile located at an angle in the ridge-straddling fence. The ridge path thereafter comes by a rocky bank and heads on over a grassy knoll, which may in fact be a whisker higher than the following knoll, which is considered to be the summit. This is where the conventional cairn is set.

Via the tumulus →6.5km/4 miles ↑250m/820ft ⏱2hr 40min
3 Follow Route **2** but instead of bearing up left on the green-way continue up the dale-floor of **Hagg Gill**. As this rises bear off left with a shepherds' track and cut back southwest over the damp tussock pasture to find a Bronze Age tumulus. Evidence of a walkers' path can be detected weaving south through the tussock grass and in time uniting with Route **2** at the wonky stile. (Let's hope it has been fixed by the time you use it!)

238

Summit cairn

The summit

They do say that if you want to enjoy a mountain you need to view it from mid-height. Well, sadly, little of what is in view looks better from this lowly station, although the wooded slopes leading up to and above the Kirkstone Road onto Dodd Hill look fine enough. As part compensation, you might have the fun of spotting Pike o'Blisco and Bowfell over the shoulder of Idle Hill, Wansfell's north ridge.

Safe descents

The regular way S is steep, so walkers new to walking should keep to the N ridge route (**2**) and, after the wonky fence-stile, find the incline green-way cutting back down into the Hagg Gill valley.

32 WANSFELL 489M/1604FT

Climb it from	Low Fold **40**, Rydal Road **41**, Town End **39**, Town Head **37** or Woundale **36**
Character	A hugely popular viewpoint (from its lower summit) above Ambleside
Fell-friendly route	7
Summit grid ref	NY 403 051

Lying right in the heart of the Lakeland fells Wansfell pays host to two of the National Park's most popular paths, and yet much of its extent is quiet unfrequented pasture. Sandwiched between the Stock Ghyll and Trout Beck valleys, and isolated from the rest of the range by the Kirkstone Road rising from Troutbeck Bridge, it is a fell apart. Along its southern apron, woods and pastures tumble to the shores of Windermere, lined with grand buildings among them the Lake District Visitor Centre at Brockhole. At the western foot of the fell lies the hub and hubbub of Ambleside, from where, since Roman times, walkers have made their way up here to marvel at its scenic setting.

Troutbeck, strung along its eastern slope, is one of the village gems of Cumbria. Composed of a succession of traditional yeoman's steadings set along a

↑ *Ridge wall running northeast to the summit*

mile-long lane, the village includes the National Trust's Town End, with its bank-barn still in use.

Good, accessible routes rise from all points south from Ambleside, Skelghyll Wood and Troutbeck but the wildest and the highest track comes down from the Kirkstone Road (8).

Ascent from Rydal Road 41

Via Stock Ghyll Force →*3.7km/2¼ miles* ↑*465m/1525ft* ⏱*2hr*

The popular route to Troutbeck via Wansfell Pike, almost invariably part of a circuit returning along Robin Lane and Skelghyll Woods

1 From the Market Place, the busy shopping heart of the town, pass up by the Town Hall into Stockghyll Lane, above Cheapside. Give yourself the early treat of visiting the impressive waterfall **Stockghyll Force**. At gates on the left enter the woodland park. Follow the eventually stepped pathway upstream to find the railed viewpoint from where the crash of the elegant falls can be admired. Bend right and rejoin Stockghyll Lane at a turnstile and then turn sharply left again to emerge into pasture. The road advances to where the Wansfell Pike path is signed right, stepping up to a stile and your climb begins in earnest. At the next gate the path in a lane from Blue Hill Road joins from the right. Above this the fellside path climbs through light woodland

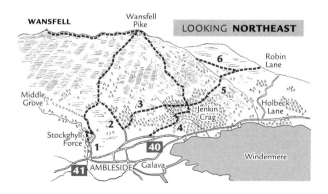

via a plank-bridge and encounters some fine stepped pitching, an essential embellishment on a path that receives such constant footfall. Wansfell Pike itself is defended by a rugged boss of rock, and the path splits to achieve the headland viewpoint by a choice of steep ways. Pass through the metal hand-gate. From here,

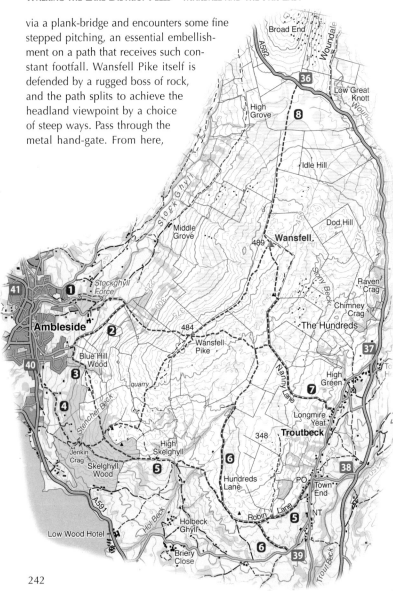

follow the path by the wall northeast, revelling in the ups and downs of the ridge, but maybe less so in the marshy hollows, to reach the true (and much-neglected) summit.

Ascent from Low Fold **40**

Start from the southern end of Ambleside for a little more solitude on your way to Wansfell.

Via Blue Hill Road →3.7km/2¼ miles ↑450m/1475ft ⊙2hr
2 Follow Old Lakes Road north and then cut through on Fisherbeck Lane to find the quiet suburban Blue Hill Road, which draws up into a lovely lane at the edge of woodland. Passing the interpretative board the lane leads by a ruin to meet up with the popular path (**1**) at a kissing-gate and join the steep southeast climb onto the rocky crest of Wansfell Pike. Follow on with the ridge wall to the true summit.

Via Blue Hill Wood →3.3km/2 miles ↑420m/1380ft ⊙2hr

A far more involved and fascinating route to the top of Wansfell Pike, with fewer walkers to disturb your solitary meanderings

3 Start out with Route **2** to the top of Blue Hill Road. A matter of 20 metres into the woodland way, turn right at the **Blue Hill Wood** National Park sign-board, passing through the wooden gate. The path levels above a wall. As a quarry nears veer left, ascending the rocky stepped path with the quarry-bounding fence right. This path leads up into the wood, passing on above the facing metal hand-gates (associated with a buried aqueduct) to go through a wooden gate up right. Enter a bracken-clad pasture. The path at once splits in two – the lower comes by a woodland wall corner to a beacon cairn with fine views. As the paths converge at the gateway contour towards a metal hand-gate that leads into **Skelghyll Wood**. Here ford **Stencher Beck** and carry on. Watch for a small National Trust waymark post indicating the key path to follow, acutely back left uphill (if an obvious fork in the path is reached, you have just passed the turning). Cross a ladder-stile out of the wood and climb on to pass a curious small fold with a tall wall-beacon inside – an observatory for the aqueduct. The path mounts low outcropping, veering right. Low wooden waymark posts consistently indicate the way. At the next rise turn left (north) heading for a sequence of two gateways. Beyond these pass to the right of a tiny **quarry** defended by a fence, with a large cairn set on the fore-spoil. Weaving up, the path splits, with the main way being the left-hand option. The paths come together and split again – one aims for a ladder-stile, while the recommended option aims for a wall-stile half-right and from there on rises with the ridge wall to the left. There is a wall-stile at the foot of the ultimate headland that provides the option of climbing the gully on the left of the wall or slanting right and keeping to grass to the top of Wansfell Pike. Join with Route **1** to follow the ridge to the summit.

Via Skelghyll Wood →3.2km/2 miles ↑420m/1380ft ⏲2hr

The ever-popular route to Troutbeck, in all probability along the line of the Roman road from Galava to Brocavum

4 From the car park find a narrow road signed 'Jenkins Crag – Skelghyll and Troutbeck (bridleway)'. Follow this uphill, passing the entrance to Broad Ings to lose the tarmac road at Skelgarth. The continuing track leads into the National Trust's **Skelghyll Wood** by a laurel fence to come by **Stencher Beck** and climbs in zig-zags, with bedrock apparent, to cross a stone bridge and complete the climb with a wall right. Watch for the path branching half-left at a National Trust 'Kelsick Scar' sign – this leads past a rock recording the gift of this land by Alfred Illingworth in 1925. The path climbs up the woodland to merge with a path coming from the right and promptly bends up obliquely right at the next fork at a low waymark post with Route **3**.

Ascent from Town End 39 or Church Bridge 38

Via High Skelghyll Farm →4.5km/2¾ miles ↑395m/1295ft ⏲2hr

Along the Roman road from the east is another scenic way to reach the intricacies of Route 3.

5 From Town End turn right (northeast) to walk up the road to the café with a letter box outside. (Reach the same spot from Church Bridge by walking steeply up the lane to the T-junction.) Bend left up **Robin Lane** beside a little

Wansfell Pike and Ambleside from Brow Head

The lovely hamlet of Troutbeck

triangle of village green. Pass a group of cottages where the tarmac ends and a loose-surfaced trail ensues. The walled lane is joined by another lane from the left. Continue, perhaps paying a visit to the small beacon cairn in the knoll up from a wall-stile. Coming to a kissing-gate go through, signed 'Skelghyll/ Jenkins Crag'. Slip through the pen by the gate and follow the regular track via a further kissing-gate, fording **Hol Beck**, and, passing a low ruin, come down

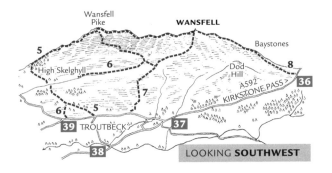

to hand-gates and a cattle grid to join a road. Rise with the fence right to **High Skelghyll** farm, discreetly passing through the yard and sheep-handling pen via gates. Passing through a gate, come by a seat with a handsome view over Windermere, and 30 metres after the metal hand-gate in the fence on the left turn off the regular path angling into the woodland on a narrow path. This duly comes over a wall, and as a path merges from the left find the low National Trust waymark post guiding up right (Route **3**).

Via Hundreds Lane →4km/2½ miles ↑325m/1065ft ⏲1hr 40min

A direct, less travelled northerly line leads to the true summit.

6 Directly opposite the layby follow the bridle-lane rising to link with **Robin Lane**. Go left, rising to reach the kissing-gate/gate where the route leaves the bridleway to High Skelghyll. Instead keep within the rough-tracked **Hundreds Lane**, which offers fine views and less disturbance, being the road less travelled. After two gates the track opens, with an attractive cascade in Hol Beck close left. Head straight on, ignoring the track bridge, with the path rising easily to a wall-stile beside a gate. Continue skipping over several damp patches and hug the wall to reach the popular path from **Nanny Lane**. Here there are two options – either go through the kissing-gate and follow the oft-pitched path climbing onto Wansfell Pike, then traverse the ridge northeast with Route **1**, or bear right with the path to a corresponding kissing-gate into Nanny Lane to join Route **7**.

Ascent from Town Head 37

Via Nanny Lane →2.3km/1½ miles ↑290m/950ft ⏲1hr 10min

The classic direct line from Troutbeck

7 Nanny Lane begins from Lanefoot Farm, situated some 400 metres south along the village street from the parking. A gate gives access into the rough-track winding walled lane, which curves above the barns and sheep-handling pens. After the third bend briefly come over bedrock. There is one gate near a bend, otherwise the lane is unhindered, arriving by the kissing-gate for Wansfell Pike. Keep within the green lane to reach a ladder-stile at its end.

Climbing over, step up onto the rigg and, passing a cairn, angle north to the summit, crossing marshy ground early on.

Ascent from Woundale 36

Via the north ridge → *1.8km/1 mile* ↑ *150m/490ft* ⏱ *40min*

A route for the purist and the loner

8 A wall-stile with mini-gate leaves the parking spot heading due south over rush-laden marshy terrain to a wall-stile. Climb **Idle Hill** and then with the wall close by on your right come onto the ridge at **Baystones**. Keep to the wall, and after the fence crossing-point bear left to complete the ascent.

The summit

A small dishevelled cairn sits upon a grassy knoll. While the many traipse over Wansfell Pike, the few come to this less-appreciated spot. Wansfell Pike has the greater diversity of scenic subjects. From there, Windermere stretches south to the islands off Bowness, and round the arch from east to west is ranged such an amalgam of fantastic fell country that it may take the breath away.

Safe descents

Nearby walls are the great asset in poor conditions. The securest line heads for Troutbeck. Follow the trace of a path ESE. This steps down in close order with the wall. The wall ushers you to the ladder-stile and so into Nanny Lane (**7**).

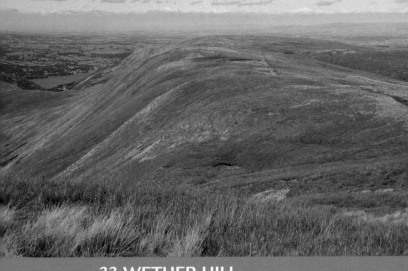

33 WETHER HILL 673M/2208FT

Climb it from	Martindale **6**, Fusedale **9**, Moorahill **16**, Bampton **15** or Burnbanks **17**
Character	Moorland ridge on Bampton Common between High Raise and Loadpot Hill
Fell-friendly route	3
Summit grid ref	NY 456 168
Link it with	High Raise or Loadpot Hill

Wether Hill, the wild home of red deer, is the perfect place for walkers with an independent spirit seeking solace and energetic days. An integral piece of jigsaw in the High Street range, Wether Hill forms the eastern horizon to Martindale and grows out of the Lowther valley by billowing moorland ridges that flank the now-peaceful but once-mined havens of Cawdale and Measand. The clutch of little hills overlooking the foot of Haweswater add a certain small-scale charm. And for an evening ramble or a place to practise navigation, the grassy hills south of Willdale are superb.

The delightful little village of Bampton makes a thoroughly grand starting point. Find here a tea room in the village shop and a lovely 'open all day' pub, the

↑ A long view of Wether Hill north from High Raise

Mardale Inn. Nearby Bampton Grange has choice walkers' accommodation in the Crown & Mitre – a strategic overnight stop on the perennially popular Coast to Coast Walk.

Take your pick from shorter, more immediately scenic routes climbing out of Martindale and Fusedale (1–4) or many generous striding routes to the top from the east (5–11).

Ascent from Martindale 6

Via Brownthwaite Crag →*4.4km/2¾ miles* ↑*510m/1675ft* ⏱*2hr 10min*

A natural line with the minimum of marshiness

1 Follow the path rising directly behind the Old Church and slanting south-east across the flanks of Steel Knotts. This leads through a hand-gate in a downward wall to reach the attractive ridge of **Brownthwaite Crag**. Heading south the path veers left under **Gowk Hill**, crosses a marshy patch and slips

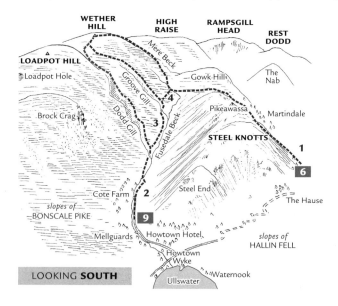

LOOKING **SOUTH**

through a gap in the wall to ford the headstream of **Fusedale Beck** between two ruined laithes or field-barns. The drove-path drifts south to embark on a steady climb across the western slopes of Wether Hill and comes up beside the ravine of **Mere Beck** to reach the saddle, where the rising wall curves south amid the peat groughs. Turn north, in the footsteps of Romans, along the gentlest of rising ridges to the summit cairn.

Ascent from Fusedale 9

There is a choice of three routes climbing out of the enclosed valley directly onto the plateau, making use of the waterways for navigation.

Via Dodd Gill →*3.2km/2 miles* ↑*505m/1655ft* ⏱*2hr*
2 Follow the concrete **Cote Farm** access road south from the verge parking. Coming to the cattle grid break right over the simple stone-flag bridge and follow the foot-path above the beck. This comes back down to cross a footbridge over **Fusedale**

The remote Carhullan

Beck and bears right. Cross the single plank-bridge over **Dodd Gill**. Here the route starts to climb left on an intermittent path up the spur. Higher up you have to tackle some stony ground. When you rise above the head of the gill cross the lateral line of a strong sheep path and continue pathless to join the ridge path. Bear right here, passing the pool in the shallow saddle and head-ing up the ridge to the summit cairn.

Via Groove Gill →*3.6km/2¼ miles* ↑*510m/1675ft* ⏱*2hr 15min*
3 Start with Route **2**, but continue to follow the path above **Fusedale Beck**, reaching a ruin about a kilometre further on. Carry on to rise to a stone-flag crossing of **Groove Gill** and later reach a path junction and two options. Choose the left one and keep uphill in harmony with the gill to reach the Roman road south of the broad saddle. Turn right to reach the summit cairn unhindered.

Howtown

Mellguards

9

St. Peter's Church

Brock Crag

Loadpot Hole

600

Loadpot Hill

671 **Loadpot Hill**

bield

Caw

6

196

Howegrain Beck

1

Steel Knotts

433 ▲ Steel Knotts

2

3

Dodd Gill

Fusedale Beck

Lowther House

Howe Grain

620

Atkinson's Grain

Seanote Grain

Lo 57

Brownthwaite Crag

Martindale

Groove Gill

4

474 ▲ Gowk Hill

Martindale Forest

673 ▲ White Bog

Wether Hill

Bampton Common

Skreel Side

Mell Beck

Mere Beck

High Kop

Keasgill Head

Fordingdale Force

Measand Beck

Measand Falls

Keasgill Sike

Red Crag

711

Redcrag Tarn

Longgrain Beck

675

Long Grain

Nook

718 ▲ Raven Howe

Bason Crag

754 ▲ Low Raise

Whelter Crags

802 ▲ **High Raise**

252

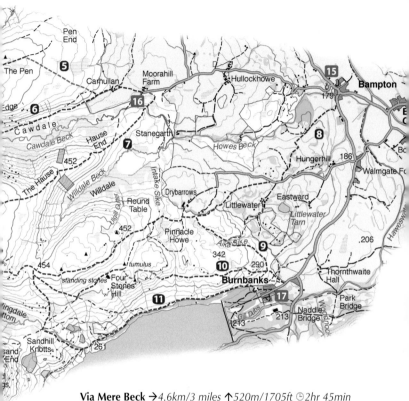

Via Mere Beck →*4.6km/3 miles* ↑*520m/1705ft* ⏱*2hr 45min*
4 Set out along Route **2** but at the decision point after Groove Gill, bear right to contour briefly to meet and join the path from Martindale (Route **1**) above the roofless stone bothy.

Ascent from Moorahill 16

Via the Pen →*5km/3 miles* ↑*360m/1180ft* ⏱*2hr 30min*
5 Follow the walled lane from the gate marked 'Carhullan'. Go to the left of the cottage and then the lovely old farmhouse along a walled passage

Slate quarry, Cawdale, in winter raiment

between stone barns to a gate. Here enter the open fell. Green paths follow the walls right and left, but your intent is up the fell straight ahead west-northwestward. There is only a tenuous hint of a path. Just avoid the bracken and aim onto **the Pen**, well above **Cawdale Edge**, to unite with the regular path near the prominent cairn. Follow this path southwest and pass beneath a bield wall. Bear off the more regular way after some 20 metres with the line of rushes that defines an old drove-path. This leads to the main ridge depression, with its large pool. Join the Roman road from Loadpot Hill and turn south to complete the ascent.

Via Cawdale →6km/3¾ miles ↑395m/1295ft ⏱2hr 45min

6 Begin with Route **5**, but after **Carhullan** keep forward alongside the wall. As the wall is lost the track begins to decline to reach the flat dale floor and advances to skip over **Cawdale Beck** at the conveniently narrow kink. The old quarry-approach track comes above a small ravine, with the ruins of a tiny bothy just above, and leads to the slate spoil bank with several more roofless ruins. Ford **Sealhole Grain** and follow the obvious path, which bends back and gains the higher portion of the quarry hollow. Backtrack and join the ascending drove, which climbs onto the ridge and is lost as the fell slope eases. Continue pathless, in a general south-southwest direction, to join the quad track leading onto **High Kop**. Seek out the crossing ridge path on the plateau and turn north to the summit.

254

Via the Hause →5.7km/3½ miles ↑380m/1245ft ◷2hr 30min

The gradient ensures a flowing stride on the old drove-path and a wonderful spacious feeling of being in a big country of far horizons.

7 Walk back along the road east towards Bampton for about 200 metres and then turn sharply right before a small fenced spring and the body of soft rushes to join a path that swings right to cross a flag-footbridge. Climb the bank and pass the mysterious low circular enclosure called Towtop Kirk. The path marches on southwest, gently rising to merge with the track from the ford. It climbs **Hause End** to level on the actual Hause, flanked by mature conifer belts, although the concept of a lateral pass seems far fetched. Coming onto **Low Kop** the ridge levels again, the path merging with a heavily used quad track (half-left you can see High Raise at the head of the Measand Beck valley). As the path comes over the ridge find a narrow trod crossing. To follow the Roman road, continue towards the wall and bear right when the main ridge path is encountered. By either path draw up and head along the featureless ridge to the cairn on the northern extremity. There is a hint of higher ground to the right, but the greater view is from the cairn.

Looking over Low Kop to Cross Fell

Ascent from Bampton 15

Via Low Kop →8km/5 miles ↑530m/1740ft ◷3hr 30min

A great long-striding route up onto Bampton Common

8 At the southern end of the village, beyond the Mardale Inn, find a footpath signposted right by a sheep pen that steps up an open track. This forms a very pleasant precursor stage to the open common and high fell. Where the adjacent fence ends, march on to go through the gate beside stone barns. Pass through the gateway and continue uphill with a field-wall close right, then go left at its corner to reach a hand-gate. Go through and traverse the open woodland pasture to a gate, and here join an open track to a gate onto a minor road. Turn right, soon finding a fence-stile left. Angle half-right through a shallow cutting to a sequence of four ladder-stiles advancing to a way-marked gap. Bear left to a hand-gate, where the open common is entered. Keep to the regular quad-bike track to come up the eastern flank of **Low Kop** by a small ruin. Soon in a grass groove leading along the plateau of Low Kop west-southwest, duly link up with Route **7**, en route to **High Kop**.

Ascent from Burnbanks 17

All three routes converge at the head of Willdale intent on Low Kop.

Via Aika Hill → *7km/4½ miles* ↑*490m/1610ft* ⏱*3hr*

9 Walk back from the car park to a gate 100 metres along the access lane. Go through and follow the path uphill beside the wall, and as the wall bears away right continue angling to the right on the hillside ahead. The path dwindles. Continue forward to join a more sure green track emerging from the gorse. This path leads alongside **Aika Sike** to link up with the field-path route from Bampton (Route **8**) near the larch copse and barn. Veer left over a flagstone spanning a marsh to meet up with the muddy track rising from Drybarrows Farm. Crossing the brow go down and ford **Intake Sike** – the unlikely, but easy ford being to the right of the pool where quad bikes have churned up the peaty basin. The continuing green-way angles half-left rising SW onto the fellside ahead. This continues at an easy gradient to come into the broad saddle at the head of Willdale, linking up with Route **8**.

Via Four Stones Hill → *7km/4½ miles* ↑*510m/1675ft* ⏱*3hr*

Best out of bracken season, the Four Stones Hill ridge deserves its own attention for its excellent views over Haweswater. The route described here is just one of many. There is plenty of scope for exploration.

10 Begin from the gate identified in Route **9**, but this time clamber up the rough path running up by the near scarp and leading ever westward. As this fades bear up onto the ridge and make for the sighter cairn, built by the reservoir engineers, perched on a forward ledge of **Four Stones Hill**. The top of Four Stones Hill has bedrock but no cairn. For rock interest venture down to stand

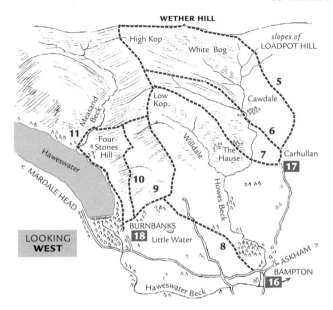

by the two stones that presumably were once a stone circle quartet, to judge by the hill name, and go back some 150 metres to the east to find a circular gathering of stones, a remnant tumulus – both features were old even when the Romans strode their High Street. The ascent route heads west, then at a faint cross-ways branch right, rising to the head of Willdale to unite with Route **8**.

Via the Forces → 7.4km/4½ miles ↑520m/1705ft ⊕3hr 15min

11 Follow the regular path along the eastern side of Haweswater to cross the footbridge spanning **Measand Beck**. Here turn up immediately right, beside the Forces ravine, a great place to observe the hydraulic energy of a mountain stream – although the best of the ravine is impossible to enter. Above, pass through the deer-fence gate (defining the new woodland compound) and cross the plank footbridge, putting you back on the east side of Measand Beck. Follow the path leading northeast over several damp patches. At the first hint of a gill bear up left, thereby avoiding the bracken, on a clear path climbing onto the ridge. On the brow this meets up with the quad track of Route **8**.

257

The summit

The plateau is extensive and undistinguished – the name White Bog provides a clue to its worst characteristic. The plain grassy setting of the cairn has no such hazard but the view will not cause you to linger long – there are better stations in line along the ridge.

Above the Forces ravine looking down on Haweswater

Safe descents

All routes up are easily retraced. The best route W is by Groove Gill (**3**), while eastwards the main routes by High Kop (**7**) and the Pen (**5**) inspire confidence on a wild day.

Ridge routes

High Raise → *3.5km/2¼ miles* ↓*30m/100ft* ↑*160m/525ft* ⏱*1hr 20min*
Two paths, one above the other, venture S. By either course come onto the eroded peaty ground above Mere Beck to run over the broken wall and connect with the ridge fence on Red Crag. Pass its namesake tarn to go through a hand-gate and unite with the continuing wall. As this ends a fence-stile is crossed and the Roman highway maintained, but briefly, as the stony crown of High Raise draws you half-left.

Loadpot Hill → *1.4km/¾ mile* ↓*55m/175ft* ↑*55m/180ft* ⏱*30min*
Head N, descending in peaty steps into the broad hollow, where languishes a lovely pool. The Roman way surges on, although you need to aim for the ruins of the old shooting box (Lowther House), from where the summit plateau comes readily to hand as you traverse to the OS column.

34 WHINFELL BEACON 472M/1549FT

Climb it from	Low Borrowbridge 29, Grayrigg 30 or Huck's Bridge 23
Character	Most prominent of four ridge summits southeast of the A6
Summit grid ref	NY 574 003
Link it with	Grayrigg Forest
Part of	Westmorland Borrowdale Round

The ridge running east along the southern side of Borrowdale from the A6 has a handsome succession of summits, five in all. There is a unity to this irregular crest whose summits beautifully coalesce into a fine end-to-end traverse. Nonetheless two summits, Whinfell Beacon and Grayrigg Forest, stand out sufficiently to merit separate fell status. Whinfell Beacon especially makes a great statement from the south while the trio of Ashstead Fell, Mabbin Crag and Castle Crag show off their individuality when viewed from the north along Borrowdale Edge. Although they are tangibly craggier in disposition, the callous imposition of conifers inhibiting the summit views takes some of the lustre from these handsome little hills.

A ragged copse of fir trees on the southern flank of Whinfell Beacon suggests that in the past trees may have been grown in this vicinity to provide a source of timber for the beacon – mentioned as such on a map of 1468.

↑ *Southern aspect of Whinfell Beacon*

Six routes are described here from which you may craft your ascent or round-ramble. They start from Low Borrowbridge (1), from the lane running north from Grayrigg (2–4) and from the A6 at Huck's Bridge (5–6).

Ascent from Low Borrowbridge 29

Via the masts →*4km/2½ miles*
↑*350m/1150ft* ⊕*1hr 40min*

A most enjoyable and straightforward climb

1 From the parking space go through the gate and follow the road along the foot of Borrowdale Wood, a lovely entrance to the valley. The road rises a little and comes to a low parapet bridge. Here a rough track departs half-left. Promptly follow this up to a gate where you join a track rising through the spacious woodland and quickly fading to a green path. This leads through a metal gate in a wall to complete the ascent to the **mast enclosure**. From here, follow the

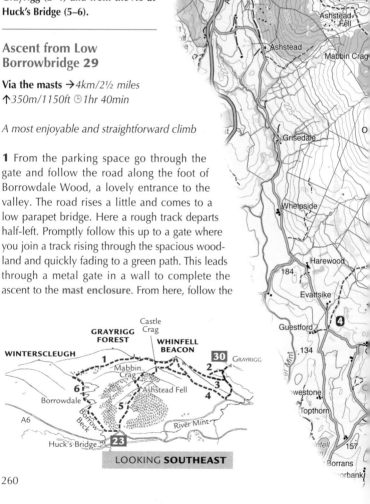

LOOKING **SOUTHEAST**

Whinash ▲ 471
Borrowdale Edge 437
Corkham

...dale

464   417
▲ **Winterscleugh**

High
Borrowdale

Roundthwaite
Common

Roundthwaite Beck

82

378 ▲ Jeffrey
Mount

Low Borrowdale

Belt Howe   Casterfell Hill

6

Castle Crag
▲ 478

Shooter Howe   419

Borrow Beck

1

29

A685

406

Whinfell Beacon

▲ 472

387   Mast
Mast 424   439

Grayrigg Forest

416   ▲ 494   478 ▲ Great Coum

338

450   ▲ Grayrigg

Agnesgill

trees

Cockin

193

261

Whinhowe Gill

Forest
Foot

Grayrigg Common

207

Deepslack   Whinhowe

3

Fellgarth

.263

Honey Moor

High Barn   227

264

232
*Grayrigg
Tarn*

177

181

2

Tarnside
House

192

30

Grayrigg
Hall

High
Mill

Sand
Beds

Peggy
Tarn

Grayrigg Hall Beck

261

A lovely hedged lane provides a southern approach

open road ahead down the short way until the reflector posts end and then bear off right to find a faint path that weaves along the damp ridge to a fence-stile in the cross-wall. Continue walking west to reach and cross a ladder-stile and climb direct to the summit.

Ascent from Grayrigg 30

Three routes lead up from the charming village of Grayrigg. Take your pick according to your time, energy and feelings about road walking!

Via field-paths to the road onto the ridge →*3.8km/2½ miles* ↑*340m/1115ft* ⊕*1hr 20min*

2 Follow the open concrete roadway north by the wall. After crossing a gill find a tractor track veering left across the pasture to and through a gate. In the next field bear half-left, passing to the left of an old quarried hollow and mature ash tree to find a wall-stile. Cross the next pasture to where a 'heck' (hanging fence) crosses a stony gill and clamber over the suitably lowered rails on the right under the bank to reach and cross a gated footbridge. Swing right, advancing to pass through the old farmyard at **Whinhowe**. Pass through a gate and rise with the track to reach a gate and then keep forward, aiming for a wall corner to the left. Cross the wall stile whose lower step is an old hurdle post with square holes. Skirt round a rushy patch and reach the open roadway. Turn right up the road with Route **3**.

Via the open road to the ridge →*4.4km/2¾ miles* ↑*360m/1180ft* ⏱*1hr 30min*

3 From the parking verge, follow the open road that swings left from the stone bridge dipping through a shallow valley in which lie High and Low Deepslack Farms. Rise to a minor cross-ways to turn right through the gate and follow a lovely hedged lane with a fine view ahead of Whinfell Beacon. After a cattle-grid meet Route **2** and pass a mature copse with a clay-pigeon shooters' cabin to the right of the roadway. Two further cattle-grids bring you to a sheepfold. Here bear off the roadway, following a green track up to the ridge and clamber over the ladder-stile by a second sheep handling pen, falling into step with Route **1** to complete the ascent to the summit cairn.

Via Evattsike →*5.4km/3 miles* ↑*365m/1200ft* ⏱*2hr*

4 A further southern ascent can be contemplated by following the narrow vergeless hedged road to the minor junction at grid ref SD 560 993. Go through the metal gate on the right and follow the green lane across from **Evattsike** to a second metal gate. Follow the wall across rough pasture to reach a third gate sheltered by a conifer copse. As you enter the high fell pasture the gorse makes the old way up by the wall impassable and a quad track is your best guide. This trends half right and ascends the slope. When it levels out you can either continue pathlessly up the bank to the left of a patch of bracken to the top, or keep with the track which eventually comes by the wall onto the ridge in a depression. Swing up right with the narrow trod to the wall-stile at the summit.

Ascent from Huck's Bridge 23

Via Ashstead Fell, Mabbin and Castle Crags →*4.4km/2¾ miles* ↑*360m/1180ft* ⏱*1hr 45min*

The primary route from the A6, great fun every step of the way and a fine ridge-top trek visiting three bonus summits en route

Shepherds' bothy on Mabbin Crag

5 From the layby walk up the A6 on the east side, slipping behind the barrier at the bend to go through the gate, where the Breasthigh Road begins. At once break right, ascending a steep path, lightly flanked by conifers on the left, to reach the cairn on **Ashstead Fell**. This definitive perch is not the summit: the ridge path continues south to cross a higher unmarked top (469m) from where the ridge bends east with views into Borrowdale. Soon the path swings south to scramble down an awkward rock-step outcrop and slip through a ridge-straddling wall. From the depression, the path follows a broad break in the conifers up to the summit of **Mabbin Crag**, the view all but blocked out by conifers.

The path finds a route down the southeast bank to pass a tiny derelict shepherds' bothy and weaves through the tangle of conifers into a marshy hollow resplendent with bog myrtle to cross a fence-stile in the depression, where open fell is regained. The thin path then rises to cross a ladder-stile, keeping with the wall over the **Old High** shoulder of **Castle Crag** (quaintly recorded as Heigh of the Hill in 1528). A detour to claim the cairn on the second proud top of this subsidiary fell is a must. Backtrack round the marsh hollow to reconnect with the progressing wall-side path, slipping through a wall gateway and easily down to a galvanised gate, from where the open path strikes up to the ridge-top wall-stile. Step up to the summit of the Beacon.

Via the Borrowdale valley →8.7km/5½ miles ↑400m/1310ft ☺2hr 40min

This scenic journey down (or up) Borrowdale makes an excellent partner for Route 5 in a fell circuit.

6 From the layby follow the Breasthigh Road as far as **Borrow Beck** but there turn right to follow the farm access track along its south side. After about 2km cross the beck to take the clear meadow way past **High Borrowdale** farm. Heading downdale pass **Low Borrowdale** Farm, now upon the farm access track which crosses Borrow Beck after 1km. Continue until 100m short of the gate – where the track becomes a tarmac road – and veer right up the prominent rough track to follow Route **1** to the summit.

The summit

Current cairn on the site of the ancient beacon

Once far more substantial, the stones in the base of the summit marker have supported a fire beacon since the mid-15th century. Tucked under the southwestern flank is a ragged larch plantation, a likely source of timber for the beacon. The remodelled summit cairn has some antique personalised inscriptions to decipher.

Safe descents

The only real caution is to avoid steep craggy ground and dense bracken on the northern flank of the long ridge. The easiest route in bad weather is the bridleway that straddles the ridge from the masts. Head NE (**1**) for Borrowdale and S to the tarmac roadway (**3**) for Grayrigg.

Ridge route

Grayrigg Forest →*3km/2 miles* ↓*120m/390ft* ↑*150m/490ft* ⏲*45min*
Descend E to cross the ladder-stile and keep along the ridge path (ignoring the inviting track right). Cross the next wall-stile and continue to join the rising open roadway briefly. Pass the repeater-station compound, keeping right with the continuing track, then veer off 30 metres short of the second mast, following a narrow trod to a wall-stile. Here go straight ahead to descend to a damp depression and then climb, pathless, onto the summit plateau.

35 WINTERSCLEUGH 464M/1522FT

Climb it from	Shap Summit **22**, Huck's Bridge **23**, Greenholme **27**, Tebay **28** or Low Borrowbridge **29**
Character	Central component of the long northern ridge from Shap Summit to Tebay
Fell-friendly route	1
Summit grid ref	NY 576 028
Part of	Westmorland Borrowdale Round

In 1763 the first six-horse Flying Machine stage-coach services began along the Kendal to Penrith road, a genuine highway which pulled over the 1400ft Shap Summit, averaging 6mph. Today you can still step off that road and trace the ridge southeast and can enjoy the freedom of the open fell upon a glorious pasture that runs for five miles to the Lune gorge, encountering red deer, skylarks and amiable fell ponies. The best section of the traverse route reaches a clear midpoint summit at Winterscleugh.

In 2003 proposals were announced for a 27-strong wind farm on this ridge. The opposition had as a champion Dr David Bellamy, who subsequently blotted

↑ *Winterscleugh from Huck's Bridge*

his copy book by claiming that climate change was not caused by human activity, but all the same, the scheme bit the dust following a public inquiry.

There are nine lines of ascent to this cairned high point. Start from Shap Summit (1), from Huck's Bridge via Breasthigh Road or Low Borrowdale Farm (2–3), from Greenholme (4), Tebay (5–6) or Low Borrowbridge (7–9). The best expeditions take the longer lines. Taking full advantage of the elevated start, the best way to enjoy the Winterscleugh ridge through to Jeffrey's Mount is as a two-car linear traverse from Shap Summit to Tebay (Routes 1 and 5).

Ascent from Shap Summit 22

Via Whinash ➔*4.5km/2¾ miles* ↑*160m/525ft* ⏱*1hr 30min*

A classic ridge walk from top to top along Borrowdale Edge

1 From the large layby at Shap Summit with its striking highway memorial stone and Shap Fell Bothy camping barn follow the broad verge south to find a hand-gate and bridleway signpost guiding left 'Bretherdale Head'. A clear path leads through the heather to a hand-gate/stile and turns right. Coming over a small outcrop called Red Crag be sure to keep right by the ridge wall spurning the clearer path down towards Bretherdale Head. The ridge dips then mounts onto **Crookdale Crag** (no crag), then runs on comparatively level until, at a slight rise, you can visit a small craggier outcrop to the left – no cairn, but a lovely spot to pause. The highest part of the entire ridge lies over the west side of the wall, a mere 5m higher but inaccessible.

Follow on, passing a rush-fringed pool short of where the wall turns south. Keep forward, dipping to cross the top of the **Breasthigh Road**. You'll easily spot the grass quad track guiding on along the broad ridge just back from Borrowdale Edge. Pass the debris

of an old anemometer on Dennison Hill (set up to measure wind velocity when 27 wind turbines were proposed before being roundly rejected at a public inquiry). A modest ten-stone cairn marks the brow of **Whinash**, from where the scarped prow of Winterscleugh is seen ahead, and the quad track leads irresistibly to the tiny outcrop and cairn.

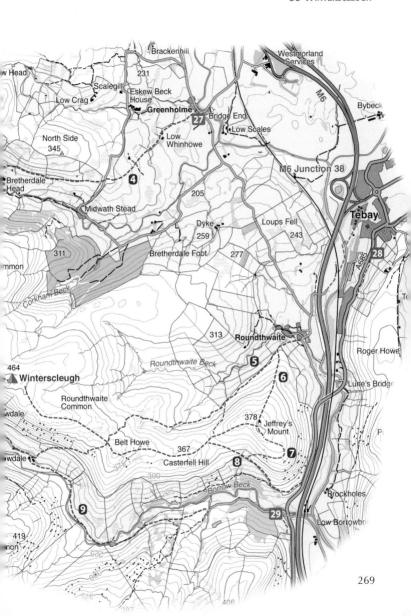

w Head
Brackenhill
Westmorland
Services
231
Scalegill
Low Crag
Eskew Beck
House
Greenholme
27
Bridge End
Low Scales
M6
Bybeck
North Side
345
Low
Whinhowe
M6 Junction 38
Bretherdale
Head
4
205
Tebay
Midwath Stead
Dyke
259
Loups Fell
243
A685
311
Bretherdale Foot
277
28
mon
Corkham Beck
313
Roundthwaite
Roger Howe
464
Winterscleugh
Roundthwaite Beck
5
Lune's Bridge
Roundthwaite
Common
6
Te
wdale
378
Jeffrey's
Mount
wdale
Belt Howe
367
7
Casterfell Hill
8
Brockholes
9
300
Borrow Beck
29
419
non
406
Low Borrowbri

Ascent from Huck's Bridge 23

Two routes that naturally combine to make a grand circuit

Via Breasthigh Road →3.9km/2½ miles ↑265m/870ft ⊕1hr 15min

2 Cross the road from the layby and keep behind the barriers to switch down through the gate to the initially untarmacked Breasthigh Road. This turns left to cross the stout stepping-stones in what could be a torrent in times of heavy rain, but is otherwise a simple hop over **Borrow Beck**. The 'road' is an all-too-popular route used by all manner of off-roaders. The Thunder Stone is a small erratic halfway up a series of hairpins. At the crest find the quad track branching right onto the open pasture ridge and turn right in company with Route **1** towards **Whinash** and Winterscleugh.

Via Low Borrowdale Farm →6km/4 miles ↑310m/1020ft ⊕2hr

This route takes advantage of the bridle-track down Borrowdale, keeping close company with the stony beck.

3 From the layby follow the Breasthigh Road as far as **Borrow Beck** but there turn right to follow the farm access track along its south side. After about 2km cross the beck to take the clear meadow way past **High Borrowdale** farm to **Low Borrowdale** farm. Here keep above the buildings in the lee of mature trees. Rise through the shelter belt to a gate, from where a green track leads

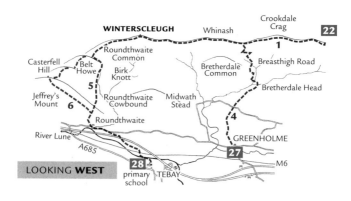

Conifer-draped Mabbin Crag and Ashstead Fell from Borrowdale Edge

up beside an enclosure wall by two further gates, gaining the open fell. A groove path unimpeded by bracken climbs the fell-side and curves onto the ridge. This old bridleway, which straddles the fell bound for Roundthwaite, gets you sweetly onto the ridge where you can turn left (northwest) to join the quad track along the spine of the broad ridge, climbing easily to the summit.

Ascent from Greenholme 27

Via Breast High →6.4km/4 miles ↑395m/1295ft ☺2hr 15min

Discover a beautiful backwater valley and follow an unadopted road onto the open ridge from where an inviting broad pasture liberates the stride and mind.

4 A bridle-track is signposted through a gate beside the old school building. It leads southwest to **Low Whinhowe**, a delightful spot in need of a little restoration. Pass on by the gate and, as the track veers left by a small ruined stone shed, a sunken way leads on by a fence. Follow the quad track. When you reach the gate in the left corner of the narrow field keep ahead up the pasture to the left of the thoroughly ruined High Whinhowe. Soon after the next gate cross an open road, with Bretherdale handsomely displayed ahead. Soon a sturdy wall comes close right. The green shelf path leads on by

271

Fell ponies on Jeffrey's Mount

several small gates, descending to a cobbled ford and stone footbridge spanning **Bretherdale Beck**. Go through the gated farmyard by the roofless ruin of **Bretherdale Head** farm. After a second galvanised gate the lane comes to a junction where you go right with the **Breasthigh Road**. Where the walled lane ends at a gate the track runs on, winding delightfully uphill, at least until the slope gathers pace and the stones unravel beneath your feet! Arrival at the ruin of **Breast High** merits a pause on this age-old trade route to Kendal. The track winds on by a traffic-torn pipe to a gate, from where the going is altogether more pleasant onto the pass. Here turn left, joining Route **1** to **Whinash** and the summit.

Ascent from Tebay 28

Via Roundthwaite →6km/4 miles ↑460m/1510ft ⏱2hr 15min

Two approaches to the eastern end of the ridge, both on clear paths but undoubtedly unpeopled

5 Walk up the road north from the parking to pass the Cross Keys Inn on the left and turn left down Church Street ('no through') which bends left into a fenced lane leading to a metal footbridge spanning the **River Lune**. Cross, admiring the riverscape if not the looming motorway flyover. Bear left and veer away from the riverbank on an open track, going by a barn and through the gated railway underpass. Now on a tarmac road proceed into the hamlet

272

of **Roundthwaite**. Cross the beck bridge and, as the road swings left, stride straight up the rough track ahead and through a gate. Continue with the bridleway up the valley of Burn Gill onto the ridge. Here turn right across **Roundthwaite Common** for the summit. **6** Alternatively, to take in the summit of **Jeffrey's Mount**, take the quad-track forking left after the gate to climb the rounded ridge to the domed top and a dishevelled cairn. To get the best view of Grayrigg Forest walk a little south and, before the ground begins to fall, appreciate its stature in relation to the traffic-thronged Lune gorge and serene Howgill Fells. Pitch off the top west, traversing **Casterfell** and **Belt Howe** to meet the bridleway (Route **5**) in a shallow col.

Ascent from Low Borrowbridge 29

Three lines of ascent are available, the basis of a compact circuit.

Via the intake drove-way →4.6km/2¾ miles ↑375m/1230ft ◷1hr 15min
7 Follow the A685 verge 500 metres northeast until the great road-engineered cliff comes close and here turn acutely left with a ramped track to a metal gate. **Jeffrey's Mount** rises abruptly right. (Out of bracken season you may be tempted to climb the steep slope to meet Route **6** a few paces before the cairn.) Follow along the wall from the gate on a green-way. When you reach a gate keep up right in a groove, keeping close to the wall to avoid the bracken as much as possible. Curving with the combe, the groove angles up from the wall. Turn right as the bracken relents to gain the high prow of the

273

ridge and, in so doing, fabulous views back to the Howgill Fells, Lune Gorge and Grayrigg Forest. **8** Alternatively, stay with the grooved path which forms the divide between bracken and grass pasture, climbing onto the main ridge of **Casterfell Hill**, the happy grazing ground of Fell Ponies and Rough Fell sheep. Turn left on the ridge path to fall into step with Route **6** to the summit.

Via Low Borrowdale Farm →*6km/4 miles* ↑*385m/1265ft* ⏲*2hr*

The final option, and perhaps the most natural, explores Borrowdale.

9 Go through the gate from the parking area and follow the open road up the valley for about three kilometres, via cattle grids, to reach **Low Borrowdale** farm. Swing right beyond the farmyard, under the canopy of trees, to a gate and ascend by a wall to a gate onto the open fell, a groove path climbing to the ridge. Break left to reach the summit with Route **5**.

Safe descents

The southern slope is steep and unpleasant, while that to the north is locked in semi-felled plantation and intractable enclosure. Keep with the ridge W for Breasthigh Road for Huck's Bridge (**2**) or Bretherdale (**4**) and E for Tebay (**5**) and Low Borrowbridge (**9**).

Summit outcrop

The summit

A small outcrop on the south side of the summit provides a pleasing break from the ubiquitous grass pasture and sufficient stones to assemble a very modest cairn. A wide view east to the Westmorland plateau and Howgills contrasts with the westward view to the delights and heights of Lakeland, perhaps the most familiar silhouette that of Ill Bell, nine miles distant as the crow flies, with Great Gable to its left and much further south, the Coniston fells.

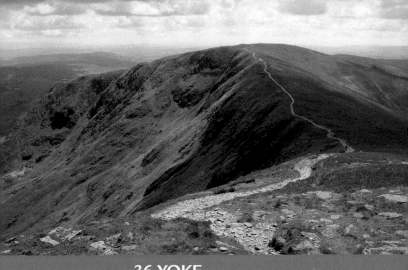

36 YOKE 706M/2316FT

Climb it from	Church Bridge **38**, Kentmere **33** or Hallow Bank **34**
Character	Blunt southern end of the Ill Bell range
Fell-friendly route	3
Summit grid ref	NY 438 067
Link it with	Ill Bell or Sallows
Part of	Kentmere Horseshoe

The most southerly sibling of Kentmere's iconic trio of shapely fells is another whose greatest attractions lie on its shady eastern side, notably in Rainsborrow Cove and Rainsborrow Crag. The latter has little of interest to a rock climber, but the cliff is hugely impressive and certainly caught the eye of quarrymen back in the day, who picked and blasted a massive cavern and a vertical cutting at the foot of the cliff and also exploited seams of the best slate up in the cove.

These workings are part of an eastward seam that runs over the Tongue and up onto the slopes of Kentmere Pike, where there is further evidence of quarrying. Below the cove the old slate workshops have been tidily converted into an outdoor centre, known as Reservoir Cottage, inspiring new generations of young walkers and climbers.

↑ *Yoke rising above Rainsborrow Cove, seen from Ill Bell*

Almost to a man and woman, walkers cross the fell on the ridge path which rises from the Garburn Pass, but Rainsborrow Crag's northern edge (5) offers easy scrambling for your delectation.

Ascent from Church Bridge 38

Via Garburn Pass →6km/3¾ miles ↑600m/1970ft ⊙2hr 30min

The western arm of the Garburn Pass is hard going underfoot but you can distract yourself with backward admiration of the idyllic valley of Troutbeck.

1 Cross the footbridge beside the road bridge, walk southwest down the road and 60 metres further along watchfully cross the A592 into the narrow walled lane. The lane (**Garburn Road**) rises by a gate and cobbled corner, marching up the slope below the old **Applethwaite Quarry**. Eventually the track levels and goes through a gate by a small conifer spinney and then comes to a right-hand bend in the track at the summit of **Garburn Pass**. At this point follow an engineered path across an otherwise damp moorland ridge north for about two kilometres. Eventually rise up by a kissing-gate. Beyond it the open track includes some fine pitched steps to a cairn, from where the summit hoves into view ahead.

Ascent from Kentmere 33 or Hallow Bank 34

Via Garburn Pass →5.2km/3¼ miles ↑545m/1790ft ⊙2hr

Another stony approach leading to the clear northerly ridge path

2 Follow the road west from Kentmere church to reach the Nook, where the Garburn Pass bridleway is signed right. The walled lane leads on below a cluster of lesser boulders in the open woodland right. After the gate the surface of the track deteriorates. The way leads up the combe where it then zig-zags up to the gate in the pass. Carry on a little further to the sharp left turn, where the engineered path departs right with Route **1**.

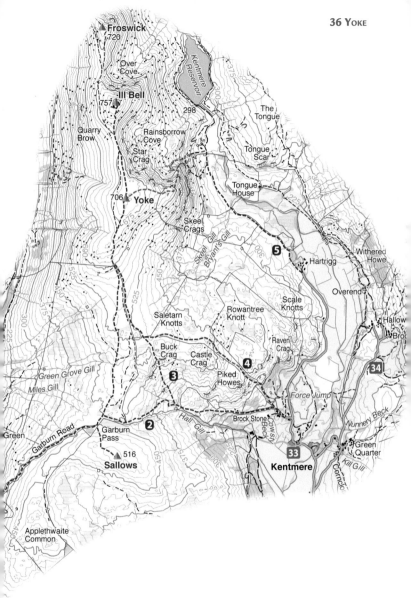

Via Buck Crag →4.2km/2½ miles ↑560m/1840ft ⏱2hr 20min

Explore the volcanic curtain overshadowing the higher reaches of the Pass.

3 Start with Route **2** but turn off just before the zig-zags up to the Pass. Follow a narrow trod which breaks from the pitched **Garburn Road** track at a ford with a fenced thorn bush right. Pass the thorn and follow the trod aiming for a weakness in the rocky facade. The grass gully leads to a peaty hollow, and the path marches on to cross a fence-stile and duly come beside the ridge wall. Follow the wall until you reach a kissing-gate. Here turn right to join Route **1** to the summit.

Via the secret drove-way →4km/2½ miles ↑540m/1770ft ⏱2hr

The impressive craggy fellside dominating the Garburn combe is unbreached by regular walkers' trods, except for one unsung drove-way that departs just short of Brock Stone.

4 Start with Route **2** but at the first left bend bear off right beside the tiny gill to go through a gate and ascend the irregular walled enclosure, climbing to a double-barred hurdle across a rock-bed and slipping under it. Where the wall comes in close on your right follow it up to step over a gill and go through a hand-gate in the upper intake wall. From here on a palpable drove-way wends up, with hints of retaining stones and juniper shrubs. This opens onto a

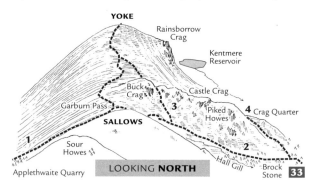

278

The secret drove-way above the Nook

broad walled pasture corridor. Hold more to the left, picking up a quad track as it joins from the left and keep to its course. (Fellwandering aficionados may prefer to wander freely over the seldom-visited pathless volcanic headlands to the left – Piked Howes and Castle Crag.)

Come up over a marsh, where the broken wall is replaced by a fence, and meets up with the Route **3** path coming in from the left at a fence-stile.

Via Rainsborrow Crag →*5.5km/3½ miles* ↑*590m/1935ft* ⏱*2hr 40min*

A sensational ascent with no exposure best tried on a clear dry day, but even on a cloudy day the intimacy with easy rocks will reward your eager hands and feet.

5 Follows the village road from Kentmere church and at the sharp left turn go straight ahead from the metal road-gate with a slate sign 'Hartrigg'. The open road leads attractively on, passing below craggy headlands, via two cattle grids, by Scales to **Hartrigg** farm. A rough surfaced track continues via gates to come under the mighty shadow of Rainsborrow Crag. With the readapted buildings of the old slate mine close ahead, bear up left beside the gill spilling from **Rainsborrow Cove**. A faint trod is discernible, rising increasingly steeply

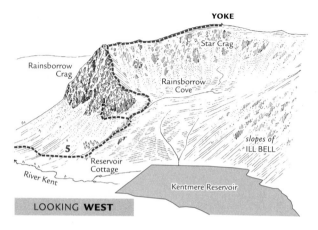

through the bracken on the north bank and leading above the copse to and above a lovely fall. (At this point a recommended detour is to ford the three strands of the gill and traverse into the slate spoil, where evidence of quarrymen's ruins are to be found below a massive quarry face. Continue, slipping down to cross a rising wall where it butts up to the foot of the cliff, then climb the grass and scree to enter the gaping mouth of a quarry cavern. There are two chambers and Tibetan prayer flags draped within so someone does visit from time to time.)

Continue the easy ascent to the upper slate workings in the cove. After inspecting the ruins bear half-left, crossing the broken wall to encounter the ridge and making steady, if steep, progress up the north ridge. Nearing the top the ridge becomes an irregular arête, so choose to either take the sporting line or keep to grass on the right-hand side to ease yourself onto the crest. Follow the ridge and come up by a lovely shelf tarn to then cross the ridge-straddling wall, completing the ascent entirely on grass.

The summit

Nature endowed cairn builders with all they needed to make their statement – a low rock rib, a clear-cut summit and a choice spot to stop and admire a spacious panorama. And stop you should. The view in the southwestern sector is quite brilliant, from Black Combe through to High Stile before Red

Screes intervenes, while further north see Helvellyn in a host of huddled fells. Close by, like a fell-festival ribbon, the ridge path beckons you on to neighbouring Ill Bell.

Safe descents

The one solid way S passes a small cairn on the plateau edge and then leads clearly down by the kissing-gate and consistent inverted substrate path to the open track at Garburn Pass – go right for Troubeck (**1**) and left for Kentmere (**2**).

Ridge routes

Ill Bell → *1km/½ mile* ↓*50m/165ft* ↑*100m/330ft* ⏱*35min*

The ridge path N has been much mended. While hasty runners have made their own contouring routes along the western slopes of Yoke, Ill Bell and Froswick, the one true ridge path provides all the scenic inducement to stick to the spine of the ridge and climb to the triple-cairned summit, with fine views into Rainsborrow Cove a special pleasure en route.

Yoke from Lingmell End

Sallows → *3km/2 miles* ↓*260m/855ft* ↑*70m/230ft* ⏱*1hr 10min*

Head S following the clear trail via the kissing-gate and easy trail down to the Garburn Pass track. Go right to the gate by the conifer spinney. Go through, turn immediately left over the stile and climb the bank ahead onto the moorland ridge of Sallows.

1 KENTMERE HORSESHOE

Start/Finish	Kentmere **33**
Distance	18km (11¼ miles)
Ascent/Descent	1080m (3540ft)
Time	8hr
Terrain	The regular Garburn track is stony and rough, but easy to follow. However, the suggested start is an off-beat pasture way with boggy patches higher up. The skyline ridge is simple all the way round, with minor outcrops either side of Nan Bield Pass and some potentially slippery rock on the final descent to Hallow Bank.
Summits	Yoke, Ill Bell, Froswick, Thornthwaite Crag, Mardale Ill Bell, Harter Fell, Kentmere Pike

In the spirit of this guide where exploring is encouraged, this clockwise circuit starts with the option of using a rarely-used sheep passage that once connected with Kentmere Hall Farm, known as Cowsty Drove (pronounced 'cowstee'). Once the main trail from Garburn Pass is joined the route is otherwise consistent with the natural skyline ridgeway. You have two options towards the end of the horseshoe. Stronger walkers will naturally include the tops of Goat Scar and

↑ *Ill Bell range from the ridge path to Mardale Ill Bell*

Shipman Knotts and are rewarded with handsome views into Longsleddale. But many will equally be content to drift down to Hallow Bank, absorbed in the wild beauty of Kentmere.

Follow the road north by Greenhead then bending west to the Nook. Here take the lane right signposted 'Restricted Byway: Garburn Pass'. After a gate the track bends left as it crosses a gill, with the Brock Stone (a large freestanding rock marked on Harvey maps as **Badger Rock** and a favourite with local boulderers) in view ahead. You can, and most walkers do, stride on along the main Garburn bridle-track – a trail heavily used these days by bikers and, for all the remedial work, inevitably there are loose sections making for uncomfortable walking. The zig-zagging track provides handsome views, notably of the crags up to the right, and rises to a gate at the top of **Garburn Pass** at the precise location suggested by the name Garburn – 'stream at the tip of the triangle of lane (parish boundary)'. The manufactured ridge path breaks off right (north) from the Pass at the left-hand bend.

Alternatively, as a natural fellranger, you might consider tracing a seldom-used sheep drove-way from that initial bend in the track short of the Brock Stone. Head off right beside the tiny gill to a wooden gate lightly tied and continue up the slope tracing the cut drove-way and keeping left with the big wall. Pass through a rock-step gateway under an ash tree, making sure you're not lured right as the wall corridor suggests, towards Cowsty Knotts. Instead keep up upon the rock-cut drove to a loose-fitting wooden hand-gate. Beyond this the groove continues on the left bank of the gill with juniper and some bracken for a short while before the path draws up to a broader, peaceful pasture, a quad track hinting at the line which drifts leftward by a broken wall with the outcropping of **Piked Howes** and **Castle Crag** dominant.

The way goes through a natural gap keeping the broken wall left heading west skirting peaty ground and slipping through the broken wall and a marshy patch to reach a fence corner and follow on with the fence and broken wall. At the light fence-stile, where a path from **Buck Crag** off the Garburn road is met, cross this path and follow on north coming by the rising wall at the top of the bank. Here join the regular ridge path immediately beside a kissing-gate.

The ridge path leads directly to the summit of **Yoke**. From this point a fence, arriving from the east, accompanies the onward route to a hand-gate after which the trail becomes open. The scenery gets more exciting as you skirt the edge of **Rainsborrow Cove** and climb to the conical top of **Ill Bell**

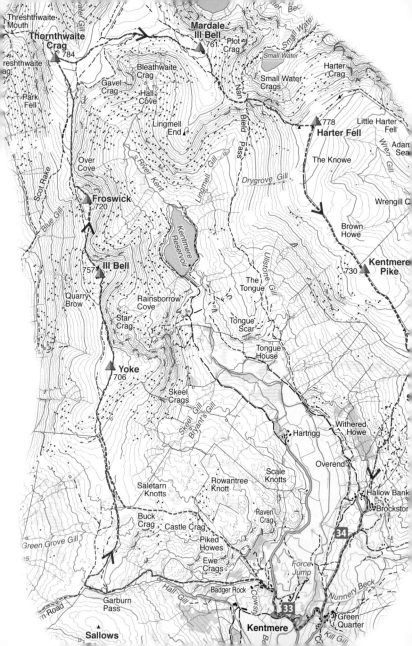

Ill Bell from the east ridge of Harter Fell

with its distinctive summit cluster of cairns. This is a revered place, loved by many for its individuality.

From here, the path scrabbles northwest down through a depression and then mounts again onto **Froswick**, where a small heap of stones with a lone metal stake constitute the summit marker. Your attention is now naturally focussed on the dale head and next objective, Thornthwaite Crag. Once more the worn path naturally swings northwest descending to a shallow depression and takes on the long gradual rise with the handmade subsoil path. Where Scot Rake (the old bridle-path coming up from Troutbeck) merges at an acute angle from the left the trail dies to the natural turf path (so as not to disturb any possible archaeology of the ancient ridge-road). A little further on, reach a metal stake set into a stone slab. Resist forking right to follow the edge. Instead, keep north-northwest to the handsome landmark beacon cairn of **Thornthwaite Crag** set impressively on a tilted slab at 784m. (Reputedly there was once a shepherds' bothy here, making it at the time the highest dwelling in England.) Take the ridge path to bear right 200 metres before you reach a broad gap in a wall straddling the ridge. Now on a lesser path head east above Hall Cove towards **Mardale Ill Bell**. Peer over the northern brink to see Blea Water and the steep face of High Street and then march on to the summit cairn, a curious stubby columnar structure.

High Street from Harter Fell

The palpable path leads on southeast with some pitching to reach the narrow defile of **Nan Bield Pass**, wherein stands a throne-like wall shelter, a popular place of refreshment shielded from southerly draughts. The eastward path mounts the rocky west ridge of **Harter Fell** in stepped stages, coming onto the plateau advancing directly east to the stake-spiked summit cairn.

Turn south accompanying the ridge fence over **The Knowe** with fine views of the Ill Bell range a constant delight. The fence is replaced by a wall before the peaty dip but it becomes a tumbled structure on the rise until pulling itself together again short of the summit of **Kentmere Pike**. Just to frustrate fell-baggers the OS column on this top stands proud as punch on the east side of the wall, requiring a stile for the sole purpose of visiting it. The cairn on the west side outcropping is quite sufficient for most visitors. Carry on with the wallside path, at one point skipping round a wide pool as you progress southeastward. Soon the path splits and you may opt to keep to the high ground beside the fence to capture the scenically spectacular top of Goat Scar with its peerless view into Longsleddale or more direct to the cairn on **Shipman Knotts** via a ladder-stile – the actual summit is inaccessible!

Most walkers will be quite content to curtail their walk at this point, taking the natural line south descending purposefully to a ladder-stile, after which the path comes and goes and is beset with damp in patches too. After crossing a broken wall it encounters rocky ground and makes hard work out of sustaining an obvious line. Passing a few thorn bushes find a more consistent grooved path that leads down to **Hallow Bank**. Pass through the wooden gate and, perhaps with some relief, step onto the tarmac beside a cottage. The simple recourse from here is to follow on the High Lane road, winding down to Bridge End, but there is also a footpath from a wall-stile by Rook Howe direct to the vicinity of the church.

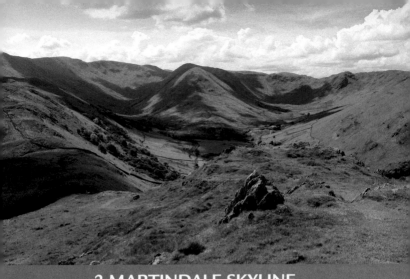

2 MARTINDALE SKYLINE

Start/Finish	The Hause **8**
Distance	20km (12½ miles)
Ascent/Descent	1215m (3990ft)
Time	8hr
Terrain	Free-flowing walking on turf most of the way, only instance of rock the section below Rest Dodd leading by Satura Crag and onto Angletarn Pikes and then the final rise onto Place Fell
Summits	Steel Knotts, High Raise, Kidsty Pike, Rampsgill Head, Rest Dodd, Angletarn Pikes, Place Fell

Ullswater contrives to give Martindale the wonderful air of cut-off seclusion, its finest qualities best observed by encircling the high skyline clockwise, with High Raise and Place Fell arguably the most scenic of seven fine summits claimed.

Pass up by the church directly southeast over the initial rise, crossing a lateral path. Head up the blunt end of the ridge in comfortable stages, initially south then southeast onto Birkie Knott – about as tough a climb as will be

↑ Head of Martindale from Steel Knotts

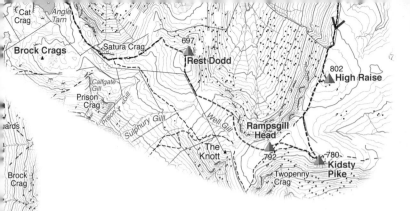

encountered on the whole walk. The grassy spine of the ridge mounts to the quirky blade of pale rock marking the summit, which fully merits a descriptive name and duly has one – **Pikeawassa**, the older name of **Steel Knotts** it would seem was the curious 'Wassa'. The ridge drops promptly south and you cross a frail wall-stile as the slope swings upward, the path wavering in its association with the wall over Brownthwaite Crag. Swing east before the moorland of **Gowk Hill** to go through a wall gateway passing between two ruined shepherds' bothies as you ford the headstream of **Fusedale Beck**.

Looking up the Howe Grain valley to the Nab with High Raise and Rampsgill Head behind

The path at once forks. Keep right gaining height gently and coming onto a distinct shelving groove pulling up to accompany the steeply climbing new fence beside the upper course of Mere Beck, high above the vivid red-roofed building (The Bungalow) down in the **Rampsgill Beck** valley. The regular path advances to the ridge-top, but the better option is to veer right through the dry gill groove to a gateway in the adjacent wall and bear back to go through the wooden gate at the corner. Keep the fence to the left to pass the modest cairn of **Red Crag** (no crag) and then a pool either side of the fence generously called **Redcrag Tarn**. On Raven Howe the fence swings left to meet a wall-end beyond the ridgeway gate. Here the path continues to merge with the main ridge path rising to a stile, where the wall gives way to a fence. Keep right to follow the regular path making sure to bear left at the brow to come onto the stony crest of **High Raise**. The views all along have been good but from here they are emphatically panoramic and will only expand as you continue.

Step back onto the old way, which was in all probability followed long before the Roman cavalry adopted it as a speedy skyline route when trees mantled the fells. The ridgeway runs on through a depression and you may again veer half-left to visit the tiny summit of **Kidsty Pike**, perhaps meeting Coast to Coast trekkers there, enjoying the view over Riggindale. Revert to the regular path curving up over the brow of **Rampsgill Head**, taking a moment to inspect the long valley trench of Rampsgill Beck running north (in the manner of High Cup in the Pennines) and the tower ridge beneath the lip of the fell.

Curve round, resisting the popular path again to keep with the grassy spur north then drift down the slope northwest to join the wall-side path again climbing onto **Rest Dodd**. The wall is lost on the final rise and there are two cairns to visit. The continuing path angles from west to northwest and then, 200 metres short of a wall-gate, pitches south-west to join the popular ridge path among the outcropping behind **Satura Crag**. Slip through a wall corner gateway and continue northwest skirting the beautiful jewel of **Angle Tarn**. Add the two tops of **Angletarn Pikes** to your tally by first breaking from the path again as it fords a tiny gill at the northern tip and ascending the bank to claim the spine of the first top. Backtrack to a short gully towards the eroded peaty hollow, but keeping left avoiding the spongy ground, then mount the more impressive of the top summit ridges from the north. Descend over the slab south with a path zig-zagging to re-join the regular way. Go right contouring and dipping to run through a small cutting to reach the broad **Boredale Hause** depression.

Head straight on from the hause passing the foundation of the **Chapel in the Hause** to join the inviting engineered path that sweeps exuberantly up the

Helvellyn range from High Raise

southern slope of **Place Fell**. A mild scramble at the top gains **Round How** and the ridge. Walk on, past some pools to reach the craggy peak with its handsome stone-built OS column. What a view, notably west to the Helvellyn range! To complete your horseshoe, follow on the main path heading northeast over the spine of **Hart Crag** easily running down the slope to Low Moss. While you can keep with the ridge, the popular path keeps to the east side of **High Dodd** onto **Sleet Fell** to meet a broken wall above **Cat Crag**. Follow it to descend northward as towards **Sandwick** but lower down veer right passing a seat to join the open road and keep right. Cross the bridge left, following a footpath sign 'St Peter's Church'. This leads by a gate, bridge and wall-stile to the banks of **Howegrain Beck** at Bridge End. Rise up the pasture to Hallin Bank by a gate and further a stiled pasture-way returning to the Hause.

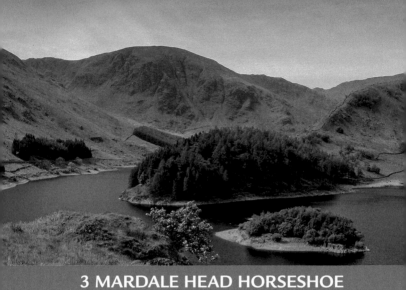

3 MARDALE HEAD HORSESHOE

Start/Finish	Mardale Head **19**
Distance	13km (8 miles)
Ascent/Descent	890m (2920ft)
Time	5hr 45min
Terrain	A steady winding climb by Gatescarth Pass onto Harter Fell, with its handsome views down Haweswater. Skipping through the rocky notch of Nan Bield onto Mardale Ill Bell and a simple open ridge way onto High Street, climaxing with the rocky crest of Long Stile and Rough Crag.
Summits	Harter Fell, Mardale Ill Bell, High Street

A compact clockwise ramble by Gatescarth Pass, Harter Fell, Mardale Ill Bell, High Street and Rough Crag features a fine succession of great viewpoints with a tremendous ridge for the finale.

Go through the tall gate that now regulates vehicular access to fragile Gatescarth Pass and set out on the track signed 'Gatescarth' heading straight on, soon running between a fence and a wall. As the track begins to zig-zag,

↑ *Harter Fell and Riggindale Crag from Haweswater*

pass through a second tall kissing-gate/gate. (Over recent years the track has been tormented by powerful vehicles whose access is now by permit only on one day a month, but the stony surface is still hard going.)

Pass a sheepfold. From here the track draws up the combe, ever more hair-pinned before levelling out at last on the broad saddle of **Gatescarth Pass**. Short of the next gate, take the made-path right, signposted 'Nan Bield Pass'. The path shortcuts to miss the top of Adam Seat, but soon draws alongside the fence on **Little Harter Fell** peering down on Gatescarth Pass. From on high, the scribbled hairpins of the climb are striking and Haweswater soons hoves into view as the path shoulders the rise and comes onto easier pasture, still near the fence.

Where the fence bends from northwest to southwest pass some rocks, one with a large benchmark, marking a grand spot to study Haweswater and the Rigg where your circuit will end. Pass a large metal stake-pierced cairn and keep on with the fence to reach the top of **Harter Fell**. Turn right (west)

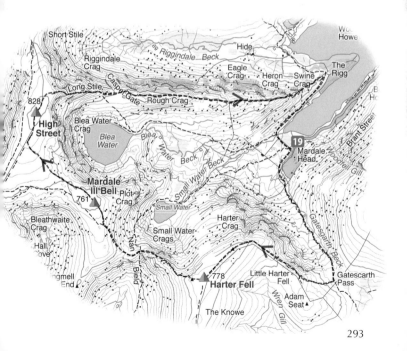

to the last cairn before the short west ridge begins, the outlook to High Street quite sumptuous, enhanced by the corrie tarns of Small and Blea Water. The path winds steadily down to **Nan Bield Pass**, a tight col with a windbreak seat. Here it slips through with views over the coiling bridle-trail dropping into the Kentmere valley so popular with mountain bikers. Curve on north-westward with stretches of path pitching en route to the summit cairn on **Mardale Ill Bell**. Keep to the ridge-top trail, taking a moment to peer over the northern edge into the vast basin occupied by Blea Water. The path gradually rises as it bends north and a newly engineered section leads to the summit crossing wall at the OS column on **High Street**.

Follow on over the gentle dome with the wall to take a prominent path turning east and leading to the brink at the top of **Long Stile**. The early stage of this stubby ridge has been intensively and superbly engineered by Fix the Fells. Enjoy breathtaking views to left and right over Riggindale and Blea Water. As the ridge levels, pass some pools in the col of **Caspel Gate** before reaching the spectacular **Rough Crag** ridge – arguably the best ridge-walk in the fells of the Far East.

Stay on the spine of the ridge on a consistent path for the best views down the cliffs into Riggindale, not long since the last stronghold and preserve of the Golden Eagle in Cumbria, passing the summit cairn. A steep abrupt

Gatescarth Pass looking back north down the hairpins

Peering over Caspel Gate from Kidsty Pike

descent marks a change in pace. The ridge path now comes beside a fenced wall leading on via a hand-gate, then briefly switching right and quickly left to avoid a crag which the wall itself manages to take in its stride. The path veers away before coming back through the bracken to complete the descent where the path to Riggindale crosses **The Rigg** headland above the conifer copse. Turn right to track back to a broad footbridge and a gate to rise to meet the outward track close to the car park.

4 WESTMORLAND BORROWDALE ROUND

Start/Finish	Huck's Bridge **23**
Distance	18km (11 miles)
Ascent/Descent	895m (2940ft)
Time	7hr 30min
Terrain	Commune with nature along two contrasting largely grassy ridges.
Summits	Ashstead Fell, Mabbin Crag, Castle Crag, Whinfell Beacon, Grayrigg Forest, Winterscleugh

A comparatively low fell expedition drawing together both sides of the Borrowdale valley, a significant part of the extension to the National Park from the A6, designated in 2016. This is predominantly grass pasture where sheep, deer and fell ponies roam and skylark soar above.

From the layby walk south along the A6 on the east side to slip behind the barrier at the bend and down to the gate where the **Breasthigh Road** begins. Through the gate, at once break right to climb a steep path, lightly flanked by conifers on the left, ultimately reaching the cairn on **Ashstead Fell** – a clear

↑ *Mabbin Crag and Ashstead Fell from Winterscleugh*

perch but not the high point of the fell. Follow the ridge path on south to cross the unmarked true top at the point where the ridge veers east for excellent views into Borrowdale.

Shortly, the path swings south to scramble down an awkward rock-step, slipping through a ridge-straddling wall to a dip. From here the path follows a broad break in the conifers up to the summit of **Mabbin Crag**, where this time the cairn does crown the highest point. Find the route down the southeast bank passing a quaint little stone bothy. Weave through the tangle of conifers into a marshy hollow to cross a fence-stile in another depression and regain the open fell. Take a thin path rising to cross a ladder-stile and keep with the wall over the **Old High** shoulder of **Castle Crag** but make sure to detour left to claim the cairn on the second proud top of this subsidiary fell. Tilted outcropping adds foreground interest to the outlook for photographers and Rough Crag shields the northeast slope below.

Backtrack round the hollow to reconnect with the ongoing wall-side path slipping through a wall gateway and easily down to a galvanised gate from where the open path strikes up to the ridge-top wall-stile and onto the fourth summit of the day, **Whinfell Beacon**. Next the ridge path angles east down to a ladder-stile by a corrugated iron sheepfold. Ignore the track right to keep on the narrow path along the broad pasture ridge to a stile in the wall and reach an open road. From here bear up left to pass to the left of the telecommunications compound.

Resist veering off the roadway half-left descending to meet the valley road and keep to the rising track towards the second mast, veering off right 30 metres short on the faint ridge path to cross an unassuming wall-stile. Go through another dip to climb pathlessly onto the plateau top of **Grayrigg Forest** and arrive at the OS column. A sketchy path eastward leads to a wall gap, where once hung a hand-gate but now a netting fence impedes only the sheeps' progress. Beyond pass a damp hollow to reach the prominent headland cairn and windbreak, with its fabulous view into the Lune gorge. The true fell-wanderer will want to detour a little further east on the faint path to a smaller cairn on **Grayrigg Pike** to

Breasthigh Road from Ashstead Fell

survey the Howgill Fells ever more gloriously. (**Do not try to descend** the abrupt grassy ridge from the cairn at 464m to reach the road above Hause Bridge. The A685 is horrid with barriers on both sides and no space for walking and traffic speeds down this stretch.) Backtrack from the Pike to slip back through the netting fencing and turn right to follow the wall as it begins a long gradual descent with a quad track. Break off half-left pathlessly to join the emerging gill and follow it down to where various streams converge and go through the intake wall by a pipe easily vaulted. Follow on down well above the west bank of the beck to steer clear of the bracken and arrive at the valley road. Turn right over the beck

The Howgill Fells from Whinfell Beacon

bridge and wander through the base of Borrowdale Wood to a gate passing the parking area to meet the **A685**. Turn left along the verge and in so doing crossing over **Borrow Beck**.

Head on beyond the mast to where the road-engineered cliff begins on the left to take a ramp track cutting acutely back to a gate. Follow on with the green-way to reach a gate and there bear up with the wall along the sunken way, which can be quite a struggle in high summer when the bracken is high. The track drifts up from the wall now forming the divide between the bracken and pasture to gain the ridge. Trace the quad-track along the ridge over **Casterfell Hill** and **Belt Howe** stepping over the ridge-straddling bridle-way from Low Borrowdale Farm and continuing unhindered to the summit cairn on **Winterscleugh**. Gaze with satisfaction into the valley below and across to the line of happy heights gathered earlier in the walk. Follow the ridge path north over **Whinash** (small cairn) to meet the Breasthigh Road. Turn left to wind down this battered off-roaders' track by its hairpins and cross the Borrow Beck stepping-stones cutting left and right up to the gate onto the A6.

MORE TO EXPLORE

Circular

- from Hartsop **3**: Gray Crag – Thornthwaite Crag – Caudale Moor – Hartstop Dodd
- from Mardale Head **19**: High Street – Rampsgill Head – Kidsty Pike
- from Mardale Head **19**: Selside Pike – Branstree – Harter Fell

Linear

- from Roehead **10** to Fusedale **9**: Arthur's Pike – Bonscale Pike – Loadpot Hill – Steel Knotts

Helvellyn from High Street

USEFUL CONTACTS

Tourist Information

Lots of information is available on the National Park website: www.lakedistrict.gov.uk. If you want to get information on your way into the National Park, the centres at Penrith (in the north) and Kendal (in the south) may be useful. If you want to talk to someone while you're there, the closest centres are in Ambleside, Ullswater and Windermere.

Ambleside

0844 225 0544
tic@thehubofambleside.com

Kendal

Made in Cumbria and Tourist Information Centre
01539 735891
kendaltic@southlakeland.gov.uk

Penrith

01768 867466
pen.tic@eden.gov.uk

Ullswater

0845 901 0845 (calls cost 2p per minute plus your phone company's access charge)
UllswaterTIC@lake-district.gov.uk

Windermere

015394 46499
bownesstic@lake-district.gov.uk

Accommodation

In addition to the tourist information centres, and the search engines, the Visit Cumbria website has a good database of local accommodation options: www.visitcumbria.com.

Weather

Consult these forecasts to gauge the best times to be on the tops.

Lake District Weatherline

0844 846 2444
www.lakedistrictweatherline.co.uk

Mountain Weather Information Service

www.mwis.org.uk (choose Lake District)

Transport

Traveline

Bus, train and coach information
www.traveline.info

Organisations

The National Trust

The National Trust owns 90% of the farms in the national park, as well as historic sites and properties, camp sites and car parks.
www.nationaltrust.org.uk
App: National Trust – Days Out

Fix the Fells

Fix the Fells repairs and maintains 330 upland paths in the national park. Read more, volunteer or donate on this website.
www.fixthefells.co.uk

Mountain Rescue

The Lake District Search and Mountain Rescue Association manages 12 teams of volunteers across the national park. The site has useful safety information Downloading the free OS Locate app will enable you to tell the team your grid ref, whether you have phone signal or not, should you need to call them.
www.ldsamra.org.uk

A FELLRANGER'S GLOSSARY

Navigational features

word	explanation
arete	knife-edge ridge
band	binding strip of land
bank-barn	barn accessible on two levels (often built on a slope or bank)
beck	main stream flowing into and through valleys to lakes and rivers
boiler-plates	non-technical term for exposed broad slabs of rock
cairn/man	small pile of loose stones indicating a path or path junction
clint	block forming part of natural limestone pavement
comb/cove	hanging valley high in the fells
common	undivided land grazed by several farmers
cop	viewpoint
crag	substantial outcrop of rock
dale	valley
dodd	rounded hilltop
drumlin	large mound accumulated beneath a melting glacier
dub	dark pool
fell	mountain pasture, frequently attributed to the whole hill
force	waterfall
garth	small enclosure close to farm-buildngs
gate	dialect term for a track
ghyll/gill	steeply sloping watercourse
glen	from British term 'glyn', meaning valley
grain	lesser watercourse above confluence
hag	eroded section of peat-moor
hause, saddle, col, dore, scarth	high gap between fells
holm	dry riverside meadow
hope	secluded valley
howe	hill or mound
ill	treacherous

intake	upper limit of valley enclosure
keld	spring
knott	compact or rugged hilltop
laithe	barn in the field or on the fell (rather than next to the farmstead)
ling	heather
lonnin	quiet lane
man	maen = stone marker (Celtic)
mell	bald hill
mere	pool or lake
mire	marshy ground
moraine	residual valley-head pillow mound debris left once a glacier melts away
nab	hill-spur or nose
ness	promontory
nether	lower
nook	secluded corner
outcrop	crag or obvious collection of rocks
out-gang	shepherd's drove lane to a particular fell pasture
park	enclosed hunting ground
pike	sharp or rocky summit
place	plot of ground
raise	heap of stones
rake	grooved track
ridding	(the action of) clearing
rigg	ridge
roche moutonnée	a distinctive section of bedrock, ice-smoothed by the abrasive action of a moving glacier
scale	summer pasture shieling (hut)
scarp/scar	steep hillside
scree	weathered rock debris beneath a crag
seat	summer pasture/high place
shaw	small wood
sheep-creep	small field-to-field access for sheep
shelter-cairn	circular windbreak wall

sike	small stream
slack	small, shallow or stony valley
sled-gate	track for pony-drawn sledges
slump	sedimentary rock that has slipped creating dykes (intrusions), fractures or ridges
stang	pole
stead	site of farm
sty	steep path
swine	pigs
tarn	small mountain pool from the Norse 'tjorn' meaning tear
thwaite	clearing
traverse	walking route across the fells
trig point	Ordnance Survey triangulation column
trod	path created by animals
wash-fold	sheepfold where sheep were once gathered for washing in the beck
water	feeder lake to river
wath	ford
whin	gorse
wick	inlet or bay or subsidiary farm
wray	secluded corner
yeat	gate

Place names

name	explanation
Artlecrag Pike	summit belonging to Arnketill (Norse family name)
Bannerdale	valley where the holly grows
Blea Water	blue tarn
Boredale	valley with a store-house
Capplebarrow	horse pasture hill
Cawdale (Beck)	valley of the crows
Dillicar Common	small field
Fusedale	dale of the cow-house
Hagg (Gill)	to hagg = to chop or coppice timber

Hullockhowe	wolves' playground hill
Mabbin (Crag)	from the personal name Mabon
Nan Bield	Anne's shelter
Smeathwaite	small clearing
Straits of Riggindale	(Norse) 'straits' = constricted current of water + 'riggin' = rigging (rope work on a ship)
Swarth Beck	dark (and forbidding) stream
Swindale	valley of the pigs
Todd Fell	the foxes' fell
Towtop (Kirk)	t'howe top = the hill top (contraction)
Truss (Gap/Lane)	cross-passage
Wath Bridge	bridge at the fording place
Whatshaw (Common)	Walter's wood
Whelter Crags	'hwilftar' (Scandinavian) = curved crags
Willdale	wild valley
Woundale	twisted valley
Wray Crag	corner cliff
(Great) Yarlside	(Norse) the Lord's high pasture

Fell names

Just the more intriguing ones…

name	explanation
Branstree	steep hillside
Grayrigg Forest	(wider area than the fell itself) forest: area under forest law where hunting rights and quarries were protected (medieval); gray: mountain limestone near Grayrigg village
Harter Fell	rutting ground of mature stags
High Raise	a place of reverence, as the term 'raise' frequently alluded to 'an ancient burial place', although the likely reference was to Low Raise, where there are the remains of a tumulus
High Street	traversed by an ancient route folklore held to be Roman, but more likely simply a native ridgeway

Ill Bell	treacherous bell-shaped hill
Kidsty Pike	the peak of the steep playground of young goats
Loadpot Hill	named after the deep hollow on the north side of the hill (lode pot) from which it was thought iron ore was once dug, now thought to be a Roman source of road-stone
Place Fell	first recorded as Plessefeld in 1256, meaning spacious field
Rest Dodd	perhaps an allusion to a regular resting place used during the ancient beating of the Martindale parish boundary but also mentioned in the late 13th century as 'Rostdode' implying a roosting place
Sallows	place of dwarf willows
Shipman Knotts	from a surname that evolved in the 14th century to describe a shepherd, surprisingly little used in Lakeland it seems
Wether Hill	upland pasture of yearling male lambs
Yoke	square-shouldered hill (looking like a yoke once used for ploughing or carrying water)

THE LAKE DISTRICT FELLS

Fell name	Height	Volume
Allen Crags	784m/2572ft	Borrowdale
Angletarn Pikes	567m/1860ft	Mardale and the Far East
Ard Crags	581m/1906ft	Buttermere
Armboth Fell	479m/1572ft	Borrowdale
Arnison Crag	434m/1424ft	Patterdale
Arthur's Pike	533m/1749ft	Mardale and the Far East
Bakestall	673m/2208ft	Keswick and the North
Bannerdale Crags	683m/2241ft	Keswick and the North
Barf	468m/1535ft	Keswick and the North
Barrow	456m/1496ft	Buttermere
Base Brown	646m/2119ft	Borrowdale
Beda Fell	509m/1670ft	Mardale and the Far East
Bell Crags	558m/1831ft	Borrowdale
Binsey	447m/1467ft	Keswick and the North
Birkhouse Moor	718m/2356ft	Patterdale
Birks	622m/2241ft	Patterdale
Black Combe	600m/1969ft	Coniston
Black Fell	323m/1060ft	Coniston
Blake Fell	573m/1880ft	Buttermere
Bleaberry Fell	589m/1932ft	Borrowdale
Blea Rigg	556m/1824ft	Langdale
Blencathra	868m/2848ft	Keswick and the North
Bonscale Pike	529m/1736ft	Mardale and the Far East
Bowfell	903m/2963ft	Langdale
Bowscale Fell	702m/2303ft	Keswick and the North
Brae Fell	586m/1923ft	Keswick and the North
Brandreth	715m/2346ft	Borrowdale
Branstree	713m/2339ft	Mardale and the Far East
Brim Fell	795m/2608ft	Coniston

Fell name	Height	Volume
Brock Crags	561m/1841ft	Mardale and the Far East
Broom Fell	511m/1676ft	Keswick and the North
Buckbarrow (Corney Fell)	549m/1801ft	Coniston
Buckbarrow (Wast Water)	430m/1411ft	Wasdale
Calf Crag	537m/1762ft	Langdale
Carl Side	746m/2448ft	Keswick and the North
Carrock Fell	662m/2172ft	Keswick and the North
Castle Crag	290m/951ft	Borrowdale
Catbells	451m/1480ft	Borrowdale
Catstycam	890m/2920ft	Patterdale
Caudale Moor	764m/2507ft	Mardale and the Far East
Causey Pike	637m/2090ft	Buttermere
Caw	529m/1736ft	Coniston
Caw Fell	697m/2287ft	Wasdale
Clough Head	726m/2386ft	Patterdale
Cold Pike	701m/2300ft	Langdale
Coniston Old Man	803m/2635ft	Coniston
Crag Fell	523m/1716ft	Wasdale
Crag Hill	839m/2753ft	Buttermere
Crinkle Crags	860m/2822ft	Langdale
Dale Head	753m/2470ft	Buttermere
Dodd	502m/1647ft	Keswick and the North
Dollywaggon Pike	858m/2815ft	Patterdale
Dove Crag	792m/2599ft	Patterdale
Dow Crag	778m/2553ft	Coniston
Eagle Crag	520m/1706ft	Borrowdale
Eskdale Moor	337m/1105ft	Wasdale
Esk Pike	885m/2904ft	Langdale
Fairfield	873m/2864ft	Patterdale

Fell name	Height	Volume
Fellbarrow	416m/1365ft	Buttermere
Fleetwith Pike	648m/2126ft	Buttermere
Froswick	720m/2362ft	Mardale and the Far East
Gavel Fell	526m/1726ft	Buttermere
Gibson Knott	421m/1381ft	Langdale
Glaramara	783m/2569ft	Borrowdale
Glenridding Dodd	442m/1450ft	Patterdale
Gowbarrow Fell	481m/1578ft	Patterdale
Grange Fell	416m/1365ft	Borrowdale
Grasmoor	852m/2795ft	Buttermere
Gray Crag	697m/2287ft	Mardale and the Far East
Grayrigg Forest	494m/1621ft	Mardale and the Far East
Graystones	456m/1496ft	Keswick and the North
Great Borne	616m/2021ft	Buttermere
Great Calva	690m/2264ft	Keswick and the North
Great Carrs	788m/2585ft	Coniston
Great Cockup	526m/1726ft	Keswick and the North
Great Crag	452m/1483ft	Borrowdale
Great Dodd	857m/2812ft	Patterdale
Great End	907m/2976ft	Borrowdale, Langdale, Wasdale
Great Gable	899m/2949ft	Borrowdale, Wasdale
Great How	523m/1716ft	Wasdale
Great Mell Fell	537m/1762ft	Patterdale
Great Rigg	767m/2516ft	Patterdale
Great Sca Fell	651m/2136ft	Keswick and the North
Great Worm Crag	427m/1401ft	Coniston
Green Crag	489m/1604ft	Coniston
Green Gable	801m/2628ft	Borrowdale
Grey Crag	638m/2093ft	Mardale and the Far East

Fell name	Height	Volume
Grey Friar	772m/2533ft	Coniston
Grey Knotts	697m/2287ft	Borrowdale
Grike	488m/1601ft	Wasdale
Grisedale Pike	791m/2595ft	Buttermere
Hallin Fell	388m/1273ft	Mardale and the Far East
Hard Knott	552m/1811ft	Coniston
Harrison Stickle	736m/2415ft	Langdale
Hart Crag	822m/2697ft	Patterdale
Harter Fell (Eskdale)	653m/2142ft	Coniston
Harter Fell (Mardale)	778m/2553ft	Mardale and the Far East
Hart Side	758m/2487ft	Patterdale
Hartsop above How	586m/1923ft	Patterdale
Hartsop Dodd	618m/2028ft	Mardale and the Far East
Haycock	798m/2618ft	Wasdale
Haystacks	598m/1962ft	Buttermere
Helm Crag	405m/1329ft	Langdale
Helvellyn	950m/3116ft	Patterdale
Hen Comb	509m/1670ft	Buttermere
Heron Pike	621m/2037ft	Patterdale
Hesk Fell	476m/1562ft	Coniston
High Crag	744m/2441ft	Buttermere
High Hartsop Dodd	519m/1703ft	Patterdale
High Pike (Caldbeck)	658m/2159ft	Keswick and the North
High Pike (Scandale Fell)	656m/2152ft	Patterdale
High Raise (Central Fells)	762m/2500ft	Langdale
High Raise (Haweswater)	802m/2631ft	Mardale and the Far East
High Rigg	355m/1165ft	Borrowdale
High Seat	608m/1995ft	Borrowdale
High Spy	653m/2142ft	Borrowdale

Fell name	Height	Volume
High Stile	807m/2648ft	Buttermere
High Street	828m/2717ft	Mardale and the Far East
High Tove	515m/1690ft	Borrowdale
Hindscarth	727m/2385ft	Buttermere
Holme Fell	317m/1040ft	Coniston
Hopegill Head	770m/2526ft	Buttermere
Ill Bell	757m/2484ft	Mardale and the Far East
Illgill Head	609m/1998ft	Wasdale
Iron Crag	640m/2100ft	Wasdale
Kentmere Pike	730m/2395ft	Mardale and the Far East
Kidsty Pike	780m/2559ft	Mardale and the Far East
Kirk Fell	802m/2631ft	Wasdale
Knock Murton	447m/1467ft	Buttermere
Knott	710m/2329ft	Keswick and the North
Knott Rigg	556m/1824ft	Buttermere
Lank Rigg	541m/1775ft	Wasdale
Latrigg	368m/1207ft	Keswick and the North
Ling Fell	373m/1224ft	Keswick and the North
Lingmell	807m/2649ft	Wasdale
Lingmoor Fell	470m/1542ft	Langdale
Little Hart Crag	637m/2090ft	Patterdale
Little Mell Fell	505m/1657ft	Patterdale
Little Stand	739m/2426ft	Langdale
Loadpot Hill	671m/2201ft	Mardale and the Far East
Loft Crag	682m/2237ft	Langdale
Longlands Fell	483m/1585ft	Keswick and the North
Long Side	734m/2408ft	Keswick and the North
Lonscale Fell	715m/2346ft	Keswick and the North
Lord's Seat	552m/1811ft	Keswick and the North

Fell name	Height	Volume
Loughrigg Fell	335m/1099ft	Langdale
Low Fell	423m/1388ft	Buttermere
Low Pike	507m/1663ft	Patterdale
Maiden Moor	576m/1890ft	Borrowdale
Mardale Ill Bell	761m/2497ft	Mardale and the Far East
Meal Fell	550m/1804ft	Keswick and the North
Mellbreak	512m/1680ft	Buttermere
Middle Dodd	653m/2143ft	Patterdale
Middle Fell	585m/1919ft	Wasdale
Muncaster Fell	231m/758ft	Coniston
Nab Scar	450m/1476ft	Patterdale
Nethermost Pike	891m/2923ft	Patterdale
Outerside	568m/1863ft	Buttermere
Pavey Ark	697m/2287ft	Langdale
Pike o'Blisco	705m/2313ft	Langdale
Pike o'Stickle	708m/2323ft	Langdale
Pillar	892m/2926ft	Wasdale
Place Fell	657m/2155ft	Mardale and the Far East
Raise	884m/2900ft	Patterdale
Rampsgill Head	792m/2598ft	Mardale and the Far East
Rannerdale Knotts	355m/1165ft	Buttermere
Raven Crag	463m/1519ft	Borrowdale
Red Pike (Buttermere)	755m/2477ft	Buttermere
Red Pike (Wasdale)	828m/2717ft	Wasdale
Red Screes	777m/2549ft	Patterdale
Rest Dodd	697m/2287ft	Mardale and the Far East
Robinson	737m/2418ft	Buttermere
Rossett Pike	651m/2136ft	Langdale
Rosthwaite Fell	551m/1808ft	Borrowdale

Fell name	Height	Volume
Sail	771m/2529ft	Buttermere
Sale Fell	359m/1178ft	Keswick and the North
Sallows	516m/1693ft	Mardale and the Far East
Scafell	964m/3163ft	Wasdale
Scafell Pike	977m/3206ft	Borrowdale, Langdale, Wasdale
Scar Crags	672m/2205ft	Buttermere
Scoat Fell	843m/2766ft	Wasdale
Seatallan	693m/2274ft	Wasdale
Seathwaite Fell	631m/2070ft	Borrowdale
Seat Sandal	736m/2415ft	Patterdale
Selside Pike	655m/2149ft	Mardale and the Far East
Sergeant Man	736m/2414ft	Langdale
Sergeant's Crag	574m/1883ft	Borrowdale
Sheffield Pike	675m/2215ft	Patterdale
Shipman Knotts	587m/1926ft	Mardale and the Far East
Silver How	395m/1296ft	Langdale
Skiddaw	931m/3054ft	Keswick and the North
Skiddaw Little Man	865m/2838ft	Keswick and the North
Slight Side	762m/2500ft	Wasdale
Souther Fell	522m/1713ft	Keswick and the North
Stainton Pike	498m/1634ft	Coniston
Starling Dodd	635m/2083ft	Buttermere
Steel Fell	553m/1814ft	Langdale
Steel Knotts	433m/1421ft	Mardale and the Far East
Steeple	819m/2687ft	Wasdale
Stickle Pike	376m/1234ft	Coniston
Stone Arthur	503m/1650ft	Patterdale
St Sunday Crag	841m/2759ft	Patterdale

Fell name	Height	Volume
Stybarrow Dodd	846m/2776ft	Patterdale
Swirl How	804m/2638ft	Coniston
Tarn Crag (Easedale)	485m/1591ft	Langdale
Tarn Crag (Longsleddale)	664m/2179ft	Mardale and the Far East
Thornthwaite Crag	784m/2572ft	Mardale and the Far East
Thunacar Knott	723m/2372ft	Langdale
Troutbeck Tongue	363m/1191ft	Mardale and the Far East
Ullock Pike	690m/2264ft	Keswick and the North
Ullscarf	726m/2382ft	Borrowdale
Walla Crag	379m/1243ft	Borrowdale
Wallowbarrow Crag	292m/958ft	Coniston
Walna Scar	621m/2037ft	Coniston
Wandope	772m/2533ft	Buttermere
Wansfell	489m/1604ft	Mardale and the Far East
Watson's Dodd	789m/2589ft	Patterdale
Wether Hill	673m/2208ft	Mardale and the Far East
Wetherlam	762m/2500ft	Coniston
Whinfell Beacon	472m/1549ft	Mardale and the Far East
Whinlatter	517m/1696ft	Keswick and the North
Whin Rigg	536m/1759ft	Wasdale
Whiteless Pike	660m/2165ft	Buttermere
Whiteside	707m/2320ft	Buttermere
White Side	863m/2831ft	Patterdale
Whitfell	573m/1880ft	Coniston
Winterscleugh	464m/1522ft	Mardale and the Far East
Yewbarrow	628m/2060ft	Wasdale
Yoadcastle	494m/1621ft	Coniston
Yoke	706m/2316ft	Mardale and the Far East

LISTING OF CICERONE GUIDES

SCOTLAND
Backpacker's Britain:
  Northern Scotland
Ben Nevis and Glen Coe
Cycle Touring in Northern Scotland
Cycling in the Hebrides
Great Mountain Days in Scotland
Mountain Biking in Southern and
  Central Scotland
Mountain Biking in West and North
  West Scotland
Not the West Highland Way
Scotland
Scotland's Best Small Mountains
Scotland's Mountain Ridges
The Ayrshire and Arran Coastal Paths
The Border Country
The Borders Abbeys Way
The Cape Wrath Trail
The Great Glen Way
The Great Glen Way Map Booklet
The Hebridean Way
The Hebrides
The Isle of Mull
The Isle of Skye
The Skye Trail
The Southern Upland Way
The Speyside Way
The Speyside Way Map Booklet
The West Highland Way
Walking Highland Perthshire
Walking in Scotland's Far North
Walking in the Angus Glens
Walking in the Cairngorms
Walking in the Ochils, Campsie Fells
  and Lomond Hills
Walking in the Pentland Hills
Walking in the Southern Uplands
Walking in Torridon
Walking Loch Lomond and
  the Trossachs
Walking on Arran
Walking on Harris and Lewis
Walking on Jura, Islay and Colonsay
Walking on Rum and the Small Isles
Walking on the Orkney and
  Shetland Isles
Walking on Uist and Barra
Walking the Corbetts
  Vol 1 South of the Great Glen
Walking the Corbetts
  Vol 2 North of the Great Glen
Walking the Galloway Hills
Walking the Munros Vol 1 – Southern,
  Central and Western Highlands
Walking the Munros Vol 2 – Northern
  Highlands and the Cairngorms
West Highland Way Map Booklet
Winter Climbs Ben Nevis and
  Glen Coe
Winter Climbs in the Cairngorms

NORTHERN ENGLAND TRAILS
Hadrian's Wall Path
Hadrian's Wall Path Map Booklet
Pennine Way Map Booklet
The Coast to Coast Map Booklet
The Coast to Coast Walk
The Dales Way
The Dales Way Map Booklet
The Pennine Way

LAKE DISTRICT
Cycling in the Lake District
Great Mountain Days in the
  Lake District
Lake District Winter Climbs
Lake District:
  High Level and Fell Walks
Lake District:
  Low Level and Lake Walks
Mountain Biking in the Lake District
Outdoor Adventures with Children –
  Lake District
Scrambles in the Lake District – North
Scrambles in the Lake District – South
Short Walks in Lakeland Book 2:
  North Lakeland
The Cumbria Way
The Southern Fells
Tour of the Lake District
Trail and Fell Running in the Lake
  District
Walking the Lake District Fells –
  Langdale
Walking the Lake District Fells –
  Wasdale

NORTH WEST ENGLAND AND
THE ISLE OF MAN
Cycling the Pennine Bridleway
Cycling the Way of the Roses
Isle of Man Coastal Path
The Lancashire Cycleway
The Lune Valley and Howgills
The Ribble Way
Walking in Cumbria's Eden Valley
Walking in Lancashire
Walking in the Forest of Bowland
  and Pendle
Walking on the Isle of Man
Walking on the West Pennine Moors
Walks in Ribble Country
Walks in Silverdale and Arnside

NORTH EAST ENGLAND,
YORKSHIRE DALES AND
PENNINES
Cycling in the Yorkshire Dales
Great Mountain Days in the Pennines
Mountain Biking in the
  Yorkshire Dales
South Pennine Walks

St Oswald's Way and St Cuthbert's
  Way
The Cleveland Way and the Yorkshire
  Wolds Way
The Cleveland Way Map Booklet
The North York Moors
The Reivers Way
The Teesdale Way
Trail and Fell Running in the
  Yorkshire Dales
Walking in County Durham
Walking in Northumberland
Walking in the North Pennines
Walking in the Yorkshire Dales:
  North and East
Walking in the Yorkshire Dales:
  South and West
Walks in the Yorkshire Dales

WALES AND WELSH BORDERS
Cycle Touring in Wales
Cycling Lon Las Cymru
Glyndwr's Way
Great Mountain Days in Snowdonia
Hillwalking in Shropshire
Hillwalking in Wales – Vol 1
Hillwalking in Wales – Vol 2
Mountain Walking in Snowdonia
Offa's Dyke Map Booklet
Offa's Dyke Path
Pembrokeshire Coast Path
  Map Booklet
Ridges of Snowdonia
Scrambles in Snowdonia
Snowdonia: Low-level and easy
  walks – North
The Cambrian Way
The Ceredigion and Snowdonia
  Coast Paths
The Pembrokeshire Coast Path
The Severn Way
The Snowdonia Way
The Wales Coast Path
The Wye Valley Walk
Walking in Carmarthenshire
Walking in Pembrokeshire
Walking in the Forest of Dean
Walking in the Wye Valley
Walking on the Brecon Beacons
Walking on the Gower
Walking the Shropshire Way

DERBYSHIRE, PEAK DISTRICT
AND MIDLANDS
Cycling in the Peak District
Dark Peak Walks
Scrambles in the Dark Peak
Walking in Derbyshire
White Peak Walks:
  The Northern Dales
White Peak Walks:
  The Southern Dales

SOUTHERN ENGLAND

20 Classic Sportive Rides in South East England
20 Classic Sportive Rides in South West England
Cycling in the Cotswolds
Mountain Biking on the North Downs
Mountain Biking on the South Downs
North Downs Way Map Booklet
South West Coast Path Map Booklet – Vol 1: Minehead to St Ives
South West Coast Path Map Booklet – Vol 2: St Ives to Plymouth
South West Coast Path Map Booklet – Vol 3: Plymouth to Poole
Suffolk Coast and Heath Walks
The Cotswold Way
The Cotswold Way Map Booklet
The Great Stones Way
The Kennet and Avon Canal
The Lea Valley Walk
The North Downs Way
The Peddars Way and Norfolk Coast path
The Pilgrims' Way
The Ridgeway Map Booklet
The Ridgeway National Trail
The South Downs Way
The South Downs Way Map Booklet
The South West Coast Path
The Thames Path
The Thames Path Map Booklet
The Two Moors Way
Two Moors Way Map Booklet
Walking Hampshire's Test Way
Walking in Cornwall
Walking in Essex
Walking in Kent
Walking in London
Walking in Norfolk
Walking in Sussex
Walking in the Chilterns
Walking in the Cotswolds
Walking in the Isles of Scilly
Walking in the New Forest
Walking in the North Wessex Downs
Walking in the Thames Valley
Walking on Dartmoor
Walking on Guernsey
Walking on Jersey
Walking on the Isle of Wight
Walking the Jurassic Coast
Walks in the South Downs National Park

BRITISH ISLES CHALLENGES, COLLECTIONS AND ACTIVITIES

The Big Rounds
The Book of the Bivvy
The Book of the Bothy
The C2C Cycle Route
The End to End Cycle Route
The End to End Trail

The Mountains of England and Wales: Vol 1 Wales
The Mountains of England and Wales: Vol 2 England
The National Trails
The UK's County Tops
Three Peaks, Ten Tors

ALPS CROSS-BORDER ROUTES

100 Hut Walks in the Alps
Across the Eastern Alps: E5
Alpine Ski Mountaineering Vol 1 – Western Alps
Alpine Ski Mountaineering Vol 2 – Central and Eastern Alps
Chamonix to Zermatt
The Karnischer Hohenweg
The Tour of the Bernina
Tour of Mont Blanc
Tour of Monte Rosa
Tour of the Matterhorn
Trail Running – Chamonix and the Mont Blanc region
Trekking in the Alps
Trekking in the Silvretta and Ratikon Alps
Trekking Munich to Venice
Walking in the Alps

PYRENEES AND FRANCE/SPAIN CROSS-BORDER ROUTES

Shorter Treks in the Pyrenees
The GR10 Trail
The GR11 Trail
The Pyrenean Haute Route
The Pyrenees
Walks and Climbs in the Pyrenees

AUSTRIA

Innsbruck Mountain Adventures
The Adlerweg
Trekking in Austria's Hohe Tauern
Trekking in the Stubai Alps
Trekking in the Zillertal Alps
Walking in Austria

SWITZERLAND

Switzerland's Jura Crest Trail
The Swiss Alpine Pass Route – Via Alpina Route 1
The Swiss Alps
Tour of the Jungfrau Region
Walking in the Bernese Oberland
Walking in the Engadine – Switzerland
Walking in the Valais

FRANCE

Chamonix Mountain Adventures
Cycle Touring in France
Cycling London to Paris
Cycling the Canal de la Garonne
Cycling the Canal du Midi
Écrins National Park

Mont Blanc Walks
Mountain Adventures in the Maurienne
The GR20 Corsica
The GR5 Trail
The GR5 Trail – Vosges and Jura
The Grand Traverse of the Massif Central
The Loire Cycle Route
The Moselle Cycle Route
The River Rhone Cycle Route
The Robert Louis Stevenson Trail
The Way of St James – Le Puy to the Pyrenees
Tour of the Oisans: The GR54
Tour of the Queyras
Vanoise Ski Touring
Via Ferratas of the French Alps
Walking in Corsica
Walking in Provence – East
Walking in Provence – West
Walking in the Auvergne
Walking in the Briançonnais
Walking in the Cevennes
Walking in the Dordogne
Walking in the Haute Savoie: North
Walking in the Haute Savoie: South
Walks in the Cathar Region

GERMANY

Hiking and Cycling in the Black Forest
The Danube Cycleway Vol 1
The Rhine Cycle Route
The Westweg
Walking in the Bavarian Alps

ICELAND AND GREENLAND

Trekking in Greenland – The Arctic Circle Trail
Walking and Trekking in Iceland

IRELAND

The Wild Atlantic Way and Western Ireland

ITALY

Italy's Sibillini National Park
Shorter Walks in the Dolomites
Ski Touring and Snowshoeing in the Dolomites
The Way of St Francis
Through the Italian Alps
Trekking in the Apennines
Trekking in the Dolomites
Via Ferratas of the Italian Dolomites Vol 1
Via Ferratas of the Italian Dolomites: Vol 2
Walking and Trekking in the Gran Paradiso
Walking in Abruzzo
Walking in Italy's Cinque Terre
Walking in Italy's Stelvio National Park

For full information on all our guides,
books and eBooks, visit our website:
www.cicerone.co.uk

Explore the world with Cicerone

walking • trekking • mountaineering • climbing • mountain biking • cycling • via ferratas • scrambling • trail running • skills and techniques

For over 50 years, Cicerone have built up an outstanding collection of nearly 400 guides, inspiring all sorts of amazing experiences.

www.cicerone.co.uk – where adventures begin

- Our **website** is a treasure-trove for every outdoor adventurer. You can buy books or read inspiring articles and trip reports, get technical advice, check for updates, and view videos, photographs and mapping for routes and treks.

- **Register this book** or any other Cicerone guide in your member's library on our website and you can choose to automatically access updates and GPX files for your books, if available.

- Our **fortnightly newsletters** will update you on new publications and articles and keep you informed of other news and events. You can also follow us on Facebook, Twitter and Instagram.

We hope you have enjoyed using this guidebook. If you have any comments you would like to share, please contact us using the form on our website or via email, so that we can provide the best experience for future customers.

CICERONE

Juniper House, Murley Moss Business Village, Oxenholme Road, Kendal LA9 7RL

✉ info@cicerone.co.uk   cicerone.co.uk